WHEN THUNDER ROLLED

An F-105 Pilot over North Vietnam

ED RASIMUS

PRESIDIO
PRESS

BALLANTINE BOOKS • NEW YORK

A Presidio Press Book
Published by The Random House Publishing Group

Published in the United States by Presidio Press, an imprint of The Random House Publishing Group, a division of Random House, Inc., New York, and simultaneously in Canada by Random House of Canada Limited, Toronto.

Presidio and colophon are trademarks of Random House, Inc.

Originally published in hardcover by Smithsonian Books in 2003.

ISBN 978-0-89141-854-2

Printed in the United States of America

This edition published by arrangement with The Smithsonian Institution.

www.presidiopress.com

First Presidio Press Mass Market Edition: October 2004

OPM 9 8 7 6 5 4 3 2

Lazy red tracks of tracer arched gracefully up from the area just to the east of the target, not apparently shooting at anyone in particular. A few black puffs of 85s detonated well above the attack, again not seeming very coordinated. The radar warning receiver continued its howling and the center of the vector scope was an angry spider indicating a mass of electronic confusion about how many radars were looking at us, but there were no SAMs airborne yet.

When I checked in the cockpit, the altimeter was passing 9,500 feet. I rolled and pulled down, watching the altitude continue to increase until the tape reversed direction at just over 12,000 feet. I kept pulling, wings-level inverted until the glowing red circle of the sight reticle rested below the dark brown roof of the largest building. Easing the back pressure off, I rolled around the point of the pipper on the ground and checked the dive angle. I was just a bit under 45 degrees, so would need to press a few hundred feet lower before releasing. Out of the corner of my eye I saw flashes and another airplane tracking level across the horizon. There's 4,000 feet, pickle, pull, roll, jink, come back the other way. Find my flight.

Sweat rolled down from under my helmet and occasionally dripped a salty fog into my eyes that I simply blinked away. Thirty seconds, or possibly the remainder of a lifetime. It didn't much matter. I was on the target and now off and sprinting to regain a position on my leader. I was alive again. Another hashmark on the trek to one hundred missions.

In memory of Vince Gianinetti,
cowboy, lawman, and fighter pilot without wings.

"If you aren't living on the edge, you're taking up
too much room."

Contents

Acknowledgments

I owe a lot to John Sherwood, official historian of the U.S. Navy and author of *Fast Movers: Jet Pilots and the Vietnam Experience,* for encouraging me to tell my stories. John made me realize the value of oral history in capturing the visceral and personal emotions of a war. History too often becomes a dry retelling of dates and statistics without the flavor of the participants' perspectives. While facts are certainly important, they lack the very important component of personality. John read the first few pages that I had haltingly assembled over several years and pushed me to get serious about the project.

Marshall Michel got me moving faster when we spent some time swapping recollections about Linebacker II at an annual Red River Valley Fighter Pilots reunion. Marshall's *Clashes* remains the definitive work on MiG engagements of the Vietnam war, and his more recent *Eleven Days of Christmas* casts new light on the Linebacker II campaign. When he convinced me that there was interest in this type of book, I finally gained confidence that it might get published.

Of course there must be recognition of the loyal wife who supported the effort. Carol, who doesn't really know which end of the airplane the hot air comes out of, took a lot of prodding before she was willing to sit down and read my draft. After years of sitting through war stories and watching a bunch of middle-aged men talking with their hands and shooting their watches, she had little interest. When she finally picked it up and pronounced it readable, I knew there was hope. As the nonaviator in the loop, she was instrumental in showing me where it didn't make sense to the average reader and where it needed more elaboration. Her insights were invaluable.

Thanks should also go to the folks who agreed to read my manuscript and offer objective criticism. Among them are Bill Stroud, F-4 WSO extraordinaire; Bob Hipps, Wolf FAC; GI Basel, Thud driver; Tom Coady, D and G Weasel pilot; Ed Cathcart, Marine F-8/F-4/A-6 pilot; Art Kramer, B-26 bombardier; and Joe Myers, ANG C-130 puke. And a special thanks to Tootie Fouratt, friend, teacher, encourager of aspiring writers, and supplier of the world's best chicken-fried steak.

For help in digging out historical details, Dennis Jenkins and his great F-105 book, *F-105 Thunderchief: Workhorse of the Vietnam War;* Jeff Koln, 421st TFS history guru; Howard Plunkett and John Revak, hoarders of details about 105 bailouts; Guy Alcala, Internet military aviation fanatic; Theo Van Geffen, Thunderchief aficionado; and Larry Davis, Wild Weasel history author.

Good stories only become good books with the help of great people. I've been fortunate to know a lot of them.

Introduction

I moved the throttle outboard and waited patiently for the afterburner to light. When the reassuring push came to the small of my back, I eased back on the stick and started a four-G pull to bring the nose up to thirty degrees. We were doing six hundred knots already, but airspeed would bleed off quickly in the pop-up, and I wanted to have better than four hundred left as I got to the top. The target was a complex of buildings off to my left and the bombs from lead were already offering an aimpoint. The pacing was almost automatic; I didn't need a stopwatch, and I didn't need to look at the altimeter tape winding up. It would take about ten seconds to reach the pull-down altitude and then another six to make the three-dimensional turn from thirty degrees nose up to a 45-degree dive. Then another six seconds or so to track the target, offset for the wind, and hopefully get the bombs off without getting hit. Make it thirty seconds from pop to pickle to descent back into the weeds. My internal clock was running smoothly.

Lazy red tracks of tracers arched gracefully up from the area just to the east of the target, apparently not shooting at anyone in particular. A few black puffs of 85s detonated well above the attack, again not seeming very coordinated. The radar warning receiver continued its howling, and the center of the vector scope was an angry spider indicating a mass of electronic confusion about how many radars were looking at us, but there were no SAMs airborne yet.

When I checked the altimeter, it was passing ninety-five hundred feet. I rolled and pulled down, watching the altitude continue to increase until the tape reversed direction at just over twelve thousand feet. I kept pulling, wings-level inverted until the glowing red circle of the sight reticle rested below the dark brown roof of the largest building. Easing the back pressure off, I rolled around the point of the pipper and checked the dive angle. I was just a bit under forty-five degrees, so I would need to press a few hundred feet lower before releasing. Out of the corner of my eye I saw flashes and another airplane tracking level across the horizon. There's four thousand feet, pickle, pull, roll, jink, come back the other way. Find my flight.

Sweat rolled down from under my helmet and occasionally dripped a salty fog into my eyes that I simply blinked away. Thirty seconds, or possibly the remainder of a lifetime. It didn't much matter. I was on the target and now off and sprinting to regain a position on my leader. I was alive again. Another hash mark on the trek to one hundred missions.

How I got to where I could do the job is the story here. No one could have anticipated the losses that the F-105 forces would suffer during the Rolling Thunder bombing campaign against North Vietnam. We couldn't know then where we fit into the big picture. We simply went because when we signed on we had held up our hands and agreed to "defend the Constitution against all enemies foreign or domestic." It turned out that there was a direct correlation between flying the most sorties and taking the most losses, and the Republic F-105 Thunderchief was the weapon of choice for the Rolling Thunder campaign. It was our job, so we did it.

Flying fighters had been my life goal; I'd done the necessary things and had made the grade. I had become a fighter pilot and looked forward to a long career of flying exciting airplanes, associating with fun people and living a great life. Then the Vietnam War flared, and flying fighters suddenly got a lot more involved. This is the story of my experiences during six months in 1966 flying the F-105 from Korat Air Base Thailand as a member of the 421st Tactical Fighter Squadron. It is the transition from fear to effectiveness as I faced the challenges of a continually changing war. It's also a thank you to the people who taught me the business and led me through a challenging time in my life.

This is a memoir, not a history. It is my recollection of the people, the places, and the events. These stories are all true. When I've been able to flesh out the stories with call signs, tail numbers, and individuals, I've included those details in brief footnotes. I'm telling you what I felt and thought. It's about what and whom I liked and disliked. Others may view the events from another perspective, but this is mine. There are good guys and bad in these stories. I owe my life to the good guys, and I overcame the bad guys who were trying to kill me. That's a happy ending.

CHAPTER 1

The Contract

How'd I get myself into this? In August 1965 when I graduated from pilot training, there was no threat. When I was in fighter checkout at Nellis, there had been only a few hints of the rising tide of the war. Now it's May 1966, and I'm riding an airliner into San Francisco, on my way to the ol' "date with destiny." Flying had been a dream since I was in the seventh grade in Chicago. If I had thought about it a little more, I would have figured out that a guy can get himself dead or even worse doing this kind of thing. Now it was getting serious. Here I was on the downhill slide into the Vietnam air war as a fully qualified F-105 pilot. Clearly an example of knowing exactly what you want until you get it and then finding out it ain't quite so good. Now the thought continually running through my mind is how do I break the chain? How do I get out of this?

I was sitting in coach on an American Airlines 707, in my freshly cleaned Air Force blue uniform. Silver wings and first lieutenant bars gleaming brightly in contrast to the sickly green of my complexion. All my worldly belongings were either in my B-4 suitcase, my helmet bag, or the leather briefcase on my lap. I was en route to Travis AFB, California, where I would catch a military contract airliner to the Philippines for jungle survival training and then continue on to Korat Royal Thai Air Base to become an instrument of national policy. That is, I was on my way to fly the Thunderchief in the air war against North Vietnam. Hell, six months earlier I didn't even know there was an air war against anybody.

To say I felt sick is an understatement. Did you ever spend

1

much time thinking about death? Not the abstract, philosophical concept. Your death. The end, nothing, darkness, eternity. The sleep from which you don't wake. And you're only twenty-three years old.

There hadn't been a doubt in my mind that I wanted to fly. It had been obvious. All I had to do was get through college, get an Air Force or Navy commission, pass the physical, and get through flight school. As with all great plans, some decision points arose along the way but no great setbacks. Everything went smoothly without much deviation from the plan. Sure, I was disappointed not to get into the Air Force Academy, but going to school in Chicago, living at home, and getting an ROTC commission was not that bad a deal. Luckily I graduated, but just barely, and luckily the ROTC unit had been short on their pilot quota for several years, so I made it into pilot training. And, miracle of miracles, I was good. Good enough to breeze through and finish in the top ten out of 350 graduates at the eight different training bases scattered across the southern United States. Good enough to get my first choice of aircraft assignments, one of nine slots for the F-105 Thunderchief.

Why the 105? It must have been an occurrence in my formative years. No, I wasn't frightened by a J-75 hardlight while in my cradle. I was older than that when I got the airplane bug. I suppose it started with model airplanes when I was about ten or twelve. Then there were the carefully collected dimes and quarters and dollars rat-holed away until I'd have a ten spot to head out to Palwaukee airport and get a flying lesson in a J-3 Cub. Which led to the desire to fly jets in the Air Force, which sort of eased into the ROTC business, which provided the opportunity to take a trip during my freshman year to Nellis AFB outside Las Vegas where some of the first Thunderchiefs were based.

I remember getting off the blue bus into the blazing Nevada sun and seeing that huge silver airplane. Standing under the wing and looking up into the wheel well thinking what it might be like to fly something this huge. Walking past the twelve-foot ladder that led to that lonely cockpit with that strange smell of hydraulic fluid and sweat and ozone. No, that wasn't it. It was the vapor. Looking into that great gaping maw of a tailpipe and smelling the lingering JP-4 from yesterday's flight. That was what did it. It must have been the vapor.

Or maybe it was that July afternoon nearly three years later. Cruising down Route 66 just west of Holbrook, on my way to start Air Force pilot training at Williams AFB outside of Phoenix. Windows open on the '63 Impala, all my worldly possessions in the trunk and the back seat, and me wondering absently about the new world I'm about to enter. Then with a blink of a shadow over the car and a nearly mind-numbing roar, two Thunderchiefs not more than a hundred feet above me blasting down straddling the highway. That's it. That's for me. I've gotta fly 105s. Life couldn't be better than that.

But the idea was to fly that incredible airplane and then go to the bar for a couple of beers. The good life had to be lived to be enjoyed. You had to see the sunshine and the blue sky and maybe get married. Get the assignment out of flying school and then spend a couple of years in Europe or maybe at Nellis. Dying wasn't part of it. Sure, there might be combat some day, but who would have thought that Mephistopheles would come to claim me so soon? I don't want to die. How do I get out of this? I'm afraid of being captured, I'm not ready to die, and I don't want to be a prisoner of war.

CHAPTER 2

Transition

She was huge, standing tall on spindly gear struts with huge intakes at the base of each wing that simply screamed *FAST*. There was a gun on the lower left side of the nose, a Vulcan 20 mm cannon that could sling six thousand rounds a minute at your adversary. The black nose cone of the aircraft shielded a powerful radar that cut through the clouds to paint a map of the ground in front of you or scan the air to find and lock on enemy aircraft. The Pratt & Whitney J-75 that provided the push was the biggest afterburning turbojet ever stuffed into a fighter with 26,500 pounds of thrust capable of launching you through the skies at more than twice the speed of sound. There's never been a more noble steed for a warrior built by man. It's beautiful no matter from what angle you look at it, with long legs, a pinched waist, sleek wings and just one seat. The perfect system for a brash twenty-three-year-old second lieutenant with a whopping 232 hours of flying time.

The instruments were a new concept. Tapes rather than round gauges. It was a simple solution to the display of information: You could quickly see a lot of data without having to interpret pointers and dials and differing units of measurement. It worked.

The rest of the cockpit was confusion. There was a radar scope and a maze of weapons selection switches. Down the left and right console panels were a mix of new strangers and old friends for communication, navigation, and identification. There were a flock of radar controls. There was a Doppler nav system and autopilot for altitude, mach and atti-

4

tude hold, as well as navigation linking. There were tail hook and drag chute handles, refueling probe controls, external fuel management and jettison circuits. There were strange lights and combination locks for nuclear weapons and dials to schedule nuclear weapon delivery and survive the experience. And there was still more, so much that all of the switches and dials wouldn't fit into the available space. Alongside each leg was an additional foldout panel with even more weapon control gadgetry. Atop all was the gun sight.

The 105 cockpit was a daunting place. The training system designers, though, had solved the problem of overload with a simple solution. Don't tell 'em what it's for until they need to use it. When the training started, the student pilot was only required to fly the airplane, not to use it as a weapon system. So, the solution is don't tell the students about the radar or the bomb bay, just tell them about the engine, the hydraulics, the electrical system, and the flight instruments. Sounds overly simple, but it worked like a charm.

Transition into the 105 from the T-38 which we had just left behind in pilot training was very much a "good news – bad news" situation. The good news was that the T-38 was excellent preparation for a high performance fighter. The takeoff and landing speeds were comparable. We had gotten used to the T-38 taking off at 155 knots, so the 105 training mission takeoff speed of around 180 wasn't a big adjustment. The T-38 flew final at about the same 155 knots, and the 'Chief came over the fence at about 190. Flight control and stall characteristics were similar. The extra weight of the 105 and its high wing-loading made it mush a little more in high-G turns and dive pull outs, but that just required a little bit of in-flight orientation.

The bad news was that transition was accomplished in the two-seat F-105F. In the two-seat 105 the visibility from the backseat was so limited that a pilot could neither take off nor land from the rear cockpit. As unbelievable as it might seem, no fighter pilot is foolish enough to get into the rear cockpit with someone at the controls who has never before flown the airplane. The solution was to have the student pilot in the rear cockpit for three flights with an instructor in the front seat demonstrating. The IP (instructor pilot) would take off and land; once safely airborne the student would fly the airplane and get the feel of the flight controls and flight characteristics. Of course because the student couldn't see out the front window while in the backseat during those three flights, he couldn't really see what the landing looked like.

The fourth flight was the initial frontseat solo ride. The bad news continued. Since the IP would not be able to see the student errors or correct them from the backseat, the student would fly without an instructor in the airplane. The IP would fly "chase" position in another aircraft and radio advice in the event of a problem. Somehow, it all came together and worked. The fact that the T-38 flew a lot like the 105 and the fact that all of the students were the product of an extremely competitive process in undergraduate pilot training (UPT) probably helped a lot. Of the nine students in my class, we all had graduated in the top three at our respective pilot training bases.

We had two F-105 training squadrons at Nellis, the 4523rd Hornets and the 4526th Cobras. Each squadron had two classes of nine UPT graduates in training. Since a class graduated from the eight UPT bases every six weeks, and since the squadrons alternated in receiving classes, the senior class in my squadron was twelve weeks ahead of me. I was in the Cobras.

The instructors were experienced fighter pilots with at least a thousand hours in the 105, and they usually had previous experience in another fighter aircraft. Each instructor had his own call sign, which was an animal. When flying, the call sign became a combination of "Cobra" identifying the squadron, and an animal name identifying the particular instructor. We had "fox" and "cat" and "lion" and "zebra," so a typical call sign would be "Cobra Cat." We all thought this was vastly superior to the other squadron whose IPs were forced to use tree names or plants. Cobra Fox had so much more panache than Hornet Redwood. The lowly students had numbers assigned, mostly for accounting purposes because very seldom would a student get to fly without an instructor present. My number was two-four. Nothing would get your head on a swivel faster than hearing a radio transmission in the traffic pattern with a number rather than an instructor call sign. It meant there was some fool running around the place at 350 knots looking for the airspeed indicator and trying to run into you. Put four or five like that in the air at one time and things get downright interesting.

I'd been through three solo flights with chase. I hadn't bent the metal or scared my instructor so I was something to reckon with. I was not only a pilot who flew jets and had Air Force wings, I was a 105 pilot. All I needed was to learn how to do something with the airplane. I wanted to drop bombs, shoot the gun, fly air-to-air. I wanted to be able to make some sense out of the radar. I was ready to get on with the business of becoming "operational." That's when more bad news arrived.

Wimpy Peake was the scheduler. No one seemed to know where the nickname came from and no one knew what his given name really was. Some speculated that he got the name from a fondness for hamburgers, like the character in the Popeye comic strip, but no one had ever seen him eat a burger. We saw Wimpy in the stag bar after duty hours drinking a beer and chain-smoking cigarettes but never eating. He wasn't a wimp either. There was no explanation, no one ever asked and hardly anyone cared what the source of the name was anyway. It simply was. The name tag said "Wimpy," he introduced himself as Wimpy, everyone called him Wimpy except for the students who called him Captain Peake, so no further discussion was needed.

In addition to being a squadron instructor pilot, Wimpy was asked to juggle the students and the airplanes and the other instructors and the range times and the syllabus requirements, tossing the whole mess into the air and getting it to land on a Plexiglas board in a pile of grease pencil that defined our lives twenty-four hours at a time. Commanders were important. Flight leaders were critical. Instructors knew everything about the airplane. But Wimpy was GOD! Nothing happened unless Wimpy willed it.

The schedule came out of a smoke-filled closet that was Wimpy's office every afternoon about five. It was preceded by an assortment of curses and crashes as Wimpy fought with the maintenance people about aircraft configuration changes — "Can you get me two tanks and a bomb dispenser for the 8 A.M. air-to-ground period?" "I need two airplanes with operational radars at three or I've got two students who won't graduate." "Hell no, I can't take an inop refueling probe light on a night tanker sortie."

He also had to sweet-talk the other squadron, wheedling range time to fill a training requirement or begging for an IP to replace someone who went DNIF (duty, not including flying — the medical shorthand for someone with a cold or a sore shoulder or an upset stomach). Phones rang in the scheduling office and were picked up and slammed down. Doors crashed and drawers banged. Shouts rang out even when there wasn't anyone else in the room with Wimpy. But every day, just like clockwork, around five o'clock it was done. There was a schedule.

If we weren't flying or in academics, we hovered between the scheduling office door and the huge board that dominated the wall behind the duty officer's desk. Students weren't allowed in Wimpy's area while the schedule was in gestation. The penalty for transgression was worse than death — it was a week or more as squadron "snacko." Taking a hot rock student fighter pilot and making him wash dishes, make coffee and, worst of all, go shopping to the commissary for lunch supplies for the squadron snack bar was the quickest way to humble him. Pushing a cart loaded with Wonder Bread and bologna in a checkout line filled with wives and screaming babies was torture. The threat of ultimate embarrassment didn't, however, keep us from lurking around the door trying to eavesdrop on Wimpy and the operations officer discussing what was going to happen tomorrow.

I'd been wading through an academics book trying to learn about a toss bomb computer radar nuclear weapons delivery, and I didn't have a clue. The diagrams didn't help and the vocabulary was ill-defined. It suddenly occurred to me that it was after five, and I needed to do two very important things. I needed to check the schedule — if I was lucky I would be getting my first visual nuclear bomb ride tomorrow. And I needed a beer. First things first. The schedule.

I headed down the hall from the flight briefing room I'd been working in toward the duty desk. My classmate, Karl Richter, was posting the names, times and working airspace for tomorrow. There it was. No visual nuclear deliveries for me tomorrow. I was scheduled for a solo. No chase, no instructor, no nothing. Just me in an airplane cruising around the Nevada skies. Who wants this kind of boredom?

Reluctantly I shuffled back down the hall to the snack bar depressed with the thought of waiting several more days before I would start to learn about the real business of flying fighters. I had just gotten my coffee cup refilled when Tom Gibbs walked in.

Tom was twelve weeks ahead of me in training. He was in the air-to-air phase and more than halfway through the program. He had been through radar and nuclear weapons deliveries as well as conventional ground attack and was just getting ready to start refueling and the tactical employment phase. Clearly, here was someone who could sympathize with my frustration and disappointment. He would understand.

"Shit, Tom. I've gotta fly an area solo tomorrow. What a damn waste of time."

"Huh? You mean you guys are getting those area solo flights? Our class had them canceled 'cause maintenance couldn't generate enough airplanes. I didn't have to worry about 'em."

"Yeah. But you know what I'm talking about. I did everything I wanted to try in pilot training. I've run a T-38 straight up and straight down. I've done eight-point rolls and double Immelmans and whatever I could think of. I wanna drop some bombs; I don't need to bore holes. What would you do if you were me? What would you do with two hours to burn in a 105?"

He looked around for just a second and then answered as though he had thought the problem through long before I asked. "I'd practice high-G barrel rolls," he said.

"Sure! That's what I can do. That's a good idea," I said as I started out the door, only to stop before my second step. "Uhhh, Tom, what's a high-G barrel roll?" Sometimes even the coolest of us has to ask a stupid question.

"A high-G barrel roll is the neatest thing you can do on defense. Say you've got this guy behind you about to gun your brains out, and you can't shake him. You just lay a high-G barrel roll on him, and he gets spit out in front. Can't miss. Works every time."

"That sounds pretty neat," I said, "but how do you do it?"

"Well," he started maneuvering with his hands, "you get going about 450 knots, and you start the nose up with a little back pressure. As soon as the nose starts moving, you real smooth bring it into buffet and full back stick and then at the same time you feed in full rudder in whatever direction you want to roll. The ol' bird kinda flat-plates into the wind, and when it comes back around to upright, you center everything up and you've lost about 200 knots. All in about three seconds. There's no way anyone can stay behind you."

"Does it hurt anything?" I had to ask.

"Naahh. Just wait till the drop tanks are empty and go for it."

Next morning I was at the ops desk checking weather and working up some takeoff data. It wasn't much of a problem. The weather was central Nevada standard, clear and dusty all the way to the horizon. My airplane was clean except for two 450-gallon wing tanks on the inboard pylons, so the takeoff wouldn't even use half of Nellis's runway. I signed the flight release form and quickly reviewed the departure procedure and the radio frequencies for Los Angeles Center. I scribbled a few memory joggers on my clipboard and then scouted up my regular instructor, Capt. Paul Daniels, to get my required pre-solo briefing. Daniels had been my IP through the first three dual rides in the two-seat airplane and had chased me through my initial solo rides. His job was to remind me not to do all the things I knew not to do, but would probably do anyway because that's the way fighter pilots are.

Paul got a cup of coffee and headed down the hall looking for an empty briefing room. He pulled up a chair and took a look at my lineup card with its frequencies and numbers. Then he looked up, laughed a little and said, "Don't bust your ass." And that ended the briefing.

I got the tail number from the duty officer, one of my classmates, then picked up my helmet, parachute and G-suit. The airplane was parked practically at the back door of the squadron building in one of the nearer rows. The sun was bright, and the morning air was surprisingly cool for September in Las Vegas. It was going to be fun, even if there weren't any bombs to be dropped. But, there was just a tinge of loneliness. It was the first time in a long time that I was going out to an airplane without an instructor or other members of a formation coming along. Oh well, it wasn't that much different than pilot training — except for the fact that the airplane was three times the size and worth fifteen million dollars.

I was lucky. The scheduled airplane was a D model, a single-seater. I wouldn't have to do a rear cockpit check and tie down. That had always been a pain in T-38s. Just do the walkaround and up the ladder and into the seat. I still was a bit awed by going up that eight-rung, twelve-foot ladder to get into a single-seat fighter.

I worked my way around the cockpit from behind my left hip, across the instrument panel and down the right console to the rear right side of the cockpit below where the water-bottle bracket was mounted on the ejection seat. Still dependent on the checklist, still having to look around to find some of the switches and gadgets, still not knowing what the hell they do. The joke was always, "Kick the tires, light the fire, and go," or "Shiny switches 'on,' red guarded switches 'off,'" but it was taking me just a bit longer.

Ready to start. Wave at the crew chief. He flips the switch on the big yellow ground-start cart. Wait for air to spin up the engine. There's 12 percent RPM, now hit the start button, then throttle comes around from cutoff to idle. Ahh, there's the light off. Engine's coming up nicely now. There's idle RPM. Okay, radios, nav, Doppler all on, radar power to standby. Ready to check flight controls. Now flaps, speed brake, bomb-bay doors. What a trip, bomb-bay doors on a fighter. Who would believe it? All looks good.

"Nellis Tower, Cobra Two-Four, taxi one."

"Roger, Cobra Two-Four, taxi two right, the wind zero five zero at eight, altimeter two nine seven five."

Power up, left out of the chocks, right on the parallel. Nice morning. The Thunderbirds are in the arming area in their F-100s headed for a practice session. I pass the parked row of red, white, and blue Thunderbird F-105B aircraft, grounded now after the disastrous accident in their debut season.[1] Too bad, everyone who saw the show said the 105s were perfect for the team, big, noisy, powerful, and impressive. But you couldn't have airplanes blowing up in the middle of air-shows. It was bad for the reputation. I sure hope they've taken care of the problems. I don't mind dying if I do the screwing up, but I hate the idea of a spontaneous blow-up.

The 'Birds are moving out. I roll into the first slot in the end-of-runway quick-check area. Follow the marshaller's instructions. Roll forward for a tire check. Hands up, resting on the top of the canopy in sight of the ground crew chief while his team roams under my airplane checking for loose panels, hydraulic leaks, and other bad stuff. All clear, he waves me off to the runway with a sharp salute. I pull out and turn left, scrambling to hold the nose gear steering with my right hand, lever the canopy down with my left, look out on final for landing traffic and mash on the mike button. For a moment there are more jobs than hands, but the sequence is

---

1. The Thunderbirds had converted from F-100s to the F-105B in 1964. During one of their first shows at Hamilton AFB, California, one of the air-craft flown by Maj. Gene Devlin broke apart during a pull-up directly in front of the crowd. The aircraft were grounded immediately and the demon-stration team reverted to F-100D aircraft, which they flew until 1968 when they transitioned to the F-4E.

over in seconds. I glance down to check that the rollers are over the latches and the canopy is secure. The rush of pressurized air makes my ears pop slightly and there's a hint of moist cold air from the air conditioning outlets.

"Nellis Tower, Cobra Two-Four, number one for two right."

"Two-Four, cleared for takeoff, the wind zero five zero at four. Change to departure control, monitor Guard."

"Roger, Nellis."

Lined up on the centerline. Pump up the brakes. Throttle coming forward. Engine checks good at just over 100 percent. EPR is on the index. Hydraulics, all three systems good. Flaps set. Looking for about a hundred ten knots at two thousand feet. Release the brakes. Throttle outboard and forward. Bang! God, I love that burner light!

Check speeds good. Coming up on nose wheel liftoff. One eighty five. Airborne. Gear up. Flaps to cruise. Three hundred knots already. Out of burner.

"Nellis Departure. Cobra Two-Four airborne. Lake One to Tonopah. Leveling six thousand five hundred."

"Roger Cobra Two-Four. Cleared Tonopah transition. Climb and maintain flight level two one zero until within the MOA, then cleared surface to FL 450. Contact Los Angeles Center on entry."

"Roger Nellis."

Okay. Climbing at four hundred knots. Ahhh. Life is good. Leveling at twenty-one thousand. Altimeter's reset. Oxygen's normal. Fuel is fine. Tanks are feeding. What to do next?

"L.A. Center, Cobra Two-Four. Flight level two one zero. Squawking two four. Entering Tonopah."[2]

"Roger Cobra Two-Four. Radar contact. Cleared to operate in Tonopah from surface to flight level four five zero until eighteen hundred Zulu. Traffic a flight of two F-4s your

---

2. Tonopah military training area located north of Nellis lies above Frenchman and Yucca Flats, the nuclear weapons test sites, as well as Groom Lake, the infamous "Area 51."

left ten at fifteen miles departing the area below you. Contact Nellis Approach on departing."

Well, here I am. What to do now? Still got fuel in the wing tanks. Can't do any acro until they burn out. Let's go fast. Burner on. Got the light. Ease off the stick a bit as she accelerates. A bit nose heavy now as she gets over point nine Mach. There it is. One point two Mach and accelerating nicely. Up to one point four and coming up on the area border. Coming left, out of burner, slowing back below supersonic. Boring.

Still got fuel in the tanks. Maybe turn on the gun sight. Reticle brilliance up. Ahh, there's the pipper. Cool. Spiral left, down from thirty-five thousand toward the desert. Trucks on the highway. Rolling in. Eighteen-wheeler in the sight. *Rat-tat-tat-tat.* Too bad about you fella. Zoom off the pass at four hundred fifty knots back up to twelve thousand. Tanks empty.

Passing twelve continuing into a big right barrel roll. Nice feeling airplane. Not as buffety and rattley as the T-38. More like a Cadillac than a Pinto. Stable. Firm. Nose down. Five hundred knots. Pulling up, five now six G, over the top inverted, rolling right. Nice Immelman. Level at twenty-six thousand.

Rolling inverted into a simulated dive bomb pass. Forty-five degrees, wings-level. Passing twenty thousand. Sixteen, fifteen, fourteen, ready pickle, pulling into the recovery. Four, five Gs. Leveling at twelve thousand. Fuel looks good. Oxygen fine. Engine good. Got about another twenty minutes before I have to start back. Maybe it's time for ol' Gibbs's high-G barrel rolls.

What did he say? About four-fifty then nose up followed by full rudder and full aft stick. Okay. Let's go for it. Airspeed's good. Smooth nose up. Coming through about 20 degrees nose high. Stick coming back. Buffeting. Full rudder. About three Gs and the nose swinging left. Heavier buffet now. Through inverted, back upright. Relax controls. Airspeed's two-thirty. Wow. It sure works as advertised.

That one was left. Gotta do one right to stay balanced. Let the nose down a bit to get some airspeed back. Passing about ten thousand. Back up to, ahh, three-fifty should be enough. Quick rollover to make sure I'm not running into someone. Now, nose coming up. Stick back. Rudder full right. Buffeting, rolling through about 90 degrees.

Sudden snap to straight down vertical. Before I can react the airplane comes back hard left and pitches up slamming my helmet against the canopy. Back right and down, but before I can tell where the horizon is I'm banged against the opposite side of the canopy. Shoulder wrenched, hand thrown off the stick. Back up again and my feet, which had been floating during the downward gyration, are now smashed back flat on the floor.

Can't read the G-meter because the tape is churning back and forth between positive and negative. All I know is there is plenty of G to go around. Master Caution light on. Can't see the warning panel long enough to read what the lights are saying. Fuel inlet pressure light is on. AC generator light, too. Stab-aug has been blown off-line.

Grabbing for controls, but the airplane appears to be through with its antics. Nose is about 60 degrees down, airspeed coming up through two-fifty, but damn, I'm low. Feeding in back pressure, keep the nose coming up. Steady, not too much. Nose wants to wander, but that's because the stab-aug is off. There, that's about level. Thirty-eight hundred on the altimeter, that's about eight hundred over the ground. Shit. What was that all about?

Enough of this. Let's just head for home.

Back in the squadron, still not quite sure what happened. Thinking about what the flight manual says about stalls. The airplane doesn't spin. At least that's what they say. But if I had started fifty knots slower than I did the first time, then when I was well into the roll, I would have been about fifty knots below stall speed with full rudder and full-back stick. I guess that's what you would call airplane abuse or at least what the aero engineers call a departure from controlled flight. Doesn't matter. It was more than enough to make the day of any pilot with ten hours in the airplane.

Sitting in the lounge trying to regain my composure. Nels Running, one of my classmates, comes in shaking his head. I've heard the complaint before.

"Shit, Raz. They've got a spare airplane this afternoon, and they're making me fly a solo. I've done everything I ever wanted to try already. I want to get to the bomb-droppin.' Hey, didn't you have to do a solo this morning? What'd you do to keep from being bored stiff?"

"Well, Nels, why don't you practice high-G barrel rolls?"

"Yeah, good idea. Uhh, just between you and me, what's a high-G barrel roll?"

Pulling some time on the duty desk about half an hour after sunset, I look up to see one of the last crews walking in the door from the flight line. His helmet bag in his hand and hunched slightly forward against the weight of his parachute, Nels still has the impression of his oxygen mask around his mouth. He's pale, even considering the blue-white glow of the fluorescents in the squadron doorway. He looks at me and the slightest twitch of a grin wrinkles the corners of his eyes.

"Did you try those high-G barrel rolls you told me about?" He stares at me waiting for the answer.

I nod slowly. He waves his right hand in a flip, flop, and fly kind of wiggle and says, "Did the bird do something sort of like . . ."

I nod a second time. "Damn," he exclaims, "that's too cool."

"Yeah," I agree, "gotta remember that one."

CHAPTER 3

The Jungle

I was in an aisle seat in about row 70 of the most cramped airliner I'd ever been in. It was a stretched DC-8 run by a contract company that was going to make a ton of money in the next couple of years hauling fresh meat to the grinder that would develop in Southeast Asia. This was an airbus before anyone ever thought of really calling an airplane an Air Bus. High density seating would be an understatement. Six abreast, as far as the eye could see and serviced by a gaggle of the ugliest stewardesses ever assembled in one place. Years later I would wonder how they could be so ugly on the way over and so beautiful on the way back. A strange phenomenon.

But for now, the only thing I'm thinking about is dying. Last night at Travis I was sitting at the Officers' Club bar trying to suck a beer down past the lump in my throat that had been there since this trip to war started, when a survivor came in wearing a flying suit and swaggering like he owned the place. A quick survey to see if there was anybody who wanted to pick a fight and then a disappointed plop onto the bar stool two seats down from mine. It was too early for fighting and besides, it seemed as though the trash-hauling Air Force didn't drink at their home base.

The place was nearly empty, so the newcomer had to talk to somebody, and it turned out the nearest person was me — the sickly looking lieutenant trying to gag down a Bud. He introduced himself and asked the standard question for Travis, "Where are you going?"

That's when I saw it. The patch on the left shoulder of his flying suit. It was a shield, a lot like an interstate highway

17

sign, blue with a red header across the top. In the red section was "North Vietnam" in white letters. In the main body of the shield, written across the blue, was "100 Missions — F-105." I'd never seen one like it, and I couldn't believe that very many existed.

Here was a survivor. Here was someone who had been there and done it. Here was someone who had fulfilled the contract, done the job, faced the threat. Did he know what I was going through? Could he tell about the empty feeling I'd had in my gut for the past two weeks as it became more and more apparent that I was going to go to war? Could he possibly know what a coward I was? How could I talk to him? What could I say? Should I ask him what it was like? I looked up at him in response to his question.

"Korat," I mumbled.

"Oh, you just coming out of Nellis? You a 105 driver?"

"Yeah. Graduated three weeks ago. Now I'm on my way to Korat." I wasn't sure how long I could make small talk with this guy before I started crying or threw up. The fact that here was a guy who had been there and met the challenge while I still had my fear in front of me wasn't doing me a lot of good.

"You'll like Korat. I was at Tahkli, the other 105 base. Korat's the better one of the two. Hell, they just put in a damn swimming pool. What a deal, huh? Did you volunteer?"

"Ah, no. They assigned my whole class to Korat — all nine of us. They started with the class before mine from the Hornets. They sent all of them to Tahkli. No more assignments to Germany or Seymour-Johnson. It's the whole output from Nellis to Thailand."

"You'll do okay. I saw a couple of those young guys. They got there just before I left. They're doing all right. You'll get by."

"Yeah."

"Yeah. Hey, here's my date coming in. I gotta run. But remember something. I think I know how you feel. Just remember this. Didja ever see one of those motorcycle guys with the tattoo that says, 'Death Before Dishonor'?"

"Yeah, what about it?"

"Well, Kid, just remember that there are a lot worse things than dying. Living with dishonor is one of them. Think about it. See ya. Good luck." And he was gone, out the door with the blonde in the red dress who had waved at him from across the room.

Now it's the middle of the night over the Pacific in this tin can with three hundred soldiers, sailors, and dependents headed for the Philippines thinking about dying. The captain just announced that we were starting our descent into Clark. We'd be landing about 11:30 at night on Monday. The time warp characteristic of a nine-hour flight was made complete by the complication of the International Date Line. That, and the uncanny ability of the Military Airlift Command to maximize the discomfort of any flight by always departing and arriving at the most ungodly hours. Two TV dinners, burned on the edges and frozen in the middle, dispensed by the surly cabin crew during the flight hadn't done anything for my appetite either. I wondered how prisoners on death row dealt with nutrition.

We landed in the dark and taxied through a mist to a parking spot nowhere near a terminal building. One of the flight attendants was standing in the front of the airplane trying to make herself heard over the din of a couple hundred people collecting jackets, carry-ons, babies, and briefcases. It didn't matter. There was only one thing to do: Head down the ramp and get on the buses waiting to take us somewhere.

Somewhere turned out to be an empty hangar converted into a half-assed passenger processing center. Finally there was something to take my mind off of my impending demise: It was hot. It was hot and humid. It was miserably, oppressively, instantly sweatingly hot. And I was suddenly very aware that wearing my blues had been a mistake. I wasn't alone either. On all sides of me soldiers in Class A greens and sailors in blue serge bellbottoms were sweating too.

At the end of the hall a passenger services representative with a bullhorn was explaining to the horde of newcomers where, when, and how they would be processed. Buses to Subic Bay would take the sailors on the rest of their journey. Buses to barracks would take the soldiers somewhere so that the Army could fully optimize their discomfort. Representatives from Family Services would aid spouses and children in finding quarters while they were separated from their sponsors for the next day or two. But the passenger rep didn't mention anything about scared shitless Air Force lieutenants going to Jungle Survival School before their date with death in a Thunderchief.

I looked around the area and found a desk marked "Information" with a slightly overweight and very sweaty Air Force staff sergeant seated behind it. I headed over and put a copy of my orders under his nose. When and where did one report for Jungle Survival?

"Oh, lemme see here. Ahh, yeah, Jungle Survival. Lemme check. Ohhh, sorry Lieutenant, you just missed a class. That course starts on Monday mornings, and this is going into Tuesday. You'll have to wait till next week to get that."

"Okay. How do I get to the BOQ?"

"You need to use the pay phone over there and call for a cab. They'll take you to the billeting office. The number's on the wall."

It wasn't a call from the governor's office. It wasn't a pardon, merely a reprieve. But it did mean I would be living at least a week longer. I could stay here waiting for class, perfectly legal, not dying or being shot or being captured. It wasn't much, but it was something. Just get a room in a nice clean air-conditioned bachelor officer's quarters, hang around the club, read a book or a magazine, maybe even meet a sweet young thing at the bar. Mainly, don't think about dying in a fireball or being interrogated by a Sessue Hayakawa clone in a North Vietnamese prison.

I headed for the pay phone. There wasn't anyone using it — who do you call at one in the morning when you've just arrived in a foreign country? Just as the sergeant promised, the number for the base taxi service was penciled on the wall. Sort of a military tradition, I guess. The taxi dispatcher said it would be about fifteen minutes, just stand out in front of the building and wait.

I grabbed my bulging B-4 bag, my briefcase, and my helmet bag and struggled for the door. Sweat was running down the small of my back as well as down my face. My blues were getting distinctly soggy, yet in a last grasp at my fighter pilot dignity, I stopped for a second to lodge my flight cap on my head with an appropriate tuck at the rear, then I moved my stuff to the side of the entryway and commenced my wait.

Three Navy officers came out the door, two ensigns and a lieutenant, junior grade, a JG. They were only slightly better suited for the Philippine night, wearing tans rather than blues. Their black shoes and slick uniform pockets, unadorned by wings or dolphins, gave them away as surface Navy rather than aviators. The ensigns had the sort of bewildered, apprehensive expression I might have seen on my own face had I checked a mirror. The JG, on the other hand, was clearly on his own turf and prepared to lead his juniors. He was in the midst of regaling his companions on the quality experience they were about to have, spending the night in an Air Force officer's quarters.

The JG waved at me and asked if I'd called for transportation. I acknowledged that I was waiting for a base taxi to take me to the billeting office, and they would be welcome to share the ride if we could all fit. They jumped at the opportunity. I was soon asked to validate the JG's opinion that AF BOQs were infinitely preferable to Navy transient quarters. I allowed that the only Navy facility I had for comparison was North Island, San Diego, which was quite comfortable, but I expected that the quarters here would be adequate for a couple of days. The sailors regretted that they could only spend one night and then needed to head to Cubi Point, where they were supposed to join their ship, a destroyer.

Our discussion of interservice quarters rivalry ended abruptly when a yellow Ford station wagon pulled up. Thankfully it wasn't one of those garish Philippine jitneys. With a bit of careful arranging, we managed to stuff the personal travel belongings of four young officers into the area behind the rear seat then wedge ourselves in. As the sole Air Force representative on an Air Force base, I didn't take a vote before commandeering the front passenger seat. We headed through the misty night with the windows rolled down and Elvis Presley's "Heartbreak Hotel" blaring on the radio. There was something prophetic about the song.

If you've been to one military billeting office, you've seen them all. A lounge that nobody would ever think of lounging in, a coffeepot that only the desperate would try, and a collection of magazines with absolutely no appeal to the typical military member. Behind the counter a civilian clerk, usually unkempt, and always presenting an impression of harried incompetence. This time it was a middle-aged Filipina, who flipped out registration cards to the four of us as though she were dealing blackjack. We went through the routine of filling out names, ranks, service numbers, units of assignment, length of stay, orders number, and everything but our mothers' maiden names.

The clerk studied the cards carefully, presumably to keep itinerant businessmen from taking advantage of the high quality facilities that the government furnished at great expense exclusively for qualified men in uniform. She wasn't about to let anyone ineligible stay in her BOQ. After grudgingly acknowledging our right to sleep, she scribbled a building number on a piece of paper. "Give this to the driver," she mumbled.

The Navy guys turned to leave. I started to follow, then stopped short. "Don't we get keys or room numbers?"

She grinned, almost laughed, and said, "No. You'll have all you need when you get there."

The four of us packed ourselves back into the station wagon, three of us confidently ignorant and one, me, developing a growing apprehension. Something strange was going on here. I couldn't quite figure it out, but two hours on foreign soil didn't make me an expert on how things were done here.

The taxi ride took about ten minutes. We were obviously

away from the main military area of the base and into what appeared to be housing. We had passed the gigantic hospital and a base gas station. Now we were in a dark, jungle area with small streetlights shedding sixty-watt circles of light on only the distant street corners. The mist seemed more oppressive than ever, and the night was definitely not getting any cooler. We pulled up in front of a jungle bungalow, a frame building on stilts with screened verandas on all visible sides. It looked vaguely reminiscent of the commander's headquarters in *Bridge on the River Kwai*. I looked for the "hot box" in the backyard. The only thing missing was a flagpole with the Rising Sun, but that might have been in the back of the building.

It was two-thirty in the morning but lights appeared to be on throughout the bungalow. The taxi driver turned to me, clicked the flag down on the meter, and said this was the place. It began to sink in that we weren't in Kansas anymore.

The Navy guys and I scrambled out of the station wagon and sorted our luggage, then grabbed it up and started toward the building. As we got closer we could see that the front veranda was filled with bunks. Two rows of simple metal cots filled the porch area, most of which were empty except for one at the far end of the screened room to our right where a guy in boxer shorts and a T-shirt sat cross-legged holding court for a group of four avid listeners. He waved as we struggled through the screen door with our bags. It was a friendly enough welcome to a strange enough place.

We dumped our bags on the floor and stared around us. The screened porch held about twelve cots, although it looked as though only two were occupied. The front door was open, revealing what once must have been a living room or parlor containing six more beds, all empty. The ceiling light was on and a ceiling fan rotated futilely trying to dissipate the humidity and bring the temperature into the livable range. Beyond were three doorways, none with doors, leading to darkened sections of the house. This was no Holiday Inn, and I strongly suspected the sailors would never again long for a night in an Air Force BOQ.

The storyteller beckoned us over, extending a mosquito-bitten arm to offer handshakes all around. Introductions completed, he waved expansively at the bunks and told us to take whichever we wanted. The three doorways to the back of the house led to rooms containing six, four, and three bunks, respectively. We could go where we wished, but he warned against the six-bunk room because an occupant back there was having recurring nightmares and didn't take kindly to roommates. The sailors and I exchanged glances and mutely agreed that we wouldn't be disturbing him. My apprehension about my impending death in combat, which I had forgotten, resurfaced when the storyteller mentioned he was an F-105 maintenance officer from Tahkli, Thailand, visiting the Philippines on R&R. If this was a vacation, how bad was it at the combat bases?

It was just past three in the morning, and the nine-hour flight combined with who knows how many time zone changes had left us exhausted. My Navy cohorts and I excused ourselves and headed toward the back of the house where the lights were out and at least the sheets would be clean. We identified the six-bed room by the snoring sounds and quickly found the four-bed facility, which seemed to have its own bathroom. We hauled our bags in and each claimed a bunk. One of the ensigns dropped on his cot only to leap up, the back of his tan shirt and pants dappled with moisture. "It's wet," he announced.

The rest of us checked and quickly confirmed that all four bunks were distinctly damp. The Philippine humidity, the lack of ventilation and the darkness of the seldom used room made the mattresses into perfect sponges. A glance under the beds didn't disclose any major reptiles but I did note that there were water stains on the rough wooden floor undoubtedly remaining from some exceptionally damp period when someone attempting to sleep in the bunk had squeezed the excess from the bedding. I began to wonder if Jungle Survival School was really just a week in the BOQ.

I didn't care. I needed a shower, and I vowed to sleep regardless of the condition of the bunk. I headed for the bathroom. The shower stall was one of those Sears catalog affairs, white enameled sheet metal nailed to the nearest wall and spouting a nozzle and two faucets. But this one was different: The customary metal floor and drain had been cut off so that the box now stood on the wooden floor of the house. No drain was necessary because the water passed through the gaps between the wooden boards onto the ground below. After another fast check for spiders and snakes, I quickly got the showering done. The relief of getting the sweat rinsed off didn't quite overcome the general discomfort of the surroundings.

The final touch was the toilet. No porcelain here. This one was galvanized tin with an overhead wooden flush box. I couldn't be certain whether this facility used the same outlet as the shower or it actually connected to real drain pipes. The *Bridge on the River Kwai* came back. Could this fixture have been cobbled together by Bataan death marchers during the Japanese occupation? It couldn't have been much newer than the forties. And it hadn't seen a Jonny Mop with any regularity.

After figuring out how to brush my teeth without setting anything down on the moldy surfaces in the bathroom, I wrapped a towel around my waist and returned to my chosen bunk. It was nearly four o'clock as I closed my eyes and tried to will the dampness away from my body. My mind was racing. Could I live here for a week waiting for Survival School? Could I live here for a night? Could I fly combat? Could I quit and survive? What could I do? I couldn't sleep.

I lay on my back for less than an hour. The first pink tinge was barely lighting the eastern sky when I rolled out of the cot and began digging through my B-4 bag for a set of summer khaki 1505s to wear. I balled up my blues and stuffed them into the suitcase, then grabbed all my belongings and edged past the sleepers to the screen porch. Unbelievably the outside air at first light was a few degrees cooler than under the ceiling fans in the BOQ from Hell. There was a pay phone on the porch with the requisite base taxi number penciled nearby on the wall. A car would be by in a half hour. It was now five-fifteen.

I was back in the MAC passenger terminal less than five hours after departing. I headed for a counter with a copy of my orders, hoping I could bluff my way out of further residence in the Philippines. If the question about Jungle Survival School wasn't asked, I wouldn't answer. The ticket agent looked at the orders, then grinned at me. "You're priority one, Lieutenant. They need you bad. F-105 pilots are a valuable commodity. I've got a C-130 leaving at 2300 tonight direct to Korat, and you could bump anyone but the president. Check-in time is two hours earlier. Here's your boarding pass."

He never even mentioned Survival School. I guess the bags under my eyes made me look like I'd been through the course. I was free. I was going to get out of the Philippines. I was on my way to Korat, to combat, to war, to dying, to being captured, to quitting, to being labeled a coward, to a destiny that I wasn't sure of, but which wasn't looking like much fun.

CHAPTER 4

Meditation

I had fifteen hours to kill until showtime for the C-130. Now that I knew I was going to get out of the Philippines I could check out of the BOQ. I wondered briefly what the nightly charge would be for such a pathetic facility and how they got away with running a place like that. I revisited the familiar wall phone and called the base taxi dispatcher whom I was now beginning to value as my only friend in the Pacific. A car would be on the way in fifteen minutes.

I stashed my B-4 bag and helmet in a terminal locker, then took my briefcase with my electric razor to the men's room, which was distinctly more serviceable than the latrine in the quarters I had left. A splash of cold water in the eyes and on the chin to cool the irritation after grinding the Remington against my sweaty beard, and I headed for the front door. The base taxi was just pulling up.

I checked out of the BOQ by paying the five-dollar fee. The clerk seemed decidedly immune to any comments about the quality of the facilities. I suspect that any sarcasm I could generate that early in the morning would pale in comparison to comments from more experienced and battle-hardened transients. I knew one thing for sure, I wouldn't rank Clark very high on my list of places to revisit.

It was nearly eight when I got to the Officers' Club. I got a newspaper — my first encounter with the *Stars and Stripes,* then headed to the dining room for breakfast. I grabbed a table in the corner and scanned the front page. The headline was not what I needed to see, "Losses Heavy in NVN Raids."

Through the day I alternated between a table outside the bar on the swimming pool patio and the same corner table in the dining room for lunch and dinner. The clock was running on me and I was going to have to do something pretty soon. I would be in Korat by tomorrow morning. When I got there, people were going to expect me to fly combat missions. Could I?

The tour of duty was different for pilots flying over North Vietnam. Those who flew in the South were assigned for a year. Those who went North would complete a tour in one hundred missions. This wasn't an arbitrary number. It recalled World War II, when B-17 crews suffered such incredible losses over Germany that they flew a limited tour of twenty-five missions. It was a reflection of losses. If danger was acceptable, you could fly for a year, taking as many missions as weather, maintenance, and the war required you to fly in 365 days. If danger was too great, if defenses were too intense, if the probability of survival wasn't high enough, then the tour required a more concrete limit. One hundred was a finite number. One hundred could be done in four or five months. One hundred could be survived. Couldn't it?

In South Vietnam the mission was close air support, the employment of tactical aircraft near friendly troops. The threat was small-arms fire and bad weather. The greatest danger was foolishness on the part of the pilot, pressing too close to the target, getting too involved with your work, getting trapped under the clouds in a canyon, running into the trees, releasing too low and being hit by your own ordnance. There were no heavy anti-aircraft guns. There were no SAMs. There were no MiGs. Rescue forces were just minutes away. If you bailed out by three you could be in the club by four, just in time for Happy Hour.

North Vietnam was a different mission. It was interdiction. It was going a long way into enemy territory against targets like bridges and railroads, factories and power plants. It meant barrages of triple-A and radar-guided SAMs and encounters with MiGs. It meant capture and torture, beatings and death. Bail out in the north and you were a long way from friendly faces.

As the day droned on I went through cycles ranging from fear to panic to cowardice to fatalism. The words of the captain I met in the bar at Travis came back, "Death before dishonor." What was worse, to be killed or wounded or captured or dishonored? Was I so valuable a commodity that the world would even miss me if I were dead? Unlikely.

Death was like sleep, I reasoned. You don't know when you go to sleep; it just happens. You don't know that you're asleep while you're asleep; it only becomes apparent after you wake up. Only if you're dead, you don't wake up. When you're dead, you don't know you're dead. I tried to gain some solace in my Catholic upbringing, but it wasn't working very well. I kept comparing dying with the old football axiom about the forward pass. When you throw a pass, three things can happen and two of them are bad. If I believed what religion told me, then in dying three things could happen, and it was the same ratio as football, two of them were bad. If there were an afterlife, I could go to heaven or hell. If there weren't an afterlife, I wouldn't know. I doubted somehow that flying fighters in Southeast Asia would move me to the head of the heaven-bound line.

Wounding seemed an unlikely outcome. Guys in foxholes got wounded. Guys in fighters either lived or died. Sure, you could get burned or banged up in an ejection, but that was the same risk as flying jets anywhere. People weren't really shooting at you; they were shooting at your airplane. They hit airplanes; they didn't hit pilots. You could get hurt, but that would be tolerable. I could live with that.

Capture was a real fear. I hadn't liked the survival and resistance training when I went to survival school at Stead Air Force Base right after pilot training. The stories from World War II and Korea were damned impressive. Torture can be administered in thousands of ways and the technology was undoubtedly improving with every new conflict. It wasn't a

Hogan's Heroes laugh riot with a bumbling Colonel Klink. The art of hurting someone without killing him was being refined continually and I was pretty sure that I wouldn't like it a bit.

As I meditated on my future I dissected the prisoner-of-war possibilities. I couldn't determine what was the most frightening aspect of that scenario. I feared being in the hands of an irate enemy. I feared torture and interrogation. I drew pictures in my mind of ejection and injury without medical care for who knew how long. I knew for certain that name, rank, and serial number weren't going to satisfy any inquisitor. I would spill my pathetic guts sooner or later, and then there would be the issue of dishonor — there's that Travis captain, again. I would be guilty of letting down my fellow prisoners, my friends, my family. I would be known as the one who gave in, who cooperated, who couldn't stand the test.

That was the issue, wasn't it? The question of honor or image or standing in society. Raise the issue in a conversation and the pedantic philosophers would lean back and rationalize how everyone understood the need to cope with the situation. They would justify going along to get along. They would describe what? Bullshit! It wasn't a hypothetical situation. It was real and in a world brought up on John Wayne and D-Day and the Long Gray Line and "Duty, Honor, Country," the individual who collaborated, who gave in, who didn't do the right thing was a coward and therefore to be shunned.

Which brought the argument back to the point of origin. If I didn't fly, I wouldn't be killed or wounded or captured. I would be alive, but I would be in that netherworld of failures and cowards. I would be disgraced without family or friends or profession. It would be a lonely world, inhabited only by that loathsome individual looking back each morning from the mirror. Which would be worse, to try and fail or not to try? What would it take to stop the process when I got to Korat? Who would I talk to first to tell them I wouldn't or couldn't risk my precious butt in combat? Whoever it was, I doubted they would be sympathetic or understanding. Then, how long would it be before I was shipped back to the States? What would those days of embarrassment be like as the word went around among those who had been my companions at Nellis and those who didn't know me at all? Was that worth it?

There might be some middle ground. I might be able to do one mission or maybe two. No one got shot down on their first mission, did they? It was possible, sure, but not likely. That would be the ultimate in bad luck. I could get by one mission. If I just flew one, that would ease the brand of cowardice. I wouldn't be a total coward. I would have tried it and then been unable to go on. That was better than a flat resignation without even attempting combat.

The argument went round and round in my head as the day went on. The one-mission solution wasn't perfect. It wasn't even good. It failed any test if I looked at it objectively, but who was objective? It didn't solve the cowardice issue. It didn't keep me from getting killed. It was a patchwork that wouldn't hold together for very long at all.

I killed time until about nine in the evening and then called for a ride from the club down to the MAC terminal. I was dog-tired, and I still had the cold lump in the pit of my stomach over what tomorrow was going to be like. I got my bags out of the locker and dragged them to the check-in counter. The two-striper behind the desk put a tag on them and tossed them unceremoniously on a pallet behind him. He told me to get a cup of coffee, we would be boarding in about an hour and a half.

The time passed quickly. The less we want something to happen, the faster the clock runs. The flight was announced and I shuffled to the bus with about ten other passengers bound for various spots in Thailand. I was the only pilot, in fact, the only officer among the group. No one spoke to me and I was just as happy they didn't.

The door of the Hercules slammed shut and the engines

began to wind up. We were scattered along the sides of the airplane in red nylon webbing jumpseats, picking the places where we could stretch our legs out between the pallets that filled the cargo area. It wasn't long before we were airborne, on our way to Thailand and my ultimate showdown with myself. I fell asleep to the drone of the turboprops.

CHAPTER 5

Arrival

The loadmaster nudged me awake. We were about a hundred miles out of Korat and they were calling the command post to announce our arrival. He wanted to know if I was going to be assigned at Korat. What was my name and rank? The flight crew would pass the word and someone would meet me when we landed. One couldn't ask for better service.

I heard the props change pitch and felt the start of an en route descent into Korat when it suddenly dawned on me. Unless we had flown a gross deviation in our course, I had just flown over Vietnam and Laos. I was "in-theater" as they say, and I had slept through the experience. We had blithely cruised through the war zone without incident. Maybe there was a possibility of survival after all.

The normal noises of approach and landing echoed through the cavernous cargo area of the Herk. Throttle adjustments and the whine of flap motors followed by the grinding and thud of the landing gear dropping into place allowed anyone to follow the progress of the approach. You didn't need to be a pilot, merely a regular airplane traveler, to know that landing was imminent.

I wondered how the squadron reacted to new guys. Throughout pilot training and during the 105 course at Nellis, the instructors who were long-experienced fighter pilots told tales of the "new guy" treatment. According to established custom green lieutenants in a fighter squadron were isolated, much like freshman pledges in a fraternity. Until you proved yourself capable you weren't given much respect, and you were only spoken to if there was no way to

Southeast Asia, showing the location of the Thailand bases in relation to Laos, Cambodia, and North and South Vietnam.

avoid it. Even among the junior members of the squadron the hierarchy was firmly entrenched. Seniority, even of a few months, was always in mind. It didn't sound fair or reasonable, but that's how it was. I steeled myself for the experience. Even if I succeeded in flying that one combat mission, I didn't expect the social arrangement to be particularly pleasant.

A minor thump indicated both our arrival and the pilot's experience level. Even if he was a trash-hauler, a grease job was worthy of note. The airplane slowed with a blast of power through reversed props and then turned off the runway. The clicking of the pavement strips and undulations of the taxiway could be felt in the back of the plane and indicated that construction standards in the Far East were just a bit different than in a stateside air base. We jolted to a stop and the engines wound down. The loadmaster was already at the back of the airplane opening the cargo ramp. The pallets were worth more to him than the passengers, and they were getting priority. We had to wait for a few seconds while a two-stripe assistant loadmaster wrestled with the door at the front of the cargo area.

My first impression of Thailand was the smell. It was a mixture of jungle mold and open sewers perfumed with jet fuel and near toxic levels of diesel exhaust. If the breeze was just right, there might have been a hint of sweat and soy sauce along with a suspicion of Brylcreem from the slick, black hair of the Thai driver who waited for the passengers by the door of the Bluebird bus parked near the wingtip of the C-130. I scanned the area and noted that this ramp area was a lot smaller than the one at Clark. The aircraft was parked a bare hundred yards from the cargo-handling pavilion. It wasn't a terminal in the strict sense of the word but rather a roofed, fenced yard where cargo pallets could be loaded and disassembled as goods arrived. There wasn't any sort of passenger lounge at all. I asked the bus driver if it was all right to just walk the hundred yards. He gave me a look that told me it wasn't at all uncommon for newcomers to skip the short bus ride.

There were two tall lieutenants in sage green unmarked

flight suits waiting by the fence. They both wore olive drab canvas hats rather than the normal uniform flight cap. With the right side of the brim turned up and snapped against the crown, the headgear looked like a cheap version of the classic Australian digger hat. I had seen similar hats a year earlier when I spent a weekend going cross-country to Florida. The Air Commando special operations unit at Hurlburt Field wore them. The lieutenants waved me over.

They were Lts. Ken Kerkering and John Russell, and they were my welcome party. While we waited for the baggage pallet to be forklifted to the cargo pavilion, they started to give me the word about my new organization. They were from the 421st Tac Fighter Squadron, one of two F-105 squadrons on the base. The other unit was the 469th. The two squadrons comprised the newly established 388th Tac Fighter Wing that had been named just three days ago to replace the temporary duty organization supporting part-time units coming and going from Japan and Okinawa. We were now a permanent unit, which indicated higher headquarters' recognition that maybe this war was going to go on for a little while.

After I retrieved my B-4 bag and helmet from the pallet, John led the way to a red Datsun pickup truck with a pair of wooden bench seats mounted in the back. We tossed my stuff in the back, Ken jumped in with the bags, and I got the shotgun seat while John drove. We took a street parallel to the flight line for about a half-mile then turned into a compound formed of single-story reddish teak buildings. Four identical buildings were on three sides of a treed square about eighty yards long by forty yards wide. On the west end of the square was a larger, H-shaped building inside a ten-foot-high, guarded chain-link fence topped with concertina wire. In the center of the square was a small, tin-roofed building shaded by a pair of huge trees. John advised me that the guarded building was the command post, and the one with the trees was the latrine. Not much else was important.

We parked the truck next to three other similar red pickups, and I followed John into one of the perimeter buildings. A four-by-six-foot plywood sign on the end of the building identified it as the 421st TFS, Fighting Cavaliers. The squadron patch was displayed on the sign, a red circle with a white French musketeer's plumed hat in the center. A sword was vertical behind the hat and white stars were arranged around the edge of the circle, grouped four, two, and one. Along the bottom of the circle, a white tab bore the legend, "421st TFS."[1]

It was just past eight in the morning, and the building was buzzing. As we came through the door, a personal equipment area was just to the right — a chute shop with racks of parachutes down the center and wooden lockers around the walls at eye level. Below the wooden lockers, which were large enough to contain a hat and personal effects with maybe a checklist bag stuffed in, there were dowels on which hung heavily loaded survival vests and G-suit chaps. On top of the lockers were flight helmets, all with red visors and with the oxygen masks neatly connected and hoses stowed identically. The room offered two aisles, one on each side of the parachute rack just wide enough for one person to pass by another. The aisles were now filled with eight or so squadron pilots wrestling with their gear.

A huge man, already arrayed in G-suit and parachute was leaning across the operations desk counter, which was just to the left of the entryway, shouting at the harried lieutenant behind the bank of telephones. I immediately recognized the lieutenant as Karl Richter, my classmate from Nellis. He glanced at me but didn't acknowledge my presence until he had responded to the shouter that he was just about to call the command post for tail numbers. Two things were obvious. One was that a mission was just suiting up to head out the door. The other was that the shouter was someone to watch out for.

With Richter on the command post phone, the big man glared at Russell who stepped forward to introduce me.

1. In later years the 421st patch changed to a black widow spider and the slogan "kiss of death," a reflection of the origin of the 421st as a night fighter squadron in World War II flying the P-61 Black Widow.

"Lieutenant Colonel Barnett, this is our new guy. Just came off the Klong from Clark. I'll get him squared away, drop off his records, get him fitted with gear, stuff like that." John seemed to shrink several inches as he attracted the attention of the squadron commander. Barnett merely glared at the two of us.

The rest of the crowd began to filter out of the chute shop, arrayed for flight and eager to get an aircraft assigned to be on their way. Several grabbed to shake my hand and introduced themselves quickly. Others I recognized from senior classes at training. All seemed genuinely happy to welcome me aboard. The command post hot line ended the reunion and welcome ceremony before it had begun. Richter was scribbling numbers on a piece of scrap paper, and the pilots were reading them upside down over the counter nearly as fast as he could write and heading out the door.

With the frenzy over, John headed me down the hall to the administration area, where he introduced me to Sergeant Morgan and Airman Lopez. Morgan took my personnel records; Lopez took my flying time forms and aeronautical orders. They seemed genuinely glad to see me too. Morgan quickly briefed John on the other stops he wanted me to make around the base today: hospital for flight surgeon clearance to fly, command post to get on the access list and get a secure area badge, life support to get issued survival gear and then check with Lieutenant Kerkering to get a room for a day or two until I could get assigned permanent quarters. He had better also get me in front of Captain Mitchell, who was going to be my flight commander, and then get me to work studying the ROEs.

John headed down the hall and out the door with me trailing. I was finding that the pace of things at Korat ranged from frantic to incredible. There were a load of questions popping up from this brief encounter as well as a clear agenda for the remainder of the day. We headed across the quadrangle to the command post, where we had to wait at the gate for someone with escort authority to bring me into the building. John's line badge could get him in, but he didn't have escort approval to bring someone else into the classified area of the command center. While we waited by the guard shack I saw two large Plexiglas-covered bulletin boards on either side of the entrance. The boards were filled with eight-by-ten, black-and-white photos depicting bomb damage from air strikes or damaged F-105s that had brought their crews back to Korat. One photo showed a grinning captain standing up through a hole in an aircraft wing while another photo displayed a small missile embedded in a tail section. If this exhibit was designed as a morale booster, it wasn't working very well for me.

We got in, did our paperwork, and with my new restricted area badge pinned to my shirt pocket flap, we continued on our rounds. Once in the truck, I asked John what a "klong" was. The answer was simple. A klong is a water-filled ditch, a rice paddy, or a small lake filled with brackish water. It was also the call sign of the C-130s that transported personnel and equipment around Southeast Asia. I had arrived on a Klong this morning. Oh, and one more thing. The klongs were the primary source of Thailand's pervasive stench.

My next question was about the welcome I'd received. What happened to the "new guy" treatment? Only Colonel Barnett seemed less than ecstatic about my arrival. The answer here was also simple, but not so benign as the definition of a klong. Korat had two F-105 squadrons. A squadron consisted of eighteen airplanes and twenty pilots. In the previous seven days Korat had lost eight aircraft and pilots, including the 421st squadron commander and the operations officer. Barnett was the days-old-and-very-temporary squadron commander. New aircraft were being ferried in daily from Yokota, Japan, and Kadena, Okinawa, but pilots were in extremely short supply. Any fresh meat was welcome. You didn't have to be good or qualified or eager; you merely had to be warm. Twenty percent of the crews had been lost during the previous week, and according to the best estimate, to fly one hundred missions would take around six months. Was my resolve to fly just one mission before quitting realistic?

We headed down the road paralleling the flight line. Aircraft could be seen off to our left taxiing out of high corrugated steel revetments that otherwise shielded them from view. As we approached an intersection, John gave me a quick tour of the important landmarks on the installation and interspersed the latest gossip. To our right was the Officers' Club, where we would eat all of our meals and do all of our socializing. Down the street was a small base exchange, where the shelves were mostly bare except for razor blades, toothpaste, and an occasional shipment of Carling's Black Label beer. The new swimming pool was next to the water tower, which Hanoi Hannah had announced on her propaganda radio show would be blown up by North Vietnamese sappers within the next few days. Like anyone new in town I listened carefully but couldn't remember much of it within half an hour. Except for the part about the impending guerrilla raid on the water tower that is.

John provided me with the breakdown on where my Nellis classmates were. Pete Foley, Nels Running, and Dick Hackford had all been assigned to our sister squadron, the 469th. They and Karl Richter had been the first to arrive about ten days ago, since they had jumped at the chance to ferry some airplanes across the Pacific. Karl was in the 421st, as I had seen when we went through the squadron. He had three combat missions already and two days ago had brought back a badly damaged airplane. John avoided the details about the incident. Either he didn't know or didn't want to talk about it. The rest of the class, Ken Hallmark, Ed Harvey, Bill Ricks, and Wayne Spelius, were all with me in the 421st. I had been the last to arrive but only by about two days. Skipping out of Jungle Survival School had caught me up with the group.

We completed a circle of the base with a stop at the clinic, where I dropped my medical records and got a quick interview with the squadron flight surgeon, Dr. Ron Goldman. If I were going to quit flying, he would be the one I would see first. But it wasn't going to be today. Things were happening too fast to think through what I wanted to say and what I wanted to do. I was being swept along by the tide of events and had pretty much decided that I would be able to face my fears and get at least one mission done. I told the doc I was feeling fine, no problems to report. He nodded, signed the clearance for flight duty, and tossed it in his out basket. I didn't even have to take off my shirt or turn my head and cough. One more obstacle out of the way.

It was just past lunchtime, so we headed to the club for a sandwich, and we caught up with Ken Kerkering. He was the squadron additional-duty housing officer and responsible for finding me a bed for the night. The squadron had four "hootches," one for each of the four flights that made up the organization. The commander and operations officer lived in a trailer down the block, adjacent to the senior officers of the wing. I would get a room in the C flight hootch in a day or two, as soon as the personal effects of one of the lost pilots could be inventoried, packed, and shipped. In the meantime I could spend the night in a hootch set aside for the temporary duty pilots. With losses as high as they were, pilots from F-105 squadrons in Japan and Okinawa were routinely sent to fill the flying schedule. They had their own building, just around the corner from the squadron area.

My head was spinning from the rush to get things done. There wasn't time to quit, and there didn't seem to be anyone who would have time to listen even if I wanted to quit. I told Russell that I was about dead on my feet, and since it was now nearly four o'clock in the afternoon what were the chances of dropping me at the hootch where I'd be sleeping? He seemed to recall his own arrival exhaustion and agreed to dump me at my room. He said he would head back down to the squadron building to check out the next day's schedule as well as my agenda. He pulled the truck up in front of a group of small teak buildings that looked a hell of a lot newer than the guest quarters in the Philippines.

The crew hootches were one-story teak structures arranged in a group of ten around a small, palm-lined square. Four buildings were on the inside of the square and six around the outside. The street was white gravel with a small white concrete curb. Each building had a central screened porch with a sitting area and an interior section housing the latrine and shower facilities. Flanking the screened lounge and facing the street were two rooms on each side with two persons per room. Nailed to the door of each room were two red tin silhouettes of F-105s, each with the name of one of the room's occupants in white lettering. Across the street, on the opposite side of the square, I could see the silhouette aircraft were green, indicating that those hootches housed our sister squadron, the 469th. The door John aimed me at had no names attached.

I opened the door and got a welcome blast of cold air-conditioned air. The drapes over the one window were drawn so the room was dim. I turned on the lights and checked the place out. The room was ample for two persons, furnished with two military single beds, two dressers, two small desks, and two side-by-side closets. The bed on my left had several pairs of shined shoes aligned under it, clearly occupied. On my right, the other neatly made bunk had no evidence of conflicting ownership. I dragged my B-4 bag off the porch, waved at Russell that I would see him in the morning, and established my claim to a sleeping space. It didn't take long to shed my uniform, brush my teeth in the central shower area, and crawl between the sheets. Exhaustion overcame apprehension and I was asleep in seconds.

The lights snapped on, and I jerked awake. It was clearly much later but I didn't have a clue what time it was other than the darkness behind the short figure standing in the open doorway. Red-haired, about five feet eight, in a flying suit and slightly flushed, the intruder stepped in, slamming the door behind him. "Why the hell aren't you at the bar, Lieutenant? Who told you you could sleep?"

I scrambled to get oriented and shake off the cobwebs. I glanced at the clock on the dresser and saw it was nearly 10:30. I'd been asleep for about four hours. The name tag on my visitor identified him as Glen Nix, and the rank on his shoulders told me he was a captain. Drawing on all the intellectual power I could muster at the moment, I said, "What?"

Things were starting to come together slowly. Blanks in the scenario were being filled as I swam to consciousness from my deep sleep. Captain Nix was obviously the owner of the other bed. Just as obviously, he had come quite recently from the club where the redness of his face was related more to his recent ingestions than his hereditary complexion. My conclusion was immediately verified.

"Why weren't you at the club with the rest of the guys from your class? There's a company rep from Seagram's there with a Crown Royal promotion. Two bits a drink and two bucks a bottle. Did you just get in today? You're gonna be in the 421st? Were you in Richter's class? What took you so long?" To suggest that he was hyper was to belabor the obvious. He was half drunk certainly, but beyond that he was flushed with adrenaline. He was wound tight with nervous energy and could barely stand still. I sat up in my bed and tried to prepare myself for this encounter. I still wasn't sure whether I was about to get punched, thrown out of his room, or dragged back to the club.

I tried to answer the questions, not necessarily in the order asked, but I was fairly certain that it wouldn't make much difference to the conversation, which had every indication of being fairly one-sided anyway. "I got in this morning. John Russell dragged me around most of the day. I was pretty beat from the trip, and I really didn't feel very hungry, so I was trying to get some sleep."

Glen didn't seem to care very much about the answers. He pulled up a desk chair and straddled it backward, closer to the bed than was really comfortable. I could smell a bit of the Crown Royal as he scanned me up and down, apparently trying to determine whether I was worthy to be here. His look wasn't quite scorn and it certainly wasn't pity; it was a bit like the hundred-mission survivor from the bar at Travis. He was special, combat proven, a survivor, maybe a hero. And he knew it. He knew who he was and what he could do. He knew he could do the job, perform the mission, face his fears, and deal with the life-and-death matters that combat flying involved. He wondered if I was a pledge for that fraternity that he was now in. He wondered if I would live or die, fly or quit, survive or perish. He'd been in the room for less than five minutes and he'd read my mind.

He didn't ask any more questions. He just started talking. It wasn't easy here. It wasn't as bad as some said. The SAMs weren't so bad. The MiGs hardly ever bothered us. You had to work hard and know your stuff. You had to stay in formation, line abreast where your leader could see you. A hundred missions wasn't so tough. It didn't take long, maybe six months. It was possible, but . . . but . . .

His eyes got glassy and I thought for a moment he might cry. He didn't, but his monologue slowed. He took a breath and then, "It's the flak. It doesn't know who you are, whether you're good or weak. It doesn't care. It's the flak. The goddamn guns. There's so many goddamn guns. They just shoot everywhere, and you get hit by the Golden B-B. You can't jink, you can't avoid it. You never know. There's so many goddamn guns. . . ."

He stood up quickly, shoving the chair back to the desk. With a deep breath, he regained his composure, then turned around, flicked off the light, and said good night. He left the room, and I heard his steps on the front veranda heading for the screen porch. I closed my eyes trying to go back to sleep, but the thoughts raced through my mind. "It's the guns . . . the goddamn guns."

CHAPTER 6

Local Preparation

John Russell was standing in the open doorway, sunlight streaming in behind him. "C'mon, get your ass moving. It's time for breakfast. I'll be back to pick you up in twenty minutes."

I rolled out of bed, glancing across the room. Nix's bed had been slept in, so he had apparently returned after I fell asleep. With nearly twelve hours sleep, I was pretty well recovered from the transpacific jet lag. I showered, shaved, and pulled a flight suit out of my B-4 bag. Suddenly remembering the flight suits I'd seen on Nix, Russell, and Kerkering the day before, I shrugged back out of the suit and set to work with a razor blade removing the Tactical Air Command and squadron patches from Nellis, leaving only my first lieutenant bars and my black leather name tag and wings. I may not be ready to fly combat, but for at least a day or two, I'd look like I was.

I was just pulling up the zipper when Russell honked the horn of the red Datsun truck in front of the hootch. Karl Richter was perched on one of the wooden benches in the back of the truck. The front passenger seat was taken, but I was a squadron new guy anyway, so I jumped in back with Karl. I asked him how things were going, and what was new. He quickly replied that we would have a chance to talk later that day, but basically he was doing all right. He was going to get his fifth mission that day, and he was eager to get moving. I quietly thought to myself that I wished I had his enthusiasm.

We headed for the club. I now was alert enough to get some feel for the place. Entry was through a covered porch

45

area, with the main club on the right and a pool table and snack bar on the left. The door to the club opened on a traditional barroom. Just inside the door stood a wooden shelf unit roughly four feet high and ten feet long and divided into small square storage chambers, each large enough to hold one of those olive-drab air commando hats that all the pilots seemed to wear. These shelves clearly served to remind patrons of the Air Force tradition that required anyone entering a bar with his hat on to buy a round of drinks for all present. You would have to be fairly well preoccupied to get past them without stowing your headgear.

Beyond the bar was the dining room. Small four- or six-person tables with red gingham table linen were dispersed through the center of the room. Three large banquet tables were placed on the left, right, and on the wall opposite the entry. One table was adorned in red, one in green, and one in blue. The red table wore a large embroidered replica of the 421st squadron patch. The green table displayed the "fighting bull" of the 469th, and the blue table had the 388th Tac Fighter Wing patch. The tables were easily twenty feet long and five feet across, so the full squadron could dine together without any danger of crowding. The segregation here was obvious. Each squadron clearly had its own place and those who were not members of one of the flying squadrons would only eat at one of the small tables unless invited to sit with the pilots.

Few seats were occupied, so we sat at the red table and ordered breakfast from the dimpled Thai girl in the pink waitress uniform who greeted us like true friends. While we ate, Karl and John gave me a list of things to get done for the day. First I had to see the life-support people and get fitted for survival gear. That was the highest priority because they planned to get me a local sortie as soon as possible, which would prepare me to fly real missions. They were certain I was eager to get on with flying combat. I nodded, somewhat glumly, not at all sure I had any such desire.

The second task on the list was to get over to the command post with any moment of my free time and start studying the

ROE, the rules of engagement. I couldn't fly combat until I had passed a test on the ROE, so they were certain I would devote myself aggressively to learning the war rules. I wondered how many weeks I could stretch the study period without seeming obvious. I didn't get to muse for long, there was no second cup of coffee. It was time to hit the road down to the squadron.

When we got to the squadron building things were a bit calmer than they had been yesterday. Karl pointed out that the morning flights had been airborne for about a half hour and wouldn't be back for another two hours. Briefings for the midday missions wouldn't start for another hour or so, and then there would be more people around, so now would be a good time to get fitted for my flying gear. Karl led me into the life-support area, where I had left my helmet and G-suit yesterday. He introduced me to Sergeant Leonard, who would take care of everything I needed.

Leonard asked me if I had any preference for parachute and locker number, since there were some vacancies and I could have a choice. I didn't make the mistake of asking why there were so many spots available. I didn't want to know. I found that twenty-four was open. That had been my number at Nellis, and I'd always considered two and four to be lucky numbers for me. Spot twenty-four would be mine.

Overnight Leonard had fitted my helmet with a red visor shell, replacing the white one that had been left from training. He had also gotten me a second G-suit in case my old one couldn't support the gear I wanted to carry, and he had scrounged me two new flying suits just in case I needed some. The Thai heat and humidity made daily changes of flight suits a definite necessity. Leonard assumed I would prefer a survival vest instead of the new chaps that had just shown up. I agreed that the vest sounded like the better option.

Then it was fitting time. The G-suit always took the longest. Laces on each side of the back at the waist controlled pressure on the abdomen, while more laces on each thigh section and each calf area made sure the legs received adequate pressure. It took about twenty minutes to fit the new G-suit, then Leonard mentioned the options. Pilots who had been flying north had gained some experience regarding what was handy during a shoot-down and rescue. Most pilots had two day/night Mk-6 flares taped to their G-suits at the narrow section of each leg alongside the knee, where they were out of the way, yet handy. On one calf section the life-support people could sew a webbing pocket that would hold two hundred feet of nylon rope for letting yourself down from the jungle canopy. On the other calf, they would attach a K-Bar Marine issue survival knife.

The vest contained most of the critical survival gear. It had one design deficiency, however. The holster, sewn under the left armpit, was too angled. It would be removed and re-sewn in a more vertical position providing better security for the Smith & Wesson .38 Combat Masterpiece during ejection and greater comfort under the parachute harness. The lower front pockets on the vest contained a UHF emergency radio and an emergency beeper. Most pilots chose to discard the beeper and carry a second complete transmit-and-receive-capable radio. Other pockets on the vest carried a signal mirror, a medical kit with drugs ranging from aspirin and salt tablets to morphine and Dexedrine, and along the top of the front of the vest were bandoleer loops for carrying an additional twenty-four rounds of .38 ammunition. Inside pockets held a wire saw, two spare radio batteries, a Day-Glo orange signal panel, a rocket-jet pen flare gun, and even a police whistle. One small box held "emergency rations," which were nothing more than a Chuckles candy bar and some vitamin tablets.

The parachute was standard except for the LPU harness worn over the survival vest and under the parachute. The LPU or life preserver, underarm, consisted of two four-by-six-inch pouches that when activated would inflate into a large orange U-shaped life preserver under each arm. I'd never worn them before, but I knew that if I managed to fly here, I'd often fly over water. As a dedicated nonswimmer, I gladly accepted the slight discomfort of the LPUs.

Was there anything I could think of that I might want to

add to my survival gear? I reached for my briefcase and pulled out my personal handgun, a Beretta .380 semiautomatic with its soft chamois holster. It was a poor effort to look like James Bond, but I thought if some of that worldly spy's confidence could rub off, it certainly wouldn't hurt. Leonard looked me over, bundled in G-suit and survival vest, LPU and parachute. He did a lap of me, then another. Finally, he grabbed a roll of masking tape and taped the holster to my right thigh, near the top of the G-suit. With the Beretta in place, he had me sit down to check whether I would be sitting on it or it would be clear to the side of my leg. Once assured the gun was clear, he quickly marked the G-suit for sewing position and promised it would be taken care of by tomorrow. I was now outfitted, at least in terms of equipment, for combat.

Down the squadron hallway to the right of the life-support area was the lounge, or you might refer to it as the main briefing area. It was a large room with a couple of couches, some nondescript tables, a dozen or so straight-backed chairs, and a refrigerator. On one wall hung a blackboard and a bulletin board. One of the tables had a coffee urn and above the table, a board with about twenty-five variously colored coffee mugs. The room was a "hanging out" place during free time and the unit's auditorium during full squadron meetings. At the back of the room, on your left as you entered from the hallway, were two small cubicles formed with an obviously temporary plywood dividing wall and swinging doors. Each cubicle was about ten by eight feet and served as briefing space for individual flights.

Richter had picked up an additional duty in the squadron as assistant stan-eval officer. Standardization and evaluation was the formal title for what any other business might call quality control. The evaluation portion was obvious. That was the system of flight proficiency checks and testing about the aircraft, procedures, and weapons. Standardization referred to the unit's procedures. It ranged from instrument approaches and departures to tactics and formations flown to things as basic as how you talked on the radio. If everyone was "standard" that meant few misunderstandings and much shorter flight briefings.

With Karl's help we went through a file cabinet collecting the bits and pieces of information necessary to fly an F-105 at Korat. We assembled a pilot's handbook with six-by-eight cards for all of the weapons we might carry on the aircraft. More cards covered things like frequency lists for the radio, emergency procedures for jettisoning ordnance, engaging a jet barrier on the runway, standard recovery procedures, location of navigational stations, and coordinates of contact points for working with forward air controllers or FACs. The stack of cards went into a blue vinyl spiral binder. When we were finished we had more than fifty pages in the book.

Then we added an instrument approach book and both a "dash 34" and a "dash 8" checklist. I already had a -1 checklist, the pocketbook-sized yellow manual that gave step by step procedures for flying the airplane. The -34 was the checklist for inspecting and then setting the cockpit switches to deliver all of the conventional weapons the airplane was capable of carrying. The -8 covered air refueling procedures. Air Force regulations required that the appropriate checklist would be open and in hand for whatever activity was taking place. In reality the books stayed in a G-suit pocket or a canvas carryall bag throughout the flight. The only time anyone ever opened up the checklist was when they were in deep shit and totally out of ideas.

While we collected my kit we caught up with what had happened since we had last seen each other more than three weeks ago in the States. I had met Karl at Stead AFB, right after finishing pilot training. We were both going through the Air Force's basic survival school and we were both headed to Nellis for 105 training, so it was natural that we should pair up. We had been in the same group of ten students during the field training and we had partnered during the two-man escape and evasion portion of the exercise. When we got to Nellis, the four bachelors in our class of nine included Karl and me, so we again spent more than our working days together. I knew him, and I trusted him. He didn't exaggerate or make up stories. And I was pretty sure that, unlike me, he had never had a moment's fear about flying combat.

The usual practice was to allow new pilots a chance to gain some experience before sending them to the heavily defended areas, but the previous week's losses had drastically shortened the time available to get newcomers up to speed. Karl had been sent on a JCS strike against a rail bridge north of Hanoi on his third mission. In the process, he had flown into the blast of a pair of 3,000-pound bombs dropped by another aircraft and had the entire left side of his aircraft stabilator blown off. He grinned as he recounted that flying the tailless bird home "took just a bit of trim." All his story meant to me was that you could get killed flying even one mission. Someone calling his name from down the hall cut the discussion short. We headed toward the ops counter to see who was looking for him.

It was nearly briefing time for Karl's mission and I was shocked when the short, gray-haired major behind the ops desk greeted me with the news that I was going to be flying that afternoon. The older fellow identified himself as Bill Sanders, "everyone calls me Sandy," the squadron operations officer. If I had been approved by the flight surgeon and had gotten my life-support equipment checked out, we were going to fly a local orientation in about two hours. The answers to both his questions were yes, so, long before I had expected to, I was going to be flying in Southeast Asia. It wasn't a combat mission, but it was a large step along what was becoming a very short and steep path. I hadn't had time to chicken out of combat since I'd arrived because no one gave me an opportunity to quit. The assumption was that I would be flying and the need, considering the loss rate of the previous few days, was so great that everyone made sure I wasn't left waiting to get into the war.

Sandy grabbed Ken Hallmark, another of my classmates from Nellis, and told him to take me to the club for lunch and be sure to get me back for a flight briefing by one o'clock. Ken was a short, prematurely balding Air Force Academy graduate who originally came from central Texas. His speech still had a most outrageous Texas twang that fascinated a Chicago product like me. Ken took a set of keys from the truck board and led me out. "Let's get you a hat before you give the squadron a bad name," was his only greeting.

A quick stop at the Thai-run tailor shop next door to the O Club left me sporting one of the olive-drab air commando hats. The issue with the hats wasn't so much style as two other factors. First, there was a bit of superstition about the hats. You needed a hat to survive was the implication. The second factor was that the hats were the "official" source for authenticating your mission count. When you flew a combat mission you inked a hash mark on the band. When you had a hundred hash marks you went home. If you didn't get a hundred hash marks, someone sent your hat home without you. By common agreement, if there was ever any question about your mission count, your hat was the primary source document. You had to have a hat.

Back at the squadron Major Sanders was waiting for me at the front desk. He confirmed that maintenance had a pair of airplanes for us this afternoon, then took me around the flight planning area to show me where everything was. Most combat mission planning would be done at Fort Apache, the command post, where classified maps, call-signs, refueling data, and intelligence information would be available. Today, however, we wouldn't be needing those details.

We went through a normal mission briefing. He pulled out the local publications to show me the layout of the airfield and taxiways, then the departure route and finally a map of Thailand showing the other tactical bases. He described the radio procedures and frequencies along with a short description of who we would be talking to during our flight. When we returned we would fly the tactical TACAN approach before getting a formation radar approach and finally a visual overhead pattern. All of this was pretty standard stuff, but there was a lot of special stuff, too.

Jet aircraft usually start with a ground power cart that generates air to spin the engine up to speed. A typical sequence was "spin 'em, spark 'em and spray 'em." The pilot would signal the crew chief for air to the engine. When the turbine was rotating at a proper speed the start button would be pressed to initiate a spark at the igniter plugs and finally at the required RPM, the throttle would be moved out of the cutoff position to provide fuel to the engine. None of that happened at Korat. All routine engine starts were done with starter cartridges, pyrotechnic devices about the size of a three-pound coffee can that burned to create expanding gases to spin the engine. Simple, yes, but also more dangerous than regular starts with potential for fires, hang fire, explosion and even pilot incapacitation from the noxious fumes. I got briefed on all of the possible occurrences that could screw up the procedure I would be using for every flight from now on.

Since all aircraft takeoffs were fully loaded with ordnance another special procedure was in effect. Water injection was used on every takeoff. Water added two thousand pounds of thrust in afterburner and made a significant difference in the long takeoff rolls. The water was carried in a 36-gallon saddle-shaped tank over the aft section of the engine. After brake release and burner light, the water injection was switched on causing the water to be sprayed into the combustion section of the engine. The water created additional mass in the exhaust which resulted in greater thrust. Because the system was designed exclusively for takeoffs, the tank was not stressed for flight loads while containing water. To ensure that no one could inadvertently wind up flying with a full water tank there was a safety interconnect dump valve that purged the water tank whenever the pressurization of the cockpit was engaged. No pressurization until after takeoff and out of afterburner also meant no air conditioning with the canopy closed and the hot, humid Thai sun beating down on you. Forgetting about the interconnect couldn't be a secret since the water dumped out in a steady stream just forward of the ventral fin looking for all the world like a urinating cow. Loss of water meant aborting the flight.

Once airborne we wouldn't be dealing with traditional air

traffic control. There were no detailed flight plans filed with Los Angeles Center. Here the control was operational, meaning we would tell the controller where we were going and the controller would warn us of other traffic. If we needed to rendezvous with someone we could get vectors from the controller until we could complete the join up visually or with our own radar. Thailand was covered by four ground control intercept (GCI) sites with large radars to direct and deconflict all of the operational traffic. Korat's site had the rather effete call-sign, Dressy Lady. Udorn to the north was named Brigham. Ubon to the east was Lion, and Nakhon Phanom, the small special operations base in Thailand's northeast corner, was Invert.

Sandy would take me for a tour of Thailand with a quick overflight of each of the bases to the east and north of Korat. We wouldn't go by Tahkli, the other F-105 base to the west since that wouldn't normally be on a route to and from a combat mission. The purpose of the flight was to familiarize me with the possible airfields for recovery with a damaged aircraft. If we were lucky, he said, we might be able to find a tanker for a quick dry hookup. During the flight we would be practicing some tactical formation turns. In short, the operations officer was going to make sure I could handle the airplane, do the job and not unnecessarily endanger any of those I flew with. It was all just one more step on the slippery slope leading to the moment of truth when I would find out if I could swallow my fear and meet the enemy.

When we had talked about everything that was going to occur and how it was supposed to happen we were ready to suit up. Unlike a combat sortie or even a stateside training sortie we weren't a scheduled flight. The airplanes were parked on the ramp and waiting for us whenever we wanted to fly them. The weather was good, the price was right, and under any other circumstances going for a joyride in a pair of Thunderchiefs would be as good as life could get.

The mission went as briefed. The cart start was uneventful although the billowing black cloud of acrid smoke that accompanied any flight at Korat was pretty impressive. I managed to make sense of all the radio calls to agencies I'd never before dealt with and not to embarrass myself with the water injection on takeoff.

We overflew Ubon and Nakhon Phanom but then cut away from our track to Udorn when Brigham advised us that a tanker was available if we wanted to tap a few thousand pounds. In the States an aerial refueling was a significant event. Coordination with Strategic Air Command, who owned the tankers, started weeks in advance. Then air traffic control needed to reserve a block of airspace, rerouting everyone in the neighborhood to allow for this critical operation. Detailed preflight briefings and a twenty-minute scripted scenario of specific radio calls and movements had to take place before fuel could flow between airplanes. Here in Thailand, though, it was like being a teen on the streets of Chicago with a length of rubber hose looking for some gas to heist. It was routine, common, no big deal.

It was no big deal until we pulled up on the wing of the tanker. There was a reason his call sign was Red 21 Papa instead of just plain old Red 21. There was a reason he was flying around the area with gas to pass to anyone who went by even though there was a war on. There was a reason he was so eager. The "papa" at the end of his call sign was for the letter P, which indicated that he was configured as a probe and drogue tanker.

There are two ways to refuel in flight. The common USAF way, the way that you see in the movies with Jimmy Stewart flying his B-47 or B-52, is called boom-receptacle. That's where the receiver aircraft opens a door or hatch or slipway and then positions behind the tanker where a boom operator maneuvers a stiff boom into the opening provided. Once you get over the aversion to letting anything come into contact with your airplane while in flight, it's easy. If you can maintain a close formation position and ignore someone poking at you with an eighteen-foot piece of pipe, it's no problem.

The other way is called probe-drogue. This is how the Navy does it, as well as some first-generation refuelable Air Force fighters. The tanker lets a hose dangle in the slipstream with a round metal basket or funnel-shaped gizmo on the end called a drogue. The receiver has a probe that extends from some part of the airplane that must be flown into the basket then pressure must be maintained for fuel to flow through the connection. Whether or not it was easy to do remained to be seen for me, since I'd never done it.

The 105 was one of only two airplanes ever built for the Air Force that had cockpit selectable inflight refueling for either boom or probe. The fact that the training program never bothered to deal with probe and drogue was a good indication that it didn't occur very often for us. While at Nellis we had four-day and one-night refueling missions, but none of them involved even practice extending the probe.

Red 21 Papa was airborne to support an EB-66 electronic countermeasure airplane that had been scheduled to support a mission going way north that afternoon. The mission had been scrubbed, and now Red 21 was trying to unload some gas before going home. Only the EB-66 and the F-100F Wild Weasel aircraft required drogue tankers and there weren't very many of either of them.

We slid up on the tanker's right wing in close formation. Brigham had handed us off to the tanker's discrete UHF refueling frequency so we could talk without restriction. Sandy asked if we could practice a few dry hookups and how much playtime the tanker could spare us. We could see the copilot looking out the cockpit window of the tanker. He waved and indicated that he could play for a lot longer than we could. If we would just wait a second he would wake the boom operator, and we could have about three thousand pounds of fuel apiece. Sandy gave me a big thumbs up, as though this were the best news we could have gotten. I was busy trying to remember whether it was pull and turn or turn and pull to get the refueling handle to change from opening the receptacle to extending the probe.

Sandy positioned behind the tanker boom with its hose extending twelve feet off of what would have been the usual business end. He glanced in the cockpit momentarily and then I saw the probe erect from its hidden compartment on the nose of the aircraft just forward of the windscreen. He moved forward and plugged in. It looked easy enough.

He moved his aircraft forward with the basket covering the nose of the refueling probe, putting a neat loop in the twelve-foot hose and pushing the probe firmly in place so that fuel could flow. About three minutes in this position and he called, "Red 21, that's enough for now. I'm disconnecting."

The boom operator cleared me into position. Out of the corner of my eye I could see Sandy moving to the tanker's far wing as I slid my aircraft back and down from the tanker's wing to a position about thirty feet behind the boom. I bobbled momentarily as I reached down and twisted the refueling handle just above my left knee. The probe came up into view, and I was ready to go. I remembered the briefing comments. All I had to do was stabilize behind the basket with my probe aligned, then look straight ahead and push the throttle forward. Don't try to fly the probe in — just line up and go forward.

Easier said than done. I lined up and moved forward. The basket smoothly moved up and left out of the path of the probe. I backed up and realigned. I moved forward. The basket moved out. Several times I just barely caught the lower right, five o'clock corner of the basket rim, which then tipped and spilled the probe out. I began to sweat. The airflow over the nose of my airplane pushed the basket away each time I got close.

Sandy called on the radio. Calm, mature, wise, he said, "Line up on the top left corner." Nothing more. No lectures, no warnings, no pressure. Just a simple pointer on how to get the job done from someone who knew exactly what I was doing.

I lined up with the probe behind the ten o'clock position on the basket. I jammed the throttle forward and as the basket started to move out of the way the probe clicked into place. I was connected. "You've got fuel flow," the boomer radioed.

I got three thousand pounds of gas and disconnected. Sandy thanked the Red 21 pilot, we switched frequencies, and in close formation dropped down and away. Brigham gave us a vector to the initial approach fix at Korat and we headed home.

We flew a TACAN approach then a GCA in formation. Finally we entered the visual traffic pattern and landed. As we taxied in, I felt a strange mixture of pride and embarrassment. I'd flown an operational sortie. It wasn't a combat flight, but it wasn't a training school mission either. I was twelve thousand miles from home in the most exciting airplane in the world doing things that most people can't even imagine. But, I was taxiing in to park in an airplane with no bomb racks, with no Sidewinders, with no contribution to what was going on in the war.

Sandy was already in the blue crew van with a white towel around his neck. The airman driving the van lifted the lid of a Coleman cooler sitting on the engine cowl of the truck and I could see the neatly rolled rows of towels inside. I grabbed one and it was icy cold. I unrolled it and wiped my face, neck, and arms. It felt good, unbelievably good. Whoever thought up this custom should get a bonus.

We went through maintenance debrief and reported the status of our aircraft. In the squadron building we finished up the paperwork, then Sandy took me back to one of the flight briefing cubicles, where he recounted the events of the mission. He seemed more than satisfied with my performance, even accepting the delays and wrestling with the probe and drogue tanker. He looked at me and said, "Get over to intel and take the ROE test by tomorrow so we can get you on the schedule." He never thought to ask me if I wanted to fly combat. It was a given. One more step on the slippery slope.

CHAPTER 7

Rules of Engagement

Yossarian knew that you had to be crazy to fly combat. But you couldn't fly combat if you were crazy. If you turned yourself in as crazy so that you couldn't fly combat that would clearly be the act of a sane person, so you couldn't really be crazy and you must fly combat. Yossarian knew all this and he recognized it as the "catch." It was Catch-22. Yossarian might have known the people who wrote the Rules of Engagement. It was many years after that fictional account of a reluctant bombardier in a B-25 squadron in Sicily, yet the insanity of the situation was as fresh during that summer in 1966 as Joseph Heller ever could have imagined.

At about six A.M. the morning after my local flight, I hopped a truck in front of the hootch. The guys scheduled for the morning missions had been long gone by the time the sun came up so there weren't many people around when I shaved, showered, and shrugged into my flying suit. I couldn't help but notice that my boots were shinier than they had ever been, the result of our Thai hootch maid's attention on the previous day. The 1505s I'd worn on the flight from Clark were also washed, pressed, and hanging in the closet. The process of dying or facing your fears in combat didn't equate with being unkempt.

I met a couple of guys from the squadron at the O Club, where they were having a second cup of coffee after having served as spares for the morning flights. Although the fear was still in the back of my mind, I was beginning to realize that activity and interaction with the others was helping me to take each successive step in this process. If I didn't have time to think about the final possibilities, the intermediate activities were all doable. I still couldn't quite hack a full breakfast, but I had a cup of coffee and then hopped in the back of the red Datsun when it pulled out for the squadron building.

Down at the compound I didn't bother to go into the squadron operations area but instead went right to the Command Post, Fort Apache. I flashed my restricted area badge to the guard at the gate and entered the sandbagged, concertina-wire-festooned complex, headed up the stairs past all the pictures of battle-damaged 105s, and took a left turn inside the door to the intelligence area. I caught the attention of one of the NCOs huddled over a multicolored map of North Vietnam and told him I needed to read the ROE and take the test. He grunted and pulled a tattered loose-leaf binder out of a bookshelf on the wall behind him and handed it to me. "Use the debrief area over there until the first missions start coming in," he said, motioning with a marker-stained index finger.

The binder was at least four inches thick and had apparently been compiled in chronological order as the "rules" evolved. Tattered sheets of slick fax paper, irregularly cut then hole-punched and now ripped loose from constant reference, were interspersed with remnants of what was once a properly printed and bound book. Most of the pages were rubber stamped in red or blue ink, denoting some level of classification, usually "Secret." Whether it was classified material or not, it quickly became apparent that there was benefit to reading the material in the secure atmosphere of the intelligence section since continual reference to the huge multicolored wall map would be necessary to decipher the restrictions.

Whenever a series of coordinates appeared in the ROE book, the quickest way to make sense of them was to find one of the points on the map. Inevitably the point would have a colored line through it, and when you followed the line to a junction or turn point, you would quickly see what the particular paragraph was describing. It was also apparent that there was considerable parochialism involved in establishing the ROE. Like medieval Europe, the Southeast Asian peninsula was divided and fenced into petty fiefdoms, some defining radar control, others operational restrictions and some sanctuaries of safety. Each sphere of control related to someone's command structure and protected his particular realm of authority. How could we fight, let alone win a war, under these rules?

Starting with what I had seen during yesterday's flight, I examined the definitions for Thailand. U.S. forces used six airbases in the country. Along with Korat were Udorn, Ubon, Tahkli, Utapao, and Nakhon Phanom. One for SAC tankers, four for fighters, and one for special operations. Four radar control centers for air traffic control and refueling coordination: Lion, Brigham, Invert, and Dressy Lady. Four dedicated refueling tracks: Red, White, Blue, and Green, each with high and low altitude reservations and all with extension tracks pointed northward over Laos, toward the area west of Hanoi. Figuring from our latitude at Korat of around 14 degrees to the limit of the tanker track extensions at 20 degrees north, I quickly calculated that we would be running about 360 miles to the point where we would be on our own.

To the east and north of Thailand was Laos. The southern half of Laos was code-named Steel Tiger, while the northern part was called Barrel Roll. A chunk of the country was cross-hatched on the maps with its own name, Tiger Hound. These names that now identified chunks of a country had once been the code names of military operations. Each of the three areas had its own chapter in the ROE book, outlining not only frequencies and controlling agencies for operations, but also providing detailed restrictions on what ordnance could be employed under what conditions and at what time of day or night.

The Laotian areas were pocked with red dots identified as Lima or Romeo sites. Some of these denoted dirt airfields for special operations aircraft. Others marked the locations of TACAN stations, the trashcan-sized radio beacons that provided navigation aid in the form of radials and distance-measuring signals for our aircraft. Some parts of the country might be controlled by good guys and some by bad guys, and judging by the number of revisions in the ROE book, that control changed almost daily.

South Vietnam was outlined on the maps in red with crosshatching on the Vietnamese side of the border with Laos, Cambodia, and North Vietnam. The paragraphs on that area were brief and to the point. Aircraft from Thai bases were forbidden to deliver any kind of ordnance for any reason. We could land at South Vietnam bases in an emergency, but we couldn't fly any combat missions "in-country." How foolish of me to think the war was there. South Vietnam was indeed defended. It was isolated, fortressed, and revetted against a fighter pilot from Thailand doing anything to support the American ground forces engaged against the Viet Cong. The battlements were bureaucratic. It was all in the ROE.

As I turned to the chapters dedicated to operations in North Vietnam, the ridiculous gave way to the absurd. I couldn't discern whether the enemy was the North Vietnamese or the U.S. Navy. The enemy might just as easily have been the State Department or even the Joint Chiefs of Staff. They all seemed to have a voice in the ROE, and the tone of the voice was seldom in favor of winning the war, defeating the enemy, or even ensuring the fighter pilot's chances of survival.

The country of North Vietnam always resembled a pork chop in my mind. The arcing coastline from China in the northeast to South Vietnam at the seventeenth parallel was the rib bone. The loin was the Red River Valley, with the meaty section stretching along the Chinese border to a peak north of Thai Nguyen then west to the mountains surrounding the famous French battlefield at Dien Bien Phu. The loin tapered south of the Black River to a shank that ran almost two hundred fifty miles past Bartholomy Pass down to Mu Gia, where the butchers of Geneva cut it off evenly at the seventeenth parallel again.

When the Pentagon whiz kids divvied up the meat between the Air Force and the Navy, they probably figured the Air

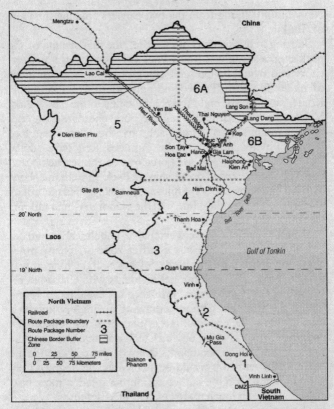

North Vietnam, depicting the six route packages, the major railroad lines to China, the border buffers, and the significant towns.

Force would be happy with lots of protein while the Navy knew the meat closest to the bone, the coastline, would be the sweetest. The whole of North Vietnam was carved into Route Packages divided between the Air Force flying from our bases in Thailand with occasional help from the guys flying out of Danang, just barely into South Vietnam, and the

Navy aircraft flying from the two carriers cruising the Gulf of Tonkin.

Starting at the seventeenth parallel, the first section of the pork chop's shank was Route Pack I. This was Air Force territory and would be the semi-benign training area for those of us going North. Proceeding northward up the rib bone, Route Packs II, III, and IV were allocated to the Navy. Pack V was the western chunk of the pork chop's meaty end, mostly mountainous terrain split by the Black and Red Rivers. Finally, there was the ominous Red River delta, Route Package VI. The Air Force owned Route Pack V exclusively, but it shared ownership of Pack VI with the Navy. The Air Force owned VI-Alpha and the Navy had control of VI-Bravo. The dividing line was the Hanoi to China rail line that ran to the northeast.

Combat restrictions were extensive, unbelievable, and decidedly illogical. There was a buffer zone of twenty miles along the entire northern border of NVN and China. It was designed to avoid international incidents with China but restricted not only delivery of ordnance but even maneuvering within the airspace. Although drawing a squiggly line on a map matching the convolutions of the boundary between the countries was easy, the obvious fact was that the airborne fighter pilot had few landmarks that would readily define the buffer. The net result would be a considerably larger safety zone for China forcing our aircraft into a smaller, more hazardous area with much more concentrated defenses.

The major cities of Hanoi and Haiphong were restricted. Each boasted a full paragraph of detailed numbers in the ROE that when plotted on a map described a circle. Hanoi got a ten-mile-radius circle, while the port city got only five.

The details of the rules for North Vietnam were the truly sticky part. Lists of coordinates described the locations of a new phenomenon in aerial warfare. Carefully plotted were the sites for surface-to-air missile batteries. The SAM sites had been bulldozed and graded then photographed by our reconnaissance aircraft. They were off-limits while under construction but could be attacked once they were completely built. To confirm that they were actually no longer under construction, the SAM site had to be observed firing a missile at you. Sure, that makes a lot of sense.

Enemy airfields, which were plainly marked on the maps and much easier to see than SAM sites, were also protected. No longer did we have the onerous restrictions that had frustrated Korean War fighter pilots. No Yalu River and China sanctuary. No, now we let the airfields within the battle area remain inviolate. Enemy aircraft could be engaged, but only after positive visual identification and only if they were definitely airborne. For us, there would be no dastardly attacks of aircraft in the traffic pattern or while parked on the ramp.[1]

The rules went on to describe the political constraints that we must abide by. Targets within Route Pack VI were strictly controlled by the National Command Authority, which is fighter pilot terminology for the president and the Joint Chiefs of Staff. The only targets we could strike in RP VI were ones that Washington had specifically approved. No targets of opportunity were allowed. Not even emergency jettison was approved. Adding insult to the blatantly obvious potential for injury was the restriction that Air Force aircraft could not drop in the VI-B area without the Navy's prior approval.

I read the rules and cross-checked with the big wall maps for several hours. A lot of it didn't make much sense, but since this was my first war I could only assume that it was typical. If Catch-22 had any basis in fact, it only could lead to the conclusion that similar restrictions and rules had existed in World War II.

My reverie, which alternated between concentrated study and stunned amazement at the convolutions of the rules, was interrupted by Kenny Hallmark coming toward my desk at a high rate of speed. He was obviously looking for me.

"Hey, Raz, get your butt in gear. Get the damn test knocked

---

1. ROE varied over time, with some of the restrictions loosened and others tightened. Rules regarding haven for enemy aircraft, for example, shifted back and forth considerably during the war.

out and get down to the main briefing room. They need you to spare a flight."

My stomach flipped and my knees went weak. I wasn't ready for my first combat mission. I had a couple of days to go before I would finish my study. I couldn't do it right now. It was too soon. I gulped and looked at Ken's smiling face. He obviously had no idea of the turmoil going on inside me. "Huh? A flight? Now?"

"Yeah, it's a four-ship. I'm flying Four, and we lost our spare. Briefing's in half an hour. Get moving. The ROE test will only take about ten minutes." He turned to the intel sergeant and said, "Hey, Sarge, lemme have the ROE test."

I swallowed hard and looked at the raggedy handful of sheets he handed me. The test had been used hard and was so heavily annotated that only a blind man could fail to distinguish the right answers for the twenty-five multiple-choice questions. The test was obviously just a square to be filled and wasn't meant to prevent anyone from flying the missions. No one would be a Rules-of-Engagement lawyer after taking the test, but someone could always say that all of the pilots were trained in the ROE. Kenny was wrong. It didn't take me ten minutes to finish the test. It only took six.

CHAPTER 8

First Counter

With the ROE test out of the way, I had nothing left to hide behind. I would either fly or I wouldn't. No one seemed to question whether I was ready or not. It was a foregone conclusion. I swallowed hard then headed down the hall to the flight planning area just outside of the main briefing room.

Bill Ricks and Kenny Hallmark were already hunched over the flight planning table. The leader of the flight was a burly mountain of a man who already had more than ninety missions, Maj. Brown Howard. The flight's element leader was my flight commander, Capt. Jim Mitchell. I would be the spare, in case one of the four primary fliers had an aircraft problem that prevented him from flying. I would brief, plan, preflight, and taxi with the flight, staying with them until all four were airborne. Then if I were not needed, I would be released to taxi back to the parking space and shut down.

Mitchell took the lead, showing me the wall bins on the west side of the planning area that held each flight's intelligence materials. For each member of the flight, the intelligence staff prepared a map with the target plotted and colored circles denoting the type and range of enemy air defenses, along with a five-by-seven-inch lineup card with the target coordinates, and the radio frequencies and code words to be used to report various occurrences. The target had a two-word identifier. If the attack was successful, a code word said so. If MiGs or SAMs were encountered, there was a code word for the event. If weather was bad, there was a word.

With a map and a card in my clammy grip, we went to the

bulletin board, where a clipboard hung. On the clipboard we found the call sign for our flight and the details such as take-off time, refueling track and tanker call sign if there was to be an air refueling available, the type and quantity of ordnance to be carried along with the fusing and any other pertinent details.

Armed with the necessary maps, cards, and data, the five of us gathered around a large, waist-high planning table. Under the Plexiglas top was a map of the entire Southeast Asian peninsula. Just as on our individual maps, the ominous colored circles denoted the coverage of anti-aircraft guns and SAMs. As the flight lead, Brownie Howard was drawing the route of flight to the target area in grease pencil on the plastic tabletop. I didn't think I could get any more frightened until I saw the black triangle that marked the target. It wasn't in Route Pack I. The flight was going to the Black River Valley, just to the east of Dien Bien Phu. We were going to Pack V, the meatier part of the pork chop.

A raspy growl from a field phone in the far corner of the room interrupted our concentration. An intel sergeant walking by picked up the receiver, listened for a moment, then called across the room, "Are you guys Maple flight?" We were. The sergeant continued, "Maintenance just told command post that you won't be getting a spare. In fact, they said you're only going to get two birds. Wanna talk to 'em?" Howard shook his head no.

Howard looked around the map table, then to Mitchell. "You want to go or do you want one of the lieutenants to take it?" Mitchell had just returned from the Fighter Weapons School at Nellis and was eager to get back into combat flying. He didn't reply, but simply motioned with his thumb in the classic umpire's gesture to the three of us. We were scrubbed. I was reprieved at least for the moment. We dumped our maps and code cards in the classified waste barrel near the door and headed out the back entrance.

In the squadron building we were met by Ken Kerkering. He notified me that since I was assigned to C flight and since there was now room in the C-flight hootch, I could move my stuff in tonight. If I wanted to share a room with Ricks, that would be fine. I looked at Bill, and he nodded his assent. We had both been in the same pilot training class at Williams, and knew each other fairly well. It would be a comfortable pairing. The duty officer behind the ops counter said he didn't have anything for us, and it was fairly late in the afternoon so we could take off and move my stuff from the temporary quarters. Somehow I didn't think I would miss the midnight wakeups from Glen Nix roaring into the room. And I certainly wouldn't miss the gloomy predictions about the Golden BB that was sure to get us all eventually.

Bill and I got keys to one of the red Datsun pickups from the duty officer then checked around to see if anyone needed a lift to the quarters area. As we walked out of the squadron building, we stepped aside to let a group of sweat-soaked guys in the door to the parachute shop. We managed to overhear their chatter. The guns had been particularly bad and the route to the target had been mandated by Seventh Air Force in Saigon. Tahkli, the other F-105 base, had lost two airplanes that morning and our sister squadron, the 469th, had lost a pilot too. It was a guy we knew from the squadron back at Nellis. Dinner would be hard to swallow again tonight.

After I got my stuff moved from the temporary room and reasonably arranged in the room that would probably be my home for the rest of my life, it was nearly five o'clock. The knowledge that an airplane being shot down was not an unusual occurrence had been pressed on me again, but brooding in the room wasn't a choice. The schedule for the next day would be posted on the bulletin board at the entrance to the Officers' Club. I might not be able to gag down dinner, but I needed to know what tomorrow held for me. Ricks and I hopped back into the Datsun and headed for the club.

The dirty purple sheet of mimeograph paper was already there under the Plexiglas just to the left of the door. Twenty sorties were listed for the 421st: four flights of four and two two-ship missions, along with spares for each of the four-ships. A Roman numeral was neatly printed after each flight call sign. It didn't take long to see that the number referred to each flight's primary target area. All four of the four-ship missions had a prominent "VI" listed — they were headed to Hanoi. The two-ships both had a single numeral, "I." The ten o'clock briefing, call sign Redwood, also had something else listed. My name.

I must have slept at least a little bit, but the impression I had was that I rolled and tossed for most of the night. At first light I got showered and slipped on a clean flight suit. It didn't take long with the door to the room open to see a couple of other guys in flying clothes gathering around one of the red Datsuns. I joined the bunch, said my good mornings, and then shut up like a good lieutenant. The truck dropped those wanting breakfast at the club then headed down to the squadron building. I wasn't up to breakfast, so I stayed aboard.

The three hours between arriving at the squadron and heading over to the command post for briefing disappeared in an instant, demonstrating once again that conundrum of time, that Christmas never comes but bad news never waits. My commitment to flying at least one mission before quitting to maintain at least a shred of honor was wavering badly as I shuffled across the quadrangle and through the chainlink fence.

My flight lead was Van Heywood, a short, blonde captain who had more than eighty missions inked onto the sweaty band of his hat. He didn't look frightened a bit. In fact he looked downright cheery. We shook hands and went through the formalities of introduction since we hadn't had much chance to associate until that moment. He then started to lead me through the same process that Jim Mitchell had started the day before.

The target was a military storage area at the north end of an abandoned airfield, Dong Hoi, in Route Pack I. We were going to be carrying two M-118 bombs each. It was a weapon I hadn't heard of before, so Heywood quickly explained that they were 3,000-pound general purpose bombs. We carried one on each wing and we would drop them simultaneously because they were so heavy that dropping just one could unbalance the aircraft and render it virtually unfly-able. We also would carry a 650-gallon centerline fuel tank. No refueling was planned for the mission.

Briefing followed map preparation and a weather check. Van didn't waste a lot of time with basics that a stateside peacetime briefing would normally have covered. He talked about the preflight of the bombs — keep your toes out from under when you shake the bomb for security on the pylon. He talked about water injection procedures — don't piss the water away by forgetting about the interconnect to the pres-surization system. He talked about formation to and from the target — stay forward where I can see you easily and don't get in the way of my maneuvering. He didn't mention dying or being a prisoner or having one last chance to quit before takeoff.

Step time, the time at which you are suited up with all your equipment and ready to step out of the building, was one hour before the scheduled takeoff time. I couldn't find a place to hide and I didn't know anyone in the building well enough to talk to about my fear, so I found myself in the parachute shop donning my G-suit, which was now weighted down with hunting knife, nylon line, day/night flares, and my personal Beretta. Next I put on the survival vest then I walked over to the open floor safe, where I picked up the Smith & Wesson Combat Masterpiece I'd been issued. Next came the LPU and parachute. Finally, I took my helmet with the suddenly gaudy, bright-red enameled visor cover and slid it into my helmet bag. Loaded down with about eighty pounds of parachute and supplemental gear, I waddled out the door in trail of my leader.

Somehow the airplane seemed bigger than it had ever been. The description of the bombs during briefing didn't re-ally prepare me for an iron shape that was eighteen feet long mounted on each wing. They were huge.

I was already pretty well soaked with sweat in the midday sun as I hustled around the airplane for preflight then up the ladder with the crew chief right behind me to help me get strapped in and ready for start. Time to quit has run out. The only possibility left is an abort, some sort of mechanical malfunction to keep the airplane from safely completing the mission. But what do you use for judging safe when the mission itself is so obviously dangerous? If safety was important, what was I doing here?

Patterns of behavior begin to take over. Setting up the cockpit gets my mind occupied. Then I hear the whistle and whine from down the row of aircraft, where Heywood has fired the start cart on his aircraft. I look back toward both wingtips to clear the area and then raise my hand to give the familiar wind up signal to the crew chief, who is waiting patiently with a fire extinguisher near the tail pipe on my left side. My airplane is now whining and the black, acrid smoke of the cart swirls around the revetment. Thirty seconds for the engine to come to idle, and now I'm up and running.

Systems are checked, radar is good, and the Doppler navigation coordinates have been set up for takeoff and the first navigation point. The radio pops, "Redwood, check," and I mechanically respond, "Two." We taxi, arm, and are on the runway for takeoff before I am fully prepared. We're going. Lead releases brakes and I'm rocked slightly by engine blast as he moves forward and his A/B lights. I'm watching the second hand of the clock, waiting for twelve seconds to pass so I can release brakes. Rolling now. Burner light. Water on. Check speed is 102 knots at two thousand feet. Nose wheel up and, after the longest takeoff roll I've ever experienced, I'm finally airborne.

Gear up, flaps to maneuver, water off, and start a turn to cut off lead. Holding the A/B until four hundred knots and turning well inside to get plenty of geometric cutoff. A good rejoin should happen within 90 degrees of turn, and I'm going to make a good rejoin.

I slide onto Heywood's inside wing in the climbing right turn. He looks at me and gives a thumbs-up meaning my airplane is okay. I flash a thumbs-up back to say he looks fine too. He taps his helmet and flashes five fingers on his right hand. I reach down and switch my UHF radio to channel five

and hear the channelization hum quit just in time to hear
"Redwood . . ." I snap, "Two."

I listen to Heywood calling Invert with our mission code as
he yaws his airplane with a quick kick of the rudder back and
forth. That's the signal to move out of close formation to a
more comfortable route position, four to six ship-widths
wide. I'm barely reestablished there when he yaws again,
meaning move out to our combat tactical spread. I look right
then roll hard and pull away. Throttle up and start edging up
to a perch position about three thousand feet wide and a
thousand above him. I'm trying to conserve energy to get
line abreast but those huge bombs make the airplane slug-
gish, even though we're climbing at 450 knots. He's given
me about 2 percent power advantage, and I shouldn't expect
more. If I really get out of position there's always afterburner, but that's bad form and means I'll be out of gas long
before my leader if I have to use it.

Once out on the perch I punch on the autopilot altitude
hold. Heywood has probably done the same thing, so all I
need to do to maintain position is move the throttle occasionally up or back a percent. If I drift in or out, I step lightly on
the rudder to yaw back into place. Heywood knows I'm on
my first mission, so he checks my position and gives a quick
radio correction. "Just a bit wider, Redwood." I adjust.

I've got time now to check my Doppler nav position
against the TACAN, which I've tuned to Ubon. It takes less
than twenty minutes to pass north of the Phantom base,
home of the 8th Tac Fighter Wing. I play with the radar,
reaching out to eighty miles in front of my airplane and seeing the dark, snakelike shape of the Mekong River, the border between Thailand and Laos. We're heading directly
toward it, level at nineteen thousand feet. I turn the heat up
with the air conditioning rheostat because my hands and feet
are ice cold, but I know it's fear not the climate. My back
feels clammy where sweat hasn't dried on my cotton flying
suit.

Minutes pass and we've overflown the brown waters of
the Mekong and passed into Laos, home of the shadow

war — the war that doesn't exist but that kills you just as dead. I'm now flying an armed aircraft in hostile territory. If I turn back now I get credit for a combat mission. It wouldn't be a North Vietnam mission, but it would be combat time. Should I? Can I find something wrong with the airplane? No. The bird is perfect. I'm still going.

We change radio channels to talk to Cricket, the airborne command and control post. Cricket is a C-130 transport loaded with radios and the war-making version of air traffic control. They've got our mission number and time logged. The controller cheerily tells us the target area weather is great and wishes us good hunting. Cricket is actually flying somewhere off our nose to the right, about thirty miles away and higher. I search the area with my radar but can't find the bogey. It occurs to me that if a transport full of controllers isn't afraid to be in this area, I shouldn't be so scared either.

Now the ground below is revealing that a war really goes on here. The jungle is broken by huge limestone karst formations rising hundreds of feet in shades of gray over the dark green of the jungle canopy. Large areas are pocked with craters that have destroyed the trees and exposed the red dirt road networks below. Like huge, complicated ant hills, the trails are blocked by water filled craters and alternate routes have been created to get by the obstructions. In one area I see a stream and the pylons of a long-destroyed bridge surrounded by more craters. The road splits at least a dozen times into detours with crossings at several spots upstream and down from the bridge site. Apparently the loss of the bridge hasn't reduced the traffic.

I'm jerked back to the job at hand as I look back at Redwood Lead to see him turning easily toward me. I grasp the stick grip and the autopilot relinquishes control. I see the reason for the turn: A towering cumulous cloud several miles ahead is blocking our route. I edge the throttle forward in anticipation of the return to course, which will be a turn away from me. The radar now shows the clear coastal outline forty miles ahead of us. We've crossed into North Vietnam. I'm in Route Pack I.

The sun is incredibly bright and the Gulf of Tonkin is deep blue. Sandy beaches and white breakers of surf line the coast. The last fifteen miles the terrain flattens out, and the mountains and limestone karst become farmland, with small villages and square fields. I'm on the right wing as we reach the coast and Heywood enters an easy turn away calling on the radio, "Redwood Two, have you got the airfield at ten o'clock low? Target is on the north end about three hundred meters west. Take thirty seconds spacing and try to hit my bomb smoke. I'll be off left." Below us, in the green flatlands less than a mile in from the beach, is the abandoned runway of Dong Hoi airfield, cratered into unusability, maybe by us in this war or maybe by the French in the fifties.

I swallow twice and acknowledge, "Redwood Two." Now I'm scrambling because I've forgotten to set my weapons switches. I take spacing off of Lead and start recalling the training sequence of switch setting — two, five, and two. I've got to set two switches on the radar to drop a bomb, set five selections on the weapons panel, and finish with two settings on the sight.

The radar is already on and in a ground-attack mode. Two down. Now I choose "conventional bombs" on the weapons selector. I punch the inboard pylon buttons in. I flip the toggle switch to "arm nose/tail" for fusing. I set the mode to manual release, then raise the red guard from the master arm switch and flip the toggle. The station buttons light up green — my bombs are ready to go. Finally I turn the sight reticle brilliance up and crank in 104 mils of depression. Two, five, and two. Done.

I roll in to the left and see Heywood's airplane tracking across the ground in a left turn across a huge circle from me. Smoke suddenly blooms just off the north end of the runway as his bombs detonate. I check the altimeter and see we've descended to just under ten thousand feet. My planned release is at thirty-five hundred feet above the ground in a 30-degree dive at five hundred knots. I put the pipper below the smoke cloud and watch the tapes spinning as the airspeed builds and the altitude decreases. That's it, pickle. The plane lurches as it releases 6,000 pounds of bombs from its wings, and I start the pullout. Nose up to the horizon and roll hard right. Stop the roll. Pull up and now come back to the left searching high for Lead. Got him in sight. Calling, "Redwood Two's off hot, Lead in sight."

Lead acknowledges, "Roger. Rolling out 260 climbing to twenty-four thousand." I've got a cutoff angle and I'm closing fast, holding 550 knots. I fan the speed brakes to stop with about fifty feet of clearance on his left wing then drift slowly into fingertip formation position. Heywood looks at me and gives a thumbs up. I return the signal and he yaws me out to route formation. We climb back toward the mountains and the jungle and the Mekong and home. I'm alive. I've flown a mission and survived. I can quit any time I want now, and no one can say I didn't try it at least once.

I'm not sure if I'm elated or relieved. After my fear, the flight was anticlimactic. It certainly wasn't filled with the sort of drama that I'd expected, but it also wasn't the type of threat that would have men like Glen Nix fearing those guns that couldn't be defeated. What could I make of the event?

After landing, one of the Datsuns meets us as we climb down the ladder. Kenny Hallmark is grinning at me from behind the wheel. With his south Texas drawl he inquires, "How'd it all go?" Did he have a similar experience a week or two ago, facing his own fear, or is he just making small talk? I mumble an "Okay" and quickly jump in the back of the tiny pickup. Ken rolls down the line of revetments and picks up Van.

The sequence after landing will always be the same. First a stop at maintenance debrief, where we fill out the aircraft log and report any discrepancies or problems. Then to the squadron building to shed our flying gear, followed by a quick walk over to the Command Post for intelligence and operations debriefing. We are asked what we saw, where we dropped, what defenses we encountered, and what results we estimate from the strike. It ends with a flight debrief in which the leader corrects, compliments, and complains about how things went within the flight.

Our airplanes were in good condition so maintenance didn't take long. Intel wasn't too worried about our little two-ship flight; they were more interested in the group just entering the building who had been on the large strike to Pack VI that morning. Two airplanes had been lost and the nervous chatter of the crews was a good indication that the adrenaline hadn't quite left their systems.

That left the flight debriefing. It wasn't very long either. Van quickly recounted the high points of the flight and corrected only a couple of things that I had or hadn't done to his satisfaction. I asked him if that was a typical mission on a typical target. He gave me the tolerant look of an old-timer guiding an ignorant child and shook his head.

"No," he said, "they're all a bit different. This was fairly easy because the weather was good and we only had each other to worry about. The target has been struck a lot, and we've lost quite a few airplanes in the area. Don't be lulled by the fact that you don't see any shooting. They're shooting at you all the time. Keep your speed up. Keep your aircraft moving. Don't be predictable. Don't be stupid. Keep your head on a swivel. They're shooting every mission."

That was all. Now the question was whether I could do it again. I thought I could. Just one more time. Two would be better than one. Just one more.

CHAPTER 9

Intrigue and Error

Bill Ricks and Karl Richter were waiting on the doorstep when I got back to the hootch. I got the obligatory handshake on successful completion of my first combat mission. Then they announced that we were invited to barbecue some steaks with three of the guys who were TDY from Kadena. The beef had come on a C-130 from their home squadron in a Styrofoam ice chest that afternoon and it would be a lot better than anything on the menu locally. The guys had flown a couple of missions with Karl, and they asked him to bring his friends over for dinner and beers. It would beat dinner at the club, and although I hadn't been at Korat long enough to wear out the menu of the O Club, Karl and Ricks both thought that a bit of variety was a good idea.

I got out of my sweaty flying suit and ran through the shower quickly. Bermuda shorts and a polo shirt were the standard off-duty outfit. We headed down the gravel street to the building where I had spent my first night. The three Kadena pilots, all captains with plenty of F-105 experience, were Glen Nix, Wayne Fullam, and Pike Grubbs. Nix I had met on that first night. Fullam was a recruiting poster version of a fighter pilot: tall, muscular, crew-cut, with a good ol' boy Georgia drawl. Pike was the spitting image of Yosemite Sam, the cartoon character with the huge red handlebar mustache. The only difference was that Pike's 'stache was blonde. In every other characteristic he was the feisty little miner. He was short, wore cowboy boots, and displayed a "call my bluff" kind of arrogance that was initially intimidating but soon dissolved into fun.

We broke out cold cans of Carlings from the hootch refrigerator and sat around on lawn chairs waiting for the charcoal hibachi to reach operating temperature. Small talk lasted about five minutes. Then the subject shifted to serious stuff like weapons and tactics and people. It appeared that the Kadena guys weren't impressed with the skills or courage of most of the folks in the 421st. No one flying 105s into North Vietnam was going to be accused of cowardice; it certainly wasn't at that level. They were concerned about sharing the load. There were clearly recognizable gradations of risk depending on where the target was and they seemed to suspect that some folks were getting more than their fair share of high-threat targets.

Most of the high mission count folks in the 421st had come from McConnell AFB in Kansas when the permanent squadron was formed. Prior to that time the war had been fought on a TDY basis — temporary duty trips for sixty or ninety days. Eager aggressive fighter pilots volunteered for the missions and less aggressive folks stayed home. There were always good reasons for not volunteering: kids in school, wife to take care of, finishing up a correspondence course for a military school, or an incipient case of the sniffles.

When the permanent units were established, the logical solution to manning them was to take qualified pilots who didn't have any missions logged. That would lead to some stability in the organizations because most of the assignees would be around for a full one-hundred-mission tour. But it also meant that the unit would be packed with some fairly reluctant warriors. The problem that the folks in the Kadena squadron had recognized was that they were being asked to shoulder more risk than the permanent party troops in the squadron. It was one thing to be courageous and another to be always placed at the pointy end of the spear. It was going to be unfair if outsiders were required to fly into the defenses around Hanoi every day while a group of folks who had been together back in Kansas took care of each other on the schedule. Bombing old craters at Dong Hoi, as I had done that morning, was not how it always was.

The night wore on, and we began to get into war stories. I had none to tell from my single milk run, so it was my uncharacteristic task to keep my big mouth shut and listen. There was plenty of excitement available, but the most interesting story was from the day before my arrival. It told the reason for Nix's flushed exuberance the night we first met, as well as the details of Richter's battle damage. It also illustrated the issue of outsiders and new arrivals being tabbed for the most hazardous missions. None of it did my self-confidence a bit of good.

The target had been the Bac Giang railroad bridge, a critical interdiction point along the northeast railroad from Hanoi to China and just a few miles from the MiG base at Kep. SAMs and flak were defending the bridge and they had claimed several 105s in the week leading up to Nix and Karl's mission. Typically the targets around Hanoi were selected in Washington by the president and secretary of defense, with occasional input from the Joint Chiefs of Staff. Once a target was assigned it was attacked daily until it was destroyed. Get the target quickly and you might get a week of respite from dangerous missions. Fail and you would go back again and again.

Despite being a temporary member of the squadron, Nix had been assigned to lead the mission. Richter had been scheduled as a spare, since he'd only had time to get three missions under his belt. In a perfect world, Karl wouldn't have been anywhere near a mission that dangerous, but with the losses of the previous week including both the squadron commander and the operations officer it was almost inevitable that he would be thrown into the cauldron. With a courage that I could only envy, both Glen and Karl showed no surprise at the scheduling. Without going into great detail, which would have been greeted with hoots and snickers from any typical group of fighter pilots, Karl simply recounted that he got the order to launch when one of the McConnell senior squadron members aborted in the arming area.

Nix had taken out the bridge. That was it; nothing fancy about it. He'd pressed the target, gotten up close so he couldn't miss, and dumped the two 3,000-pounders on the bridge. The flak was heavy, SAMs were fired, and two airplanes were lost on the mission. On the return, while over the Gulf of Tonkin during poststrike refueling, Nix had reported success code words, and he was immediately ordered to divert to Saigon, where he could report directly to the intelligence people at Seventh Air Force headquarters. His element leader would take the rest of the flight back to Korat. Nix had just returned to the base on the evening I arrived, flush with the celebration of being surprisingly decorated with the Silver Star while in Saigon.

Karl had performed well, but had lost track of the other aircraft in his flight while maneuvering to attack the bridge. With SAMs airborne and intense flak, he dropped his bombs and then found an F-105 heading away from the target. He rushed to join up, but suddenly realized something was wrong. The aircraft ahead of him, heading away from the target was still bomb laden. Karl stroked the afterburner and started to close on the fleeing aircraft at low altitude when suddenly the airplane jettisoned both of the 3,000-pound bombs. He told how he had seen the bombs come off the airplane in level flight and start to arc slowly to the ground. He hadn't yet realized that the time of flight of the bombs was more than enough to arm them. Without thinking he flew straight ahead over the bombs, just as they impacted the jungle and detonated below his aircraft. The blast rocked the airplane upward from the tail section, momentarily causing it to pitch nose down. Reacting to the surge, Karl pulled back on the stick and felt the airplane start to level, then roll slightly to the left. Acting instinctively he clicked the trim button several times back to the right and leveled his wings. High to the right he saw three other 105s climbing out of the area and heading toward the Gulf of Tonkin. He headed toward them to rejoin with some friendlies.

When he got closer he recognized Nix's tail number and slid into fingertip position. That was when a visual check by his flight leader told Karl the result of the bomb blast. All of the left side of the slab but a small stub of twisted metal had been blown away. Shrapnel holes peppered the underside of

the engine's afterburner section. There was no fluid streaming from the holes, which would have been the telltale sign
of hydraulic system damage. As he recounted the story,
Karl's voice got louder and the tale was punctuated with
more and more profanity regarding the heritage, parentage,
pedigree, and sexual proclivities of the guy who had dropped
the bombs.

Getting shot down by the enemy was certainly terrifying
enough, but being killed by someone on the same side was
arguably worse. Fortunately, the sizzle of the steaks ended
the elaboration of possible squadron cowardice and changed
the conversation back to less emotional topics. That's when
Pike told us about his mission the previous day.

He'd had the common load of two three-thousand bombs.
The target was a lightly defended storage area near Dong
Hoi — practically the same area I'd hit on my first mission.
That wasn't much problem for an experienced pilot like
Grubbs, until he'd pickled the bombs off and started his recovery from the 45-degree dive-bomb pass. Without thinking he had simply pickled and pulled back on the stick in the
standard four- to five-G pullout. Things went bad in a hurry
then, as the airplane snapped into a hard right roll to inverted.
Already in a steep dive, the snap caused the airplane to lose
still more altitude and to Pike's surprise when he tried to roll
back to wings-level, the airplane seemed to resist the roll. It
only took a second or two to realize that one of the two huge
bombs had failed to release. The combination of drag and
weight on the one wing was severely accentuated when he'd
started the pullout. The solution was one that none of us low-
time lieutenants would have thought of. When he realized
the cause of the problem, he simply reversed his roll to go
in the direction of the bomb-loaded wing, then after passing
through inverted he continued rolling until he could slowly
reapply back pressure to complete the pullout.

"Watch your step guys, and make sure you be ready to jettison the remaining bomb if one of those big muthas hangs
up on you. You won't have time to do much if you start

pulling with one hung," he counseled. The three of us lieutenants nodded in assent as we added one more thing to the long list of possible ways to die in an F-105.

Mission number two was another piece of cake and with no excitement other than what was generated by my own imagination, it seemed only reasonable to fly another one. The fear was always there, but the pace of events helped to subdue it for a few hours as I planned, briefed, flew, and finished a flight.

The next day I wasn't on the schedule. Things seemed quiet until Karl came down the hall of the squadron from the duty desk to the lounge area. "Grab your shit, Raz. We're both up to spare a couple of add-on flights."

As the cold slam to the pit of stomach returned, he told me about the mission. "Gary Willard, one of the F-100 Wild Weasels, found a SAM site in Pack II this morning. He's going to lead the first of two flights of four 105s this afternoon to kill it. I'm sparing his flight and you'll spare the second one with Major Howard leading."

I couldn't think of a response, other than to express amazement that Willard was able to go back and forth between the F-100 and the 105. I knew a little bit about the three F-100F two-seater aircraft parked out on the ramp. They carried an electronic warfare specialist in the back seat and were outfitted with some special gear to detect the radar emissions that the SA-2 used to detect our aircraft and guide the missiles toward us. I hadn't had time to learn much more than that, but I was pretty sure that any airplane assigned the task of detecting SAM sites and attacking them was probably one that I didn't want to get too close to.

There were ten pilots in the briefing. The two flights would take off ten minutes apart and proceed directly to the coordinates that Major Willard had jotted on the briefing blackboard. He wasn't sure exactly where the site was, nor did he have any information on what it might look like. He had gotten several radar signals from the area that morning and by a process of triangulation he felt fairly certain about the general location. We'd each be carrying the standard pair of 3,000-pound bombs.

Because most of the crews were highly experienced and had been at Korat for a while, most of the usual flight-briefing details were omitted. Richter would be spare for Oak, the first flight, and I'd spare Redwood, the second four-ship. Our job was to preflight, start engines, and taxi with the flight out to the arming area. If anyone had a problem with an aircraft before the change to Brigham control, the air traffic control agency that deconflicted airspace east of Korat, we would fill in with our aircraft. The odds were that we wouldn't be needed. I breathed a sigh of relief.

Things went smoothly through taxi and arming. Oak flight was already airborne about five minutes ahead of us. As Redwood flight moved forward out of quick-check and onto the active runway, I spotted Karl's aircraft sitting just short of the taxiway waiting for a break in traffic to taxi back to the parking area. Then the radio crackled. "Redwood, this is Three. I've got a problem with the TACAN. It looks like it won't lock on, so I won't have any nav." The hairs on the back of my neck tingled and jumped to attention.

"Roger, Three. You're cleared to abort. I'll take Oak Spare. Redwood Four, you're now Three. Oak Spare, you're Redwood Four. Acknowledge." I took a deep breath. Apparently Brown Howard thought the additional experience Karl had gained with five missions was superior to my two missions. I certainly wasn't about to disagree. The new lineup smartly acknowledged their positions — "Two . . . Three . . . Four."

They taxied onto the runway, lined up, closed their canopies, and got clearance from tower for takeoff. I followed through the radio channel changes as they went about their business. Lead started rolling, followed at twelve-second intervals by Two, Three, and then Karl. I felt my airplane vibrating from the jet blast of the afterburners. I was relieved. For thirty seconds, anyway. That was when Redwood Three called out that he'd lost his P-1 primary hydraulic system. "Roger that. Redwood Spare, you on the channel?"

"Roger, Redwood. Spare's up."

"Spare, you're now Redwood Four. Get a move on."

"Korat Tower, Redwood Spare's now Redwood Four and number one for takeoff."

"Roger, Redwood Four. Cleared for takeoff. The winds are two-one-zero at eight, altimeter two niner eight eight. Change to departure control when airborne. Your flight is now 050 at twelve miles passing six thousand for flight level 190 assigned."

"Roger, Korat. Redwood Four cleared for takeoff."

I came out of afterburner at four hundred knots and started the right turn to chase the flight. The airplane rumbled with the drag of the two big bombs and the centerline 650-gallon fuel tank. I let the speed build to five hundred before I started the nose up to climb. My left hand dropped off the throttle to the radar antenna tilt control and started the process of gradually running the antenna up and down slowly searching the area ahead of me for the three airplanes. I saw them just to the left of the nose and a bit above the horizon before the radar could do me any good.

"Redwood Four is visual, about six miles in trail," I called. The flight was climbing gradually at 420 knots and I'd make up the distance in about three minutes with the speed I was holding. Richter would be on the left wing from his rejoin in the turn out of traffic, so I planned to join on his left.

The flight switched channels to Brigham control, and we leveled at nineteen thousand feet in a spread formation with about four thousand feet between aircraft. The afternoon sun was bright, and the glare reflected off the towering white cumulous clouds ahead made me keep my dark helmet visor down. I punched on the autopilot in altitude hold and tried to relax and get my head into the mission. This was a four-ship, not two, and it was headed into suspected SAM country. Hell, the target was a SAM site! I nudged the throttle slightly forward to keep my position as close to line abreast with Karl as I could manage, while my brain was scrambling for an excuse.

"Redwood, Brigham, cleared outbound. Go strike primary," broke into my mental funk. We were crossing the Mekong River, headed northeast toward a wall of clouds.

"Roger, Brigham. Redwood Flight, channel fourteen, go!"

We snapped our numbers and switched channels. The UHF radio ground for a second or two finding the four-digit frequency then Brown Howard's voice growled, "Redwood, check." I swallowed and consciously tried to lower my tone from a petrified tenor to a more mature bass as I sequenced my check-in, "Four."

Now the pressure was rising. I needed out. I needed an excuse. I needed an alternative. I needed something wrong with my airplane. How's the hydraulic pressure? Is the oil okay? What's my fuel? Why is everything still working? Doesn't this damn airplane know that I need an excuse? The J-75 behind me wasn't exactly purring, but the throaty roar was exactly what it was supposed to sound like. The airplane was solid as a rock. It was eager, even if I wasn't.

Lead's airplane rocked left and right in the visual signal to rejoin into close formation. We were approaching the clouds now, and Major Howard was looking for a way through the buildups. I hit the paddle switch, just below the stick grip, to pop the autopilot off and banked toward my leader while pushing the throttle up a bit. That's when the radio went wild.

"Oak Lead, move it, they're shootin'," came through almost as a scream.

"Rog, I've got guns all over me."

"Shit, they're mad."

"Let's get out of here."

The chatter went on, most of it without call signs, and none of it with the maturity and calmness that you would have expected from an experienced flight of four. These were guys with more than eighty missions each, and they were screaming like panicked children. It wasn't supposed to be like this.

Howard waited for a break in the chatter, knowing that Oak flight would calm a bit once they got clear of the target area. He also knew that Oak would want to sound a lot steadier when they realized that Redwood was on the frequency with them. "Oak, Redwood's inbound. What's the weather like? And did you find the site?" There was a decidedly pregnant pause before Oak Lead responded.

"Roger, Redwood. It's towering cumulus all around the valley. Lots of shooting. The best way in is from the south end. No activity from the site."

The brief conversation presented me with a bucket full of "good news—bad news." The good news was that the SAM site hadn't fired. The bad news was that the site hadn't been hit. Good news was that the weather was bad. Bad news was that it wasn't bad enough to keep us from continuing. Good news was that we had a clear route into the target area. Bad news was that the area was defended and even worse news was that the defenders were now very unhappy with the U.S. Air Force. And through it all, my airplane kept purring like a kitten. No alibis, no excuses, no aborts.

"Redwood Two has traffic, left ten o'clock high, opposite direction, looks like Oak." I craned back over my left shoulder, looking away from Karl's wing to catch just a glimpse of four 105s in route formation climbing westbound back to Thailand. I wished I were one of them.

We maneuvered left around a thunderhead, then swung to the north. I glanced in my cockpit to check the distance to the target area coordinates. The DME was winding down through fifteen miles meaning less than two minutes to go. Major Howard snapped the left wing of his aircraft down in the signal to move into left echelon with all three of the flight members on the same side. That meant we'd be rolling in on the target to the right. "Green 'em up, Redwood," was the radio call. I started flipping and twisting the various weapons switches until the green lights of the two inboard pylon stations glowed. I took a quick look at my lineup card on my knee for the release altitude and sight settings for a 30- and

45-degree dive-bomb pass and momentarily had a thought about Pike Grubb's tale of a hung-up 3,000-pound bomb.

It was getting darker as we entered a canyon of clouds. Towering cumulus rose above us to the left and right, and the cloud canyon closed off about ten miles to the north. We were over a valley roughly the same shape as the storm cloud formation, ten miles long and half as wide. I was breathing a lot faster as I scrambled to keep wide enough on Richter's airplane without getting scraped off into the black clouds. I knew we had reached the target, but I didn't have a clue what it was. The lead aircraft broke hard to his right away from us with the call, "Redwood Lead is in. I'll be off left then back to south."

Less than five seconds later, the second aircraft rolled into a dive from our twelve-thousand-foot altitude. Now there were just the two of us, Karl Richter and me. Karl veered slightly away giving me a bit more space off the cloudbank. Then I saw a quick wave of his left hand as he rolled into his bomb run. Rather than fly straight ahead to get some spacing, I pulled up slightly and watched Karl's airplane plunging toward the ground. That's when I really saw the valley floor.

It was mostly rice paddies with dirt trails between the fields and scattered clusters of huts. But that wasn't what was remarkable. The valley floor was flickering like the flashbulbs of the Washington, D.C., press corps meeting the president's plane at night. Ten miles long by five miles wide was a sea of white flashes interspersed with a half dozen circular formations regularly emitting rings of dark red fireballs surrounded by puffs of black smoke. It was amazing. I'd never seen so many flashbulbs going off at one time. I rolled to my right into the dive, watching Karl start his pulloff below me. I still didn't know what the target was.

Then the two M-118s from Karl's airplane detonated like a mini-A-bomb in the center of one of the circles of flashing red. The humidity caused a sudden dome of white vapor over the bomb explosion, immediately followed by a huge white flash and then a cloud of black smoke and dirt rising from the crater. Karl had dropped on one of the circles. I banked

quickly to find another circle and put the pipper of the gun-
sight just below the outer ring of dirt. I checked altitude and
thought again of Pike's warning about hung bombs. As the
airplane dove, the red dot in the center of the gunsight reticle
drifted toward the center of the ring on the ground. As the
ring cycled through another series of blackish-red flashes, I
pickled and started a pull out, squeezing against my G-suit
pressure and feeling the airplane buffet as the nose started to
rise.

I pulled left as the nose came to the horizon, then reversed
back to my right and looked south to see where the rest of
Redwood flight was. In the right turn a dozen white puffballs
appeared right where I was headed. Shit! How stupid could I
be? The flashbulbs, the fireballs, the twinkling circles . . .
they were guns! This was flak. They were shooting. They
were shooting at me!

I snapped the airplane back to the left and headed right into
the nearest black cumulus cloud. Surrounded by the dingy
gray, I didn't mind the bouncing turbulence. Suddenly I felt a
secure blanket around me. I got on instruments and started to
reach for the radar antenna tilt wheel when a half dozen
glowering red flashes dazzled me just outside the right
quarter-panel of the windscreen. They were still shooting at
me, even in the clouds. There was no hiding from radar-
directed 85-mm guns. I churned the stick left away from the
flashes then started a pull up. I pushed forward after a few
seconds then banked back right. Nothing in instrument training in flight school ever referred to jinking from guns on the
gauges.

The throttle was at full military power and my head was
spinning. I had good airspeed and was trying to work toward
higher altitudes. I slid down in my seat and tried to fight the
vertigo and believe my instruments rather than my inner ear.
At better than five hundred knots it couldn't take too long to
get clear of that cursed valley. Then, suddenly and without a
warning, I was in the clear. Out of the clouds and with a
check of my Doppler telling me I was twenty miles south of
the target area, I tried to calm myself. I took a slow deep

breath and started scanning the area in front of me. Within seconds I found two members of Redwood flight, side-by-side, about five miles ahead. Then I saw Redwood Three, not more than two miles away, so close that someone who didn't know better would think we had planned it. I banked slightly toward Karl and closed up to normal tactical spread position. He saw me almost immediately and gave me a thumbs up. I returned it, acknowledging that I was okay.

The flight back to Korat was uneventful. The sky was blue, the setting sun bathed the Thai landscape in jewellike greens, and there was little other air traffic to worry about. As we cleared the active runway and jettisoned our drag chutes, I took a deep breath and popped the canopy open. I'd made it. I now had three missions, and I'd seen some serious shooting. I could do this. I was part of this group, and I'd glimpsed maybe just a bit of fear in the other pilots. I wasn't the only one afraid when the shooting started but because I'd kept my mouth shut and done my job, no one would know about my fear. I could fly just one more.

Turning into the revetment, I was surprised at the sudden gathering of blue maintenance trucks. It wasn't uncommon to have a line chief park his pickup in front of an arriving airplane as the engine was shut down, but I had four vehicles surrounding the nose of my airplane. The crew chief hoisted the big yellow ladder up and hung it from the cockpit rail then came up to take my helmet. He grinned and said, "Sure must have been hot when you punched off your tank, Lieutenant."

I was confused. "My tank? The centerline tank is gone?"

"Yessir. The pylons are gone off the wings too."

"The pylons?"

"Yep. You cleaned 'er off slick as the day she was built. Is she okay? Were you hit?"

Could I have pulled so hard off the target that I ripped the 650-gallon tank off its attachment points on the bomb bay doors? If I did, why were the pylons missing too? The pylons couldn't be torn off by G forces. What happened? What did I do? Had I been hit?

As I climbed down the ladder, it dawned on me. I'd

screwed up. There wasn't any other answer. I'd been thinking about Pike Grubb's hung bomb, hadn't I? I'd consciously
looked for the guarded-red master jettison button just before
I'd rolled in on the target, and I'd reminded myself of the
danger of a bomb that didn't release. I'd been engrossed in
all of the shooting and radio chatter, and I had tracked the
target to release then mechanically, in a three-step ballet of
green lieutenant incompetence, pickled the bombs, punched
the jettison button, and pulled out of the dive-bomb run. My
elation at having survived the tough mission was deflated
and replaced with embarrassment at being a screwup.

The maintenance supervisor got out of his truck and came
toward me with a clipboard. "Sign right here, sir," he said,
pointing to the bottom line on a card listing the equipment I
had jettisoned: two inboard, special-weapon pylons valued at
$6,000, and one 650-gallon centerline fuel tank at $1,850.

I took the offered pen, but hesitated. "Am I going to be
charged for this?" It would take years at a first lieutenant's
pay to clear the account.

"No sir, it's simply routine. Happens all the time."

The crew van had pulled to the front of the revetment, and
Karl was hanging out the back of the truck yelling for me to
hurry up. I signed my name, took my helmet bag from the
crew chief, and jumped aboard the van. No one mentioned
the missing equipment, and I didn't bring it up.

CHAPTER 10

Weasels and Weapons

To my surprise, the debriefing never mentioned my jettison nor my excursion off the target into billowing thunder-clouds. In fact, no one had noticed. The discussion centered on the defensive reaction we had encountered, the reliability of the electronic signals encountered that morning, and whether or not a SAM site existed as far south as Route Pack II, where we had dropped our bombs. The North Vietnamese were undoubtedly defending something at Ha Tinh, but most agreed that it was more likely a supply transshipment point than a missile site. Surely if there had been a SAM site, the bad weather that had forced us into a narrow canyon of clouds and the poorly planned tactics that had brought us in at high altitude would have made our flights a very attractive target for a launch.

It didn't take long for me to relate the debrief comments from the other guys to what I had seen during the mission. The white flashes on the ground were 37- and 57-mm guns. They fired a projectile that exploded at altitudes of five to ten thousand feet in white puffs about a foot in diameter. They were usually aimed by a gunner looking through a gun sight at the aircraft overhead. Sometimes the guns were coordinated by radar, but most often they were fired as a barrage at a designated section of the sky without much aiming. Unaimed fire sounded at first like a good deal for the F-105 driver, but that was the worst situation. When flak gunners aimed at 105s, they usually underestimated the aircraft's speed and, like a shotgunner shooting at doves or quail, the gunners would underlead and shoot behind the target. When they simply shot at a sector of sky, the exploding flak created a wall of shrapnel that the target aircraft had to fly through. Aimed fire was actually easier for us to defend against than a barrage. Random changes in heading and altitude could defeat it.

The circles I had seen with the deep red flashes and black clouds of smoke were batteries of 85- and 100-mm guns. Typically, six or eight of these large artillery pieces would be arrayed around a Fire Can radar. The radar would detect the aircraft and provide direction and range information to the guns, which would then be fired in salvos. The large projectiles were much slower than the 37- and 57-mm guns, but they could reach a much higher altitude and with the ranging provided by the Fire Can radar, the shells would burst very close to the target's predicted position. The red explosions and large black puffs at altitude were almost thirty feet across and created serious blast and fragmentation threats.

When our debriefing was over I grabbed Richter by the shoulder before he could follow the others out. "Got a minute?" I asked. I needed more information about what I'd just been through, and although Karl had only three missions more than I did, he was someone I could turn to without the risk of blurting out my fear. Was this as bad as it got? What was going on with all that screaming on the radios? Was that what it was like in Pack VI?

Karl turned back into the flight planning area and headed toward the Coke machine. "I'll match you," he said, pulling out a quarter. We flipped, he matched my heads, and I bought. We moved down the long hall toward a study area and pulled up chairs at a desk in one of the cubicles.

"Did you notice my airplane was clean?" I asked him.

"Huh? No shit?"

"Yeah, I must have punched off the stuff in the target area like Grubb was talking about the other night. I thought sure you would have seen it on the flight home."

"No, I just looked at your airplane when you came aboard

to make sure the bombs were gone and you didn't look like you were on fire or anything. I didn't think of looking for anything else," he admitted a little sheepishly.

If Karl hadn't noticed, then it wasn't likely the other flight members would have either. I wouldn't hear anything more about it. What about the shooting then? How was the best way to handle it? What did Karl think about the mission?

We spent about an hour talking about what we'd seen in the target area. The flashes on the ground were unusual, Karl said, because on most days the bright sunshine made them less obvious. Apparently the towering, dark storm clouds surrounding the valley had made the muzzle flashes a lot brighter. Most of the time the only evidence of the shooting would be air bursts at altitude, white puffballs for the 37- and 57-mm guns and black clouds from the 85s and larger artillery. At least that's all that he was familiar with.

"What about SAMs?" I wanted to know. They were the new wrinkle in this air war. Enemy aircraft could be fought. They were simply men in machines like my own and even though I had my fears, I was confident that I could hold my own against another pilot. Flak had been around for a long time as well and could be countered by jinking to foil a lead prediction or by maintaining high speed through the barrage areas. But SAMs were something different. They were faster than enemy planes and carried a much larger bang than anti-aircraft fire. They were guided by radar and homed in on you as the target. They chased you down to kill you. What about SAMs?

Karl had seen a couple of SAMs during his mission to Bac Giang with Nix. It had all happened quickly, and he suggested that whether or not you got targeted depended on something between luck and magic. It didn't take long for the two of us to realize that we didn't know much about the missiles, and it might be damned important for us to get smart in a hurry. We finished our Cokes and went down the hall to the intelligence officers' area, where we hoped a couple of first lieutenant intel types might be able to give us more information.

We were in luck. Two of the young lieutenants, Paul Heimbach and Mark Wilcox, were killing time in their office waiting for the next day's mission frag to come in on the secure Teletype. They were eager to share their knowledge with a couple of young aviators who had broken the "know-it-all" mold of most fighter pilots and were humbly asking for their help.

Paul began by describing what we knew about the missile that the North Vietnamese were using. It was the SA-2 Guideline, a Russian product that had first gained notoriety in 1960 when it had shot down Francis Gary Powers's U-2 spy plane. It could reach out nearly thirty miles from its launch site at speed nearly two and a half times the speed of sound. It was command guided by a radar called the Fan Song and could be detonated by contact — hitting you, by command from the ground when the operator thought the missile was close to the target, or by a proximity fuse that sensed the passage of a mass of metal like a targeted airplane. Obviously, since it had downed the U-2, the heavily laden F-105s wouldn't be able to fly above the missile's maximum altitude.

But it had limitations too. The missile depended upon line-of-sight guidance by the Fan Song radar, so you could get low enough to hide your aircraft in ground clutter. You could duck behind hills or mountain ridges to break a radar lock-on and the Fan Song antenna could be tilted only so far to follow you down. Most analysts thought that dropping down to between a thousand and fifteen hundred feet should break the radar lock. Paul didn't have to add that the "analysts" didn't have their butts in a jet over bad guy country.

Paul also noted that the missile had a nitric-acid-oxidized booster. When launched, the missile couldn't be guided until the booster burned out and dropped away. That meant that inside of a mile and a half radius of the launch site, the missile was purely ballistic — an unguided dart. I chalked that up to a mixed blessing. I liked the idea of the missile not being guidable, but didn't think I wanted to spend a lot of time rooting around within a short distance of the site. It was the coming and going from the sanctuary inside minimum range that was a problem. Paul went on to mention that the booster created a bright orange cloud of smoke when the missile was launched, offering a clear marker for the location of the SAM site as well as a trail to define the missile's initial flight path. If you could see the missile coming, you had a good chance of evading it.

Once the booster had dropped off, the sustainer motor displayed only a bright white flame and produced much less smoke. It would be harder to see, particularly during bright daylight. All reports said that the ground radar guided the missile using both azimuth and elevation information on the targeted aircraft. It chased you rather than trying to meet your aircraft at a point in space. Pure pursuit by an airplane in combat was almost always a mistake for the attacker, but with a missile traveling three or more times faster than the target it could be more effective.

The missile's high speed and its tiny wings made large maneuvers difficult, so the best defense that had been devised by crews that had successfully countered the threat was a last-second hard turn up and into the missile's flight path, forcing it to overshoot. Heimbach suggested a multiple-step defensive plan. Your first move should be a rapid descent to try to get below the Fan Song's antenna angle or to get into the radar's ground clutter. Terrain masking, putting a hill between you and the radar, would work. Reports were that if you could see the missile following your maneuvering, you could tell when it lost radar guidance because the missile would level off. If you were unable to break the radar lock, then the best tactic was to continue descending to get the missile to commit its nose down, then "when you just can't stand it any longer," to pull up sharply over the missile, which can't make the close-in turn. Do it too early, and the missile still has turning room to chase you. Do it too late, and the missile hits you.

In a court of law, I thought, this testimony would be dismissed as hearsay evidence. Paul may have read all of the classified reports on the SA-2, but he didn't wear wings, and he hadn't been there. He had related what he had heard from crews during debrief. But the only crews that debriefed were the ones who had survived. What about the guys who had been downed by the SAMs? What hadn't they done? What mistakes had they made?

Mark Wilcox had been working with the F-100F Wild Weasels, so he had more information about the SAMs. The three, two-seater aircraft had been modified with a number of antennas and a backseat display that provided information about the Fan Song radar. The pilot would maneuver the aircraft while an electronic warfare officer, or EWO, in the rear would monitor and interpret the signals. He could tell the difference between a Fan Song and a Fire Can, the radar used to guide the anti-aircraft guns. The equipment could supposedly tell whether the radar was simply searching or fully locked on and tracking you as a target. When the missile was about to launch, the EWO picked up the change in electronic emissions; when the missile was fired and guidance signals were broadcast, the EWO would receive a "launch" light.

What was more important to us, Mark confided, was that a system similar to this first generation radar warning equipment was being installed in our F-105D aircraft as quickly as possible. We already had eight airplanes on station with the APR-25/26 radar homing and warning system or RHAW gear. The full fleet would have it within about a month. We wouldn't have an EWO, but the equipment displays for the 105 would be fairly easy to understand.

He pulled out a classified manual and showed us the two RHAW components. We would be getting a small display that looked like a miniature radarscope, roughly two inches in diameter. This would show a relative-strength vector arrow pointing toward the signal source. The stronger the signal, the longer the strobe that would be generated. A quick glance at the tiny box would tell you where a radar threat was located. Tiny rings etched on the scope helped to measure the difference in length of the strobes.

The second component was a flat rectangular box about six inches wide by two inches high. Called a TDU or threat display unit, this box was divided like an egg crate into small square lights, labeled to identify the types of radar signals being detected. Colored lights told you when a Fire Can or Fan Song was emitting nearby and even if a MiG's radar was scanning you. A separate light labeled "activity" told when a signal indicating launch preparation was received and an ominous red "launch" light needed no further explanation. Wilcox enthusiastically added that the whole package would alert us to whatever was displayed with audio in our headsets. Buzzes and beeps would correlate with the strobes on the scope and lights of the TDU.

It was hard to know whether or not to feel reassured. On the one hand, knowing more about the defensive environment would be helpful. Knowledge of what types of radar were around you and what they might be doing was valuable. But implicit in the installation was the idea that there was going to be a lot more activity in SAM country. The targets were going to be increasingly in SAM-defended territory, and there could be little doubt that the enemy was going to be getting lots more of the missiles. So Santa was bringing us new toys to play with. The problem would be keeping the little guys up North from breaking them when we came to visit.

Mark wanted us to know about one more thing: the Shrike. The Weasel aircraft did more than just detect electronic activity from the North Vietnamese missile sites. It carried a bite as well. The Shrike missile was built on the body of the AIM-7 Sparrow, a radar guided missile that the F-4 Phantom carried to shoot against enemy aircraft. The Shrike replaced the seeker head of the Sparrow, which guided on reflected radar energy from the shooting aircraft, with a radar homing antenna that guided the missile right to the source of any detected enemy radar. When a Fan Song had the temerity to broadcast its radar signal, a Shrike would follow the beam right to the center of the antenna. At least that was what the advertising promised. I wasn't sure I wanted to be part of the test program.

A weasel, of course, was a tiny but ferocious animal that went down rat holes to dig out rodents and other vermin. A shrike was a hunting bird that circled over fields watching for mice to kill with a rapid blow from the sky. In a particularly vicious bit of behavior, the shrike was known for impaling its prey on sharp sticks creating meals for later consumption. The naming of these weapons seemed appropriate. I liked the idea of vicious carnivores attacking the enemy that was trying to kill me. I just wondered if they worked. Karl didn't know, and the intel guys weren't very convincing. We stood up and headed out of the command post. A wall of hot, humid air hit us as we opened the door of the air-conditioned building. Lightning to the east indicated it was going to rain soon.

The rain poured down for the next two days. Several flights each day were canceled and others that managed to get airborne went to secondary targets in the lower route packages or even tertiary targets, flying armed reconnaissance along road segments in Laos. The rain each night created massive mud puddles that sucked at your boots as you tried to walk and doubly endangered pedestrians as trucks passed by, sliding, barely in control and splashing walls of water in the dark, predawn murk. When the rain stopped, the sun drove the humidity to a misty saturation point and dried the red clay in less than an hour so that dust would blow and stick to your wet skin. Somehow you could be dripping wet while the ground was talcum powder dust.

In the mornings as we opened the doors of our hootches to catch a ride to the squadron, we would see dozens of flashlights bobbing around the edges of buildings. Thai workers would emerge from the dark corners of the base brown paper bags clutched happily along with their stacked lunch pails. They were harvesting giant rice beetles. These three-inch-long, roach-like insects, flushed out by the torrential rains, were considered a culinary delight by the Thais and a skin-crawling horror by the Americans. With only a bit of encouragement, the Thais would gladly demonstrate the proper way to eat the bugs by biting off the head and sucking out the insides much like a Cajun feasting on a crawdad.

Some workers had them with lunch, while others took them to downtown Korat where they sold the bugs for a baht each, about a nickel in the Thai currency.

My mission count was building slowly, and with the bad weather the threat of dangerous missions to Pack VI was low. On days that I didn't fly I handled squadron duties, such as a stint as duty officer at the front desk or a few hours out by the runway in the mobile control unit, a small structure about the size of a telephone booth where a pilot observed takeoffs and landings for proper configuration. With binoculars, a UHF radio to monitor, and a pair of flare guns to alert landing aircraft of problems, the duty was boring but considered essential.

On my sixth mission I was flying in a two-ship with Bill Loyd into Laos. The mission wouldn't count toward my one-hundred-mission tour credit, but it added combat hours and operational experience. Major Loyd had arrived at Nellis from Germany just as our class was graduating and had led the deployment of eight aircraft to Korat with Richter, Running, Foley, and Hackford, four of the members of my training class accompanying him on the long flight across the Pacific. Bill was a burly guy, looking like a center linebacker for a pro football team and with a huge black handlebar mustache. He was well-known in the 105 community and had lots of time in the airplane acquired flying in Europe. Best of all, he genuinely liked lieutenants, or so it seemed. A welcome change from the likes of Lieutenant Colonel Barnett or even my flight commander, Jim Mitchell.

Since his arrival at Korat about a week before mine, Loyd had been working at the Wing Headquarters and flying as an attached pilot with the 421st. He knew his business and had the kind of personality that everyone instinctively liked. We had heard rumors that as vacancies occurred with the Mc-Connell leadership in our squadron that there was a good chance that Bill would become the operations officer. Whether that came to pass or not, I welcomed the opportunity to fly with him. He had a reputation for teaching his wingmen the necessary skills to survive, taking care of them in dangerous situations, and getting the job done.

We were tasked to recce a section of highway from Mu Gia Pass into Laos down toward Tchepone in the area called Steel Tiger. Each airplane carried a new weapons load that took advantage of our normally unused outboard pylons but unfortunately placed us above the maximum allowable gross weight for take off. Only by consuming fuel during taxi and arming did we finally reach an allowable flying weight just prior to takeoff. We had a centerline 650-gallon tank, two M-118 bombs, and each outboard carried a LAU-3 rocket pod with nineteen 2.75-inch folding-fin rockets.

Finding a target for the bombs was easy. We found a place where the road crossed a small river and dropped them on the narrow, rickety bridge. Then, at a better weight for maneuvering, Loyd began an examination of the road seeking trucks or storage areas that might be suitable for the rockets. We flew a fast but smooth ballet over the road, essing back and forth, continually turning and seldom offering a wings-level target for any gunners. It was an exercise in practical formation flying, and I found myself enjoying the hunt. Keeping Loyd in sight, watching the ground for trucks or a target, staying alert for defensive fire and throughout the process maintaining airspeed and maneuvering potential was a challenge.

The radio crackled on guard channel with words I'd never heard before in anything but a B movie. "Mayday, Mayday, Mayday. Elm Two is hit. I've got a fire light and am climbing out westbound." It was Dick Hackford's voice. The first of my class of nine from Nellis was in serious trouble.

Loyd immediately took control of the situation. Even before the transmission ended, he had started turning to the west and began climbing to conserve fuel. I maneuvered to get to a line-abreast spread position and checked my TACAN to see where we were. "Pine, go guard," was Loyd's next call as he took us to the emergency frequency.

"Pine, check."

"Two," I responded.

"Elm, this is Pine. Say your position."

"Roger, Pine. Elm is zero-seven-zero at ninety-five off channel fifty-one. Climbing through eight thousand."

I checked my position and saw we were about fifteen miles east of Elm. "Elm, we're right behind you. Pine has a pair of 105s with rockets and twenty mike-mike and we've got about thirty minutes of playtime," Loyd advised. We didn't know what ordnance Elm might have or what their fuel state was, but Bill had just told them what help we could provide.

Hackford called again. "Elm Two has a definite fire. I'm going to have to get out. Have you got me in sight, Lead?" There was a brief pause, not long enough for his leader to reply. Then he continued. "Elm Two is bailing out. . . . Oh, shit."

A flash of fire against the dark jungle backdrop caught my eye. It was an airplane. It seemed to be climbing slowly, then more fire was streaming from the tail section. Steadily the airplane nosed over and gracefully arced downward. It didn't take more than twenty seconds to hit. The explosion was small, shielded by the thick canopy, and only a thin dark tendril of smoke marked the point of impact. We were closing on the area fast, and before long I saw the chute. The howling of the emergency beeper in the parachute made guard channel virtually useless. I closed on Loyd's wing and saw him flash two fingers at me. I changed to channel two on the radio and turned off the guard receiver to quiet the incessant whooping of the emergency transmitter. "Pine Two, are you up?" I checked in. "Okay, have you got the chute in sight?" I acknowledged. "Let's go rescue secondary." I flipped my radio to 346.2 and kept watching the chute, thinking how easily that could be me swinging over the jungle.

We checked in on the secondary rescue frequency and began circling the wreckage. Elm Lead was calling King, the rescue command post, to get a helicopter and search aircraft into the area. Dick was fortunate that we weren't far from Ubon or Nakhon Phanom. Both bases had rescue forces on alert to recover downed crews. Things were working smoothly.

We circled overhead waiting for Dick to get on the ground and hoping he would be able to collect his gear, get under cover, and talk to us.

I was beginning to worry. We hadn't heard anything from the ground. Was he okay? Had there been Pathet Lao troops or other hostiles nearby, waiting to capture him? Why hadn't he checked in on his emergency radio? Then it dawned on me. I'd turned off my guard receiver to quiet the parachute beeper. I dropped my left hand down off the throttle and flipped the radio back to main and guard. I came into the middle of the conversation. " . . . the ground. Can't see anybody. How long 'til the choppers get here?"

"Roger, Elm Two. We've got Jolly Green 21 inbound along with Sandy 11. They're estimating overhead in about twenty minutes. Get under cover and stay quiet. Turn your radio off to conserve the battery and come up in fifteen minutes. Understand?"

He was on the ground and okay. I watched as Loyd adjusted our orbit to avoid direct overflight of Dick's position. We eased off to the west in anticipation of meeting the big Jolly Green rescue helicopter and his two A-1 propeller-driven escorts. The A-1s dated back to the Korean War, but their low-speed compatibility with the Jolly and their endurance made them ideal for search and rescue missions. Typically, they carried a wide range of ordnance on their fourteen wing stations, ranging from bombs to marking rockets, flares, and even nausea gas designed to incapacitate anyone on the ground threatening the aircrew survivor.

Cricket, the airborne command post, broke into the scenario. "Pine, this is Cricket. We've got Buick flight, a pair of F-4s coming into the area with full fuel and ordnance. You're cleared to depart the area and RTB. Thanks for your help."

I was reluctant to leave my friend on the ground, but a check of my fuel gauge showed that we couldn't have stayed more than another five minutes. Bill acknowledged Cricket's instructions, and we turned toward Korat and started climbing. The last thing I heard on the rescue frequency was Buick flight checking in, followed almost immediately by Sandy

11, announcing that he was assuming control as the on-scene commander. If the shooting and shouting a week earlier at Ha Tinh had been an exercise in pandemonium, the coordination of this rescue effort was an example of professionalism and cool competence. They were going to get Dick out.

As soon as we landed, we got on the command post radio from the flight-line truck to ask about the status of Elm Two. He was safe. He was in the chopper and just touching down at Ubon. He would be back at Korat later that afternoon. Loyd looked at me and winked. We had been first on the scene to help a friend, and we'd been part of a successful effort. That's what you're supposed to do.

The intel portion of the debrief took longer than usual because we tried to provide as much information as possible about Hackford's bailout. Then Loyd took me back to the squadron, where we headed for one of the flight briefing cubicles. We sat and talked for more than an hour as he detailed the entire mission, starting with explanations of his decision process in finding a target for the bombs, then drawing up our road recce formation and maneuvers. He went through a list of possible scenarios and tactics options that we could have used for attacking targets that we might have found. Clearly, Bill Loyd had a different attitude about flying fighters and leadership than the others I'd flown with in the squadron. There was no question about treating me as an equal. I wasn't. He was a senior, experienced fighter pilot, and I was a neophyte lieutenant. But I was going to be a wingman for him during a very dangerous combat tour, and he wanted to be certain that I had all the information necessary to be the best wingman possible. Whether my skills and courage would rise to the task remained to be seen, but Loyd was going to be sure I didn't lack for tactical knowledge. If the information helped me to survive, that was simply a dividend.

Then he described the rescue operations. Speed was critical for the guy on the ground. When someone was hit, you had to start the rescue effort moving and take charge of the situation. The flight lead of the guy who had been hit would most likely take charge and if a flight leader was hit, the second in command, usually the number three aircraft would organize the effort. They were nearby, they knew the location, and they knew how much fuel and ordnance they had remaining to support the downed crewman. They would be first on the scene and would need to locate the pilot on the ground after ejection as well as contact the closest rescue forces. If the enemy was nearby, they had to employ their ordnance as effectively as possible while maintaining the safety of the evading pilot.

Today, Elm Lead had been first on the scene when his wingman was hit, and we had provided support. Loyd emphasized the need to keep the radio frequencies clear for critical communication. We had used hand signals and our squadron local frequency for passing information, and then we had contacted Elm Lead to quickly offer our assistance. When directed by King, the rescue command post, we had complied with orders and cleared the area, even though it was someone we knew and cared about on the ground. We had not flown directly over the position of the downed crewman to avoid giving away his location, and we had oriented ourselves to support the slow and vulnerable Jolly Green and A-1 Sandys. Defenses weren't very heavy in the area we had been in, but they had been heavy enough to down Elm Two. If we faced a rescue situation up north in Pack VI, we would have to execute these principles perfectly to get our guys out.

As I stood up to leave the briefing table, Major Loyd looked up and added, "Oh, and one more thing, Raz. Grow a mustache."

"Sir?"

"I said, grow a mustache. Get started in the morning. It's a fighter pilot tradition. It makes you bulletproof."

For a split second I stared at his thick black handlebar, then saluted smartly, and said, "yes, sir!"

With the debrief over, I knew a lot more than when I'd started the day. Certainly the instruction on being an effective fighter pilot was a big part of it, but I also knew some other things. I knew that Bill Loyd would be a leader in our organization. I knew that men like Loyd would guide my development as a fighter pilot and maybe even give me a chance to survive the whole hundred-mission tour. He was different in his outlook and approach than what I had seen from the senior guys in the squadron, who seemed much more intent on adding to their mission count and taking care of themselves. If he had any fear about the job at hand, he certainly didn't show it. And he didn't ask if I was afraid. He simply assumed I would do what was asked of me. I had also learned that when necessary, I could forget about myself and focus on doing what was required to get another fighter pilot out of a bad situation.

Experience had shown that the first ten missions were the most dangerous for new pilots. No one knew whether that applied equally to new lieutenants just out of training as well as to senior flight leads, but the policy was to avoid sending new guys to Pack VI until they had completed their first ten missions. That hadn't worked for Richter, but the combination of bad weather and pressure among the established ex–McConnell pilots to finish up their tours had kept me from the final test. I didn't question the schedule but merely followed through on my now well-established plan to eke one more mission out before quitting. I had gotten the full ten counters before my number came up for Pack VI.

This was the major leagues. I was flying number Four on the wing of the squadron assistant operations officer, Maj. John Shay in an Iron Hand flight. Iron Hand was a Navy code word for the SAM-suppression mission, but USAF crews had adopted it as well. We were tasked to support a bombing strike on a military storage area at Thai Nguyen, an industrial city north of Hanoi. Our flight lead was Capt. "Buns" Frazier, a portly senior fighter pilot flying an F-100F Wild Weasel.

The mass briefing was my first look at a big show. Flight crews assembled in the command post planning area three hours before takeoff. A huge wall map depicted the target area as well as locations of refueling tracks, MiG combat air patrol flights (MigCAP), electronic warfare EB-66 orbits, and prepositioning of search and rescue (SAR) assets. Beside the map, a listing of takeoff times, assigned tankers, tanker drop-off time, and time-on-target (TOT) showed the sequence of events. On another bulletin board was a listing of call signs, ordnance loads, radio frequencies for the day, and code words to relay information about the mission back to command and control centers.

The Iron Hand flight was Cactus. The Weasel would be carrying two AGM-45 Shrike missiles as would John Russell, who was flying the number two position. The second element, Shay and I, would be armed with four CBU-24 cluster bomb units on the centerline rack. All of this was new to me. It was the first time I became aware that the F-105D could carry the Shrike, and it would be my first encounter with the CBU. It was a perfect ordnance for attacking soft targets like SAM sites. About the size of a 750-pound bomb, the CBU consisted of two clamshell sections that looked like a bomb that had been sawed in half from nose to tail. Inside the shell were several hundred baseball-sized bomblets. A timer fuse in the nose fired a preset number of seconds after release, allowing the weapon to function above the ground. As the weapon fell and when the preset time was reached, a primacord seam blew, separating the two halves and dispersing the bomblets. When they hit the ground the bomblets blew up like several hundred hand grenades. The CBU was delivered pretty much the same way as an iron bomb, with the big advantage that you didn't have to be quite as accurate.

A compartmentalized distribution box next to the wall map had sections labeled with each flight's call sign. Within each cubicle were five maps and five mimeographed cards with the code words and frequencies, one for each flight member and the flight spare. I found the box labeled "Cactus," picked up one of the maps, then went looking for Major Shay. I found him at one of the planning tables with Frazier and his EWO. I started to fill out my lineup card, copying information from the one that Shay had shoved under my nose.

Other crews were gathered around the planning room, roaming to the wall charts to copy coordinates or tanker information, or clustering by flight to talk about tactics or defenses. I finished filling out my card, somewhat astonished at the complexity of the information compared to the single-flight missions I'd already flown. Shay and Frazier had little to say to me, and I couldn't think of anything to ask them. I checked my watch; it was five minutes to the scheduled briefing time. Pilots were already shuffling into the main briefing room and settling into the theater style, fold-down seats. Aligned in the front center was a row of four large armchairs upholstered in red leather, each with a table on the right side holding a black loose-leaf binder. These chairs were reserved for the wing commander, deputy commander for operations, the mission commander for the day, and any visiting dignitaries that might be on base.

A raised stage dominated the front of the room with a speaker's podium on the left side, a large projection screen lowered to cover the back wall, and an overhead slide projector on a small table in the center. An American flag stood in a floor stand to the left of the podium, which displayed the crest of the 388th Tactical Fighter Wing on the front. On the wall on each side of the screen hung a large framed poster in stark black lettering on a plain, unadorned white background. The message was simple and, I thought, stunningly redundant. "The Mission of the United States Air Force Is to Fly & Fight. Don't You Ever Forget It!" How the hell could anyone forget that we were here to fight? I devoutly wished I could forget it, at least for an hour or two.

The lights dimmed, the chatter hushed, and a major in tans climbed the three stairs to the stage and stood behind the podium. An airman with a stack of viewgraph slides sat in a chair next to the projector. He turned on the light and the briefing agenda splashed onto the screen. The major offered a terse "Good morning," then went through the routine of a time hack.

"The target for today is the Thai Nguyen military storage area, located 4.3 miles southwest of the center of Thai Nguyen city. The strike package includes four flights of four F-105s from here at Korat: Pine, Elm, Redwood, and Maple.

You'll be supported by Cactus flight for Iron Hand, and Teal 35, an EB-66 jammer. MiGCAP will be flown by Buick and Cadillac flights, F-4s out of Udorn. Refueling for Korat forces will be on Red Anchor extension with flights assigned to the tankers as noted on the chart. SAR forces will be Jolly Green 21 and Sandy 31, flight of four A-1s on orbit over Lima 85 in northern Laos."

A slide with a map displayed the tanker tracks, each with a flight call sign neatly printed next to it, as well as the SAR orbit just short of the North Vietnam – Laos border. Grease-penciled onto the slide was the recommended route. A straight line extended from the usual refueling orbit in Thailand to a drop-off point at 20 degrees north latitude. From there the line proceeded nearly straight north across the Black River in North Vietnam to a point along the Red River just north of a town called Yen Bai. From there the track headed east, directly across a prominent mountain ridge to the target triangle, which was superimposed on the city of Thai Nguyen.

Small silhouette icons dotted the map showing the location of defenses. Tiny airplanes showed the location of MiG bases at Phuc Yen, Kep, Hanoi's Gia Lam, and even at Yen Bai. Little red missile outlines showed possible SAM locations, each with a thirty-mile-radius circle around it in black to denote the missile's maximum reach. To minimize confusion, the circles weren't completed, but only displayed the total coverage of the missile sites as a composite outline. All of Route Pack VI was effectively covered by the missile rings. Various-caliber anti-aircraft guns were shown in color-coded circles as well. Those rings made little difference to the whole picture because they were everywhere too.

Next came the intelligence portion of the briefing. A lieutenant from intel whom I hadn't previously encountered approached the screen with a long wooden pointer. Mechanically, he noted what the slide had already made apparent. The target was heavily defended. There were SAMs, MiGs, and lots of guns.

Weather came next. A chart showed the airfield temperature and wind direction for the launch period. A map of Southeast Asia showed expected cloud coverage and winds at altitude. Finally, a target-area map showed the expected weather conditions and winds at various bombing release altitudes. The farther north we went, the worse the weather was supposed to be. By the time we got to the Red River, the weather was forecast to be broken to overcast, with areas of heavy rain. It wasn't a pretty forecast, so it gave me some hope that we wouldn't have to go.

When the weatherman finished, the major from operations returned to the podium, asked for any questions, and when there were none, dismissed the group. Silently, we all stood and moved out of the auditorium. Several groups of four returned to the squadron buildings for their individual flight briefings. Russell waved me over to one of the planning tables, where Frazier and Shay were spreading maps and lineup cards.

As the flight lead, Frazier started through the flight briefing checklist, making sure we all had a good time hack and the required details of the mission. Our job was to protect the strike force from any SAM sites. The Weasel would monitor the radars on the air and would try to locate them on the ground. If a radar stayed on the air long enough, he would fire a Shrike. If the rest of the flight could see the Shrike impact, we would attack the location. If we could follow the radar vectors on the APR-25/26, we would try to acquire the SAM site visually and then attack it. If the SAM site fired a missile at us, we would first evade the missile, then attack the site that fired it. "If the sonofabitch comes up on us, we're gonna kill him," Frazier concluded.

Frazier and his EWO left. With less than half an hour remaining until we would have to head out to the aircraft, Major Shay reviewed the flight details. I was awed by the choreography required to bring more than fifty aircraft together from several different bases in an integrated attack plan. We needed to fit into a scenario that already had the tankers airborne from Kadena Air Base on Okinawa and Don Muang airport at Bangkok. We had to start engines in a sequence, taxi in the proper order, take off on time, and even make our radio channel changes and check-ins in the proper sequence with other flights.

Once again I was caught in that downhill slide of expectation. If I'd wanted to quit before facing the defenses of Pack VI, I should have done it yesterday. I was now part of a tightly knit package and giving up would not only mark me as a coward, it would, more importantly, endanger a large and complex operation. It was too late to get a replacement to fly my position, and Shay couldn't go without me on his wing. Without the element, the Weasel couldn't go and, without the Weasel, the strike package would be in much greater danger. I was going, whether I liked it or not.

The parachute room was as congested as it had been on the day I arrived. Several flights were all vying for space as they zipped G-suits, donned survival vests, checked their emergency radios, collected their guns from the safe, and swung the heavy parachutes onto their backs. Conversation was subdued, with none of the joking or sarcasm that usually characterized the preflight period. Guys that had completed suiting up were quietly clustered at the ops counter waiting for the duty officer to get aircraft tail numbers from maintenance.

The phone from maintenance rang at almost the same time as the field phone growled. Sergeant Morgan grabbed the maintenance phone, while the duty officer took the field phone call from the command post. Morgan scribbled numbers in grease pencil on the schedule board next to our flight lineup, while the duty officer nodded his head and waved a thumbs up to us. We had a go for the mission.

Pilots in flight gear poured out of the squadron buildings and jumped into the fleet of multicolored Datsuns. Green trucks turned toward the 469th revetments, the blue pickup from the Weasel detachment headed toward the three F-100s, and our three red trucks roared off to the 421st aircraft. Each of us jumped from the still-moving truck as it passed almost under the long nose and pitot tube of our assigned aircraft.

Preflight and strap-in went quickly, and it seemed like only seconds later that the first hiss and whine of a start cart firing indicated the time for me to push the button on my aircraft. Barely three minutes later came the first litany of call signs that would characterize all Pack VI missions.

"Cactus, check."

"Two." "Three." "Four."

"Pine." "Two." "Three." "Four."

"Elm." "Twoop." "Three." "Fourp."

"Redwood." "Two." "Three." "Four."

"Maple." "Two." "Three." "Four." It took less than ten seconds.

"Korat, Cactus, taxi," came at the same time I heard the throttle move up on John Russell's bird in the revetment next to mine. He needed to start early to meet the F-100 at the main taxiway. I signaled the crew chief to pull the chocks then started forward. The hot exhaust from Russell's airplane was still swirling down the ramp as I turned to fall into position behind Shay, who was already aligned on the taxiway. I was almost elated to be part of such a large package of men and machines.

Arming was quick, and we were lining up on the runway. The three F-105s dwarfed the Weasel. As Frazier released brakes and lit the afterburner, the Super Sabre's J-57 engine seemed almost puny. We gave him twenty seconds rather than the usual twelve to get spacing before Russell rolled. Shay released brakes after twelve seconds, and then I rolled. I felt the bang of the AB light, then the comforting shove of the extra two thousand pounds of thrust when the water injection came on. The airplane lifted off at just under two hundred knots, and I left the burner in as the gear came up and I started a right turn to rejoin.

We contacted Brigham and got a vector to Red 21 Papa, orbiting near Nakhon Phanom. The flight settled into a comfortable route formation, with Russell on the right wing and Shay's element on the left. Other flights were checking in as they got airborne, following us from Korat to the cell of five Red track tankers stacked at thousand-foot intervals and roughly a mile in trail of each other. Brigham's radio chatter reflected the difficulty of running five separate flights of four fighters each toward five separate tankers in close proximity of each other.

The tanker orbit was an elongated racetrack flown between two anchor points defined by the Udorn TACAN. The lead tanker was at FL 160 or sixteen thousand feet, with each successive tanker in the cell maintaining altitude at one thousand feet higher. Legs of the orbit were forty miles long with the tankers holding 280 knots until the fighters joined up, then the tanker would push up his speed to 325 for refueling. Depending on where in the orbit the cell was when the fighters completed their rendezvous, the maneuvers could range from mild to wild. A good flight lead could be a big help in holding his flight together, planning ahead for the rejoin and keeping clear of all the other flights converging on the tanker cell from various directions and altitudes. Frazier had done this before.

With a wing dip to the right, he echeloned the formation to his right wing. We were in an easy left turn to fall in behind the first tanker. As number Four, I could look through the other three aircraft in the flight and watch the closure on the KC-135 as we converged and smoothly eased into formation on the tanker's right wing. At the end of the tanker's extended boom, the drogue basket bobbed along almost tauntingly on its twelve-foot hose. With five flights converging on five different tankers, all on a single radio frequency, the sequence of "mandatory" radio calls was thrown out the window. The boom operator simply called, "Cactus, cleared in."

It looked easy as the F-100 smoothly banked left, then immediately reversed right and swayed into position behind the basket. The probe was not retractable, as on the 105, but permanently fixed on the right wing. Hookup was quick, virtually effortless, because the probe's wing position eliminated the over-the-nose airflow interference that I'd encountered two weeks earlier. As Cactus Lead took his fuel, the radio was busy with the other flights checking in on the frequency, rejoining on their respective tankers, and starting their refueling.

The tanker reached the south end of the orbit as lead finished taking fuel. He moved to the left wing as Russell slid into position behind the basket. The turning tanker made it more difficult for John, but after two pokes he hooked up and took his gas. Shay followed on the northbound leg, and I was up just after the turn at the north end of the track. I could feel the tension increase as I slid into position. I extended the probe and tried to recall the lessons that Bill Sanders had taught me. I stabilized behind the basket, aimed for the ten o'clock corner, then looked forward as I cobbed the throttle to 100 percent. Amazingly, the probe slid smoothly into the drogue. I was taking gas.

The secret, I was told, was to fly formation on the knuckle. The twelve-foot hose was connected to the refueling boom with a large aluminum fitting. All I had to do was fly close formation with that fitting. Move the airplane forward to double up the hose, placing the basket next to the knuckle, then stay there with small control movements, correcting position as though I were flying wing on another airplane. Simple enough, but easier said than done. I dropped a bit low and eased in a bit of back pressure to correct. I was moving left toward the knuckle and pressed the rudder to get away a bit. I was coming up high and overshooting the position I wanted, so I clicked the nose-down trim and let the aircraft drop slightly. Oops. Too low, pull back. Now roll right to get closer. The oscillations were getting bigger and I was sweating like a pig. Up, down, now back up. I was churning the stick around like I was mixing a bowl of cake batter. If there'd been a generator attached I could've lit the city of Los Angeles. My overshoots were getting bigger, and then I was in a classic PIO. A pilot-induced oscillation. One pitch overshoot after another, each one requiring a larger correction, and each one being a split second too late. I dropped off the basket before I either ripped it off or broke my probe.

I'd taken about forty-five-hundred pounds of fuel. The lead tanker called that we had to depart the refueling orbit now and start our extension run up to 20 degrees north latitude, where the strike force would drop off and head to the

Cockpit photo taken with Joe Vojir's helmet, and no survival vest was displayed on the squadron wall. Losses made keeping the photos up to date a difficult task.

Major Bill Loyd, squadron operations officer, relaxes at his desk.

Capt. Bob Loken at the duty desk a few weeks prior to his shootdown.

CINCPAC Adm. U.S. Grant Sharp presents me with the Air Medal for my first ten combat missions.

Lts. Karl Richter and Ed Harvey at the 421st.

MiG Killers, Maj. Fred Tracy and Lt. Karl Richter, celebrate Tracy's one-hundredth mission. Courtesy Jeff Koln.

A-1E Sandy starting his engine in a cloud of oil smoke. Courtesy Wayne Mutza.

Spider Spelius, author, and roommate Bill Ricks celebrate on landing from our one-hundredth combat mission.

Six years later, still with a bulletproof mustache, I lean against the bombs on an F-4E at Korat prior to heading back north to the same targets.

The Bat Bird gets a night runup to make sure the engine is in peak condition. Courtesy David Hansen.

The Bat Bird loaded with eight 750-pound bombs. Note the unpainted 450-gallon tanks indicating that the pace of operations didn't allow time for painting prior to use. 62-4334 Courtesy Col. Bob Krone via Theo Van Geffen/IAAP.

Two aircraft loaded with M-118 three-thousand-pound bombs refuel en route to the target area. Courtesy USAF via Theo Van Geffen/IAAP.

Roscoe lived at Korat from 1966 until he quietly passed away in September 1975. He was laid to rest in front of the Korat Officers' Club with a plaque marking his grave. Few doubt that he wags his tail and walks beside Ray Lewis in a fighter pilot's heaven. Courtesy Col. Lucky Ekman via Theo Van Geffen/IAAP.

Jet exhaust creates a haze over the taxiway as the strike force forms up prior to takeoff. Courtesy Theo Van Geffen.

A pair of 105s with finned napalm cruise amid the typical cloud layers. Courtesy USAF.

A bomb-loaded airplane slides into contact position. Several birds were not yet camouflaged at Korat when I arrived. Courtesy USAF.

Capt. Tom Coady about to roll in his Suzi Baby. Coady would eventually log more combat time in the F-105 than any other pilot. Courtesy Col. Tom Coady.

Headed north with eight M-117s, this Tahkli airplane tops off one last time. Courtesy Col. Tom Coady.

Loaded with six M-117 bombs, a single-seat
F-105D taxis. Courtesy Larsen/Remington via
the Air Force Museum.

Cart start of this Wild Weasel two-seater fills
the air with black smoke. Courtesy USAF.

A-1E and
HH-3, the
rescue team
in flight.
Courtesy
USAF.

This photo of a damaged aircraft is typical of the "morale" photos on the wall at the entrance to the command post. An Atoll missile from a MiG engagement caused this damage. Courtesy Republic Aviation via Dennis Jenkins.

Taxiing in at the end of a combat tour, it became a 105 tradition to give the world the "finger" with an extended refueling probe. Courtesy Bill Erickson.

Bill Loyd's grin on completion of his one hundredth mission shows that even experienced fighter pilots can feel a sense of relief. Loyd also had one hundred missions and a MiG kill during the Korean conflict.

target area. I had about eight minutes to get back on the damn drogue and get another three thousand pounds. I pushed the throttle up and banged past the drogue. Then I eased off and stabilized. I moved forward again. Contact. Taking gas again. "Cactus Four, let's get going." Frazier sounded less than encouraging. He needed to top off to replace the fuel he'd been burning, and the rest of the flight needed to cycle through for one more transfer. I glanced out of the corner of my eye to see how close my fuel gauge was to full. I was within a thousand pounds. I eased off the drogue and slid onto Shay's wing, on the left side of the tanker.

We reached 20 degrees north before I could get back on the tanker. Shay was just hooking up when Red 21 called his left turn south. Ahead of us in the distance, a wall of towering black cumulus spread from east to west. Below us the broad, cratered expanse of the Plain of Jars in central Laos, the fabled PDJ, showed that this land had been at war for a long time. I was about fifteen hundred pounds below the rest of the flight when Frazier called for an ops check. I hoped it wouldn't matter.

"Cactus, strike primary," started the call-sign litany that would get the whole package from refueling frequency to the discrete channel for the day's mission. We checked in and almost immediately saw the F-100's wings rock signaling our flight to close up our tactical spread as we neared the wall of clouds. This was going to be a problem. As I was closing on Shay's wing, I dropped my left hand off the throttle to the radar control panel. I slowly tilted the antenna up and down and watched as greenish blobs bloomed on the scope in front of me signifying thunderstorm cells ahead. We had space enough to pick our way between the cells, just to the left of our track, but the F-100 leading us didn't have our radar. Once the 105s moved into close formation on our leader's wing, we wouldn't be able to watch our own scopes.

"Buick, Cactus. How's it look ahead?" Frazier was calling the MiGCAP F-4 flight to check on the weather conditions. The F-4 had better air-to-air radar than our Thunderchiefs and also had a second pilot to operate it, so the aircraft commander could concentrate on flying instruments in bad weather.

"Cactus, Buick Lead. I'm leveling at thirty-one thousand and it's solid in front of me. We're edging to the west to see if we can get around."

That didn't do us much good. The 105s with bombs couldn't get much above twenty thousand feet and our flight, on the wing of the Weasel, was slogging into the weather at sixteen thousand. The Weasel was working hard to provide a stable platform for us to fly formation off of in the clouds, but his best cruising speed with full fuel tanks and the Shrike missiles was just 360 knots. We would have been a lot happier at 420, and I knew that when we got closer to the target area I'd be wishing for 500 knots or faster. We were wallowing in the sky, and now that we were fully into the clouds, I could just barely see past Shay's airplane to make out the gray outline of the F-100F's canopy. It was dark, but so far we hadn't encountered much turbulence.

I kept glancing at the flight instruments while trying to maintain position on my element lead. He was flying formation off the F-100, fighting his own aircraft to keep position, while I was flying off of his bouncing airplane trying desperately to smooth out the gyrations. In the clouds the only reference I had was to keep Shay's wingtip aligned with the star in the USAF decal on his aft fuselage. Keep those two points aligned left and right, up and down, and I would be going wherever his airplane went. It wouldn't matter if he climbed or dived, turned left or right, sped up or slowed down. I'd be in formation. But my head might not agree with what was going on. The inner ear knows when you turn and roll and it viciously attempts to override your brain. Your eyes see one thing and your ear tells your mind another. Checking the attitude indicator could add the tiebreaking vote and help stabilize my head. I checked the Doppler distance to the turning point north of Yen Bai, wondering if we'd still be in the weather when we got there. Sixty miles to go, but Frazier didn't know that. His F-100 didn't have a

Doppler or an inertial nav system either. He was flying time and distance on a precomputed heading. State-of-the-1940s-art dead reckoning.

"Buick, Cadillac." The second MiGCAP flight was calling.

"Roger, Cadillac. Buick's going company." The leads of the two Phantom flights that were to defend us against enemy aircraft were switching to their squadron frequency to talk over the weather situation and what to do about it. From their higher altitude and with their longer range radar, I was hoping they might call this whole thing off before we got much further. Cactus was pressing on. We were lower, and we were slower, but we were at least thirty miles ahead of everyone else. They would close that distance by the time we got to the target area, where we were scheduled to be just a few minutes ahead of the first bombing flight.

Before long Buick and Cadillac returned to the strike frequency. "Cactus, Pine, Elm. This is Buick Lead. Cadillac reports the weather is towering to over forty thousand from his position, and I don't see anything better where I am. I'm aborting for weather. Recommend you do the same." It looked like I was going to get a reprieve.

Frazier's response was cryptic. "Roger, Buick." He acknowledged but didn't indicate what he was going to do about it. We were still in the clouds and my DME was showing about thirty miles to the turn point over the Red River, which was about 10 degrees to the left of our present heading. I wasn't sure whether I wanted to keep going straight and level or hang onto the wing in the clouds for a 180-degree turn. It wasn't my choice anyway. We were still going north.

The dark gray murk began to thin and lighten. I could see the other three airplanes entirely, and ahead of us the sky was considerably brighter. We were almost out of the clouds . . . then I could see ground. A valley. Dark and overcast. Deep gray granite outcroppings on the hills and very dark green foliage. Steep but not too narrow, maybe ten or twelve miles across. I almost miss the rudder wag as Frazier signals the formation to move out of close and get to a two-ship-width route. Then I'm looking at the entire top of Shay's airplane. He's coming at me and obviously getting to tactical spread not route. I slam the stick into my left knee while pushing forward, and I'm nearly blinded by a rising wave of sand, dust, bits of paper, and two old cigarette butts that the negative Gs have unloaded from beneath the cockpit floorboards. I'm inverted, but haven't been hit, so I continue through the complete roll to see Shay's airplane still headed west above me. He doesn't know where I am, and I've got a strong feeling he doesn't much care. I pull across below him and take advantage of the descent to get up to five hundred knots. When I'm clear to his left I pull up into line-abreast spread, and he probably thinks I was there all the time.

"Cactus has Fire Cans on the nose. Two rings. Green 'em up." I can see more of the valley now. There's a river below, maybe two hundred yards across. It stretches from northwest to southeast, meandering along the valley floor. It's got to be the Red. I check my Doppler and notice that we're a good ten miles south of where we had planned to cross and that means . . . awww, shit. We're going to pass right over Yen Bai. Shay's airplane is inverted now, and he's pulling down. Frazier and Russell are spread out in line abreast about a mile right of us. Before I can match my leader's descent, he's back turning right and the vapor trails off the wings tell me he's got a lot of G on the airplane. I'm pulling right to stay with him, and I've simply planted the throttle against the forward stop wondering if I'm going to need afterburner to follow these gyrations. I've got the switches set for the CBU and the sight set. The whole flight has edged downward so that now we're dancing at about five or six thousand feet above the ground.

"Cactus has a Fan Song now. Just looking at us. We're getting some 85s." Yeah, right. The common sense of Shay's wild gyrations now becomes very apparent as the black puffs of the big guns start popping up behind us. There's a whole block of little white popcorn balls, maybe a full mile across and a thousand feet deep, just to the right of Russell's position across the formation. Frazier doesn't seem to notice all the flak, as he points his airplane toward the rising terrain east of us. Several rows of foothills cross our line of flight and then the real mountain range rises into the dark overcast. The target lies on the other side of that range. The F-100 doesn't seem able to go much faster than four hundred knots and our three F-105s don't want to slow down to that speed.

"Cactus, Teal 35."

"Roger Teal, are you on station?"

"That's negative, Cactus; we got off late, and we can't get through the weather. Are you aware that Buick aborted?"

We're well across the Red now and out of range of Yen Bai's guns. Now the EB-66 isn't here, and we're definitely within range of the SAMs. The Weasel is steadily headed east while our aircraft violently S-turn trying to keep a reasonable speed and not overrun him. It's as though our birds won't let us slow down. I haven't pulled my throttle back from full military power since we popped out of the clouds, and it's all I can do to stay somewhere close to my tactical spread position on the jinking Shay. Russell is keeping line abreast of Frazier by working in and out. None of us seems capable of even thinking about slowing.

"Cactus is approaching the second turn point, coming onto the ridge. Pine, are you inbound yet?" All I can think about is wanting to get out of here. When are we going to get back across the river? What's wrong with Frazier? Doesn't he know this whole package is coming apart? The MigCAP aborted, the jammer aborted, and we haven't talked to the strikers in days. Where the hell are we going and why?

"Cactus, Pine. What's your position?"

"Roger, Pine. Cactus is almost to the ridge. We've got a Fan Song up, and we're getting ready to work him. The weather breaks up over the river, but there's cloud cover all over the top of the ridge. Don't know if you can make it. . . . Cactus is coming left. . . . We've got three rings on the nose now . . ."

"Rog, Cactus. Pine's breaking out now and it's totally

socked a few miles in front of us. I'm calling this thing off.
We won't be able to get through. Copy that Elm, Redwood,
and Maple?"

Thank God, someone has some sense. Now, how long is it
going to take for Frazier to get turned around and get us out
of here? We're down to about two thousand feet above the
jungle, and the clouds above us are restricting our vertical
movements. Every time Shay comes toward me I have to roll
away from him and yank into a turn. When I roll out he's
usually reversed again and I pull back. The four bomb-
carrying flights have all acknowledged the weather abort and
are on their way back south to alternate targets in Laos.
We're now defending a nonexistent strike package against
some very real SAM sites. This is beginning to look just
plain dumb.

"So long Pine. Cactus is coming easy left. Three rings on
the nose. Watch yourself guys. Steady zero six five. Steady."

We're still pressing on against a SAM site. Frazier is fix-
ated on the attack. I check my heading and glance at my fuel
gauge. The short refueling and the violent maneuvering
since we crossed the Red have taken a toll. I'm below bingo
fuel by five hundred pounds. We aren't all the way to the target area so there is a little pad in the gas required to get back
home safely, and everyone expects the number four aircraft
to use a little more gas. Should I call bingo and get us out of
here or should I press a little bit to let Frazier continue? The
strike force is gone. The weather is crap. Bullshit! "Cactus
Four is bingo."

Frazier is obviously pissed. He's got some kind of grudge
against this SAM site, and my fuel state is going to keep him
from pressing the attack. Worse yet is the problem of how to
disengage from the SAM that has been watching our approach. With the SAM in front of us, we've got a good defensive posture, but when we try to turn to leave the area, the
SAM may well fire if he's got a good shot. Before I realize
what's happening, I see the F-100's nose come up, and with a
bright flash, a Shrike comes off the rail. "Cactus, come left to
240," is Lead's call.

With the lead element coming hard into us, Shay eases off his jinking and makes the first reasonable move since we broke out of the clouds over Yen Bai. He floats across behind the other aircraft allowing us to maintain our high speed. We're slightly above our leader when the reversal is finished, just below the cloud layer. Frazier is going to cut the corner and pass southeast of Yen Bai, hopefully avoiding another flak barrage on our way outbound. The Shrike has done its job of keeping the Fan Song radar off the air as we head for home.

Across the Red we climb to thirty-one thousand feet and cruise home between the tops of the storm clouds. We track southbound to TACAN channel 36 in central Laos, then directly to Korat. The weather improves all the way, and by the time we cross the Mekong into northern Thailand, the sun is shining brightly. After landing, debriefing doesn't take long because most of the flights have not yet returned from their alternate drop areas. Frazier has little to say about the flight, and Shay doesn't offer any critiques either.

When I left the squadron building the sun was setting. I heard the whine of taxiing J-75s and looked out on the flight line to see six airplanes in a row with the lead airplane just turning off the parallel toward a crew chief with two flashlights raised to guide him into a parking spot. Each of the aircraft had the refueling probe extended, figuratively giving the finger to anyone who might notice. They were F-105s, but they were different. As they pulled into a neatly aligned row and shut down, each airplane in sequence opened its canopies. Two of them per aircraft. They were F-105Fs. They were the first of the 105 Wild Weasels. Things were going to be changing rapidly.

Ten missions over North Vietnam got you an Air Medal. It didn't take any bravery or special success; merely survive the challenge of poking your nose across the border ten times and you get a medal. When you got to one hundred, you'd have ten of the things; well, not really ten medals, just one medal and a bunch of tiny metal oak-leaf clusters denoting multiple awards of the gong. It was all automatic. Sergeant Morgan's office processed the paperwork about once a week. If you had passed the ten-mission mark during the previous couple of days, he put you in for the award.

I was walking down the hall after a mission debrief when Morgan asked me to step into the admin office. "Take a look at this form, and see if we've got all the right information on you." Morgan shoved a medal recommendation across the desk. I scanned it quickly, checking my name, address, service number, and date of rank. It all seemed correct. Then I checked the section on schools completed and noted that I had successfully completed Jungle Survival School during May. Amazing, I thought. The mere flick of a pencil on a training square is as good as a week among the lizards and snakes in the Philippines. I didn't complain. I'd rather fly combat than go back to the house of horrors at Clark.

Less than a week later, it was announced that we were going to be visited by CINCPAC, the commander-in-chief of all U.S. forces in the Pacific. This is the guy running the war, the tallest dog in the pack after the president, SecDef, and chairman of the JCS. I was told to be available at three in the afternoon on Friday in 1505s for a presentation of awards by the CINC, Adm. U. S. Grant Sharp. I was going to get my Air Medal pinned on by the big boss.

Actually, he turned out to be a small boss. Admiral Sharp was a short, spare, gray-haired gentleman. He presided over a brief ceremony in which he thanked a small group of us for service to our country, then walked down the row and pinned a medal on us one by one. There was a pause for a handshake and a picture with every recipient. Admiral Sharp's remarks caused considerable discussion among those of us in attendance after the presentation. He didn't seem to have any knowledge of what we did at Korat or why we got the medals. He didn't seem to understand that we were bombing North Vietnam or that we were suffering serious losses. He didn't acknowledge that he knew about a bomb shortage or that anything was being done about ordnance availability. He seemed blithely ignorant that there was even a war going on.

Either he had the ability to take the denial of operations from Thai bases to new levels of secrecy, or he was totally clueless. The small, elderly man certainly didn't motivate or offer anything that might have been construed as leadership. I couldn't picture him striding purposefully ashore like MacArthur at Leyte or walking among the paratroops like Eisenhower on the eve of D-Day. If medals ceremonies are meant to express the gratitude of a nation and to encourage the recipients to further sacrifice, the Air Medal ceremony with Admiral Sharp was a dismal failure. We hurried from the command post back to our quarters to get out of the uniforms and back into more comfortable flying clothes. A cold drink at the club was a better reward and a damn sight more motivating.

CHAPTER 11

Changing of the Guard

It didn't happen overnight, obviously, but it happened with surprising speed. One day I was part of a group of young lieutenants, recent arrivals from training who were outsiders of a closed group. The next, we were part of a new, exciting and seriously changed team. The McConnell guys finished their tours. They didn't all do it on the same day and maybe not in the same week, but they finished. By ones and twos they flew their final, hundredth missions, and with little fanfare they departed the base. For some there was a welcome home ceremony, quickly mustered at the foot of the ladder as they dismounted from their last flights. A yell would ring down the hall from the duty desk, and everyone available in the squadron was expected to head out the door, jump in the back of one of the Datsuns, and ride down the flight line to offer congratulations. Since few of them had offered much to us in the way of support, friendship or even leadership, we didn't add much to the celebration. Joy was for those who had finished the tour, and sharing the joy was for those who expected to follow the same path shortly. We dutifully rode out to the parking spot, stood around and mumbled to each other, shook hands when our turn came, then waited for the trucks to return to the squadron building. There may have been celebrations at the O Club later, but they were hardly noticed and any invitations for new guys to join the festivities were backhanded at best.

Departures were balanced by arrivals, of course. Hardly a day went by without one or two new pilots arriving at the squadron on the morning Klong. The majority of the inbounds were experienced F-105 pilots, but they differed considerably from the somewhat reluctant warriors we had never quite become accustomed to. These were guys from the other side of the world who had been flying the big bird in Europe, doing the peacetime nuclear-alert mission while their brothers-in-arms had been involved in a shooting war. While Tactical Air Command had been sending volunteers on temporary duty to the war, the troops in USAFE (USAF Europe) had been locked in place in Germany. Now the clock had rolled far enough forward that they could begin rotating back home, or, for those who wanted to be a part of the war, to Thailand. Like the initial cadre, these guys were eager and aggressive. They were well trained, experienced, and willing to get the job done. Bill Loyd was joined by old squadron mates from Bitburg and Spangdahlem so that the squadron quickly became a new machine assembled from well-oiled parts, smoothed and trued by careful use.

At a Friday afternoon squadron meeting the new leadership of the 421st was announced. Lieutenant Colonel Barnett was leaving, along with Bill Sanders and John Shay. Of the three, the only one that I'd had any good experiences with was Sanders. I'd miss him and his quiet, almost grandfatherly patience. The other two were not going to be missed. Replacing Barnett was Maj. Fred Tracy, recently arrived from Bitburg. Loyd would be the squadron operations officer, the number two man. Having a major as squadron commander was extremely unusual. It wasn't quite the same as the twenty-one-year-old boy colonels in the World War II bomb groups, but it was close. There was a shortage of F-105 pilots, and although Tracy couldn't yet get the rank to be a squadron commander, he could definitely get the responsibility.

The instructor force from the training unit at Nellis was also inbound to the war. As 105 pilots completed their tours, many were routed back to the training squadrons to provide a combat-experienced flavor to the training. With instructor replacements arriving, that meant IPs with lots of flying time could go to war. Captains and majors that we had met during our qualification in the airplane were now joining their former students. We knew them and they knew us. There was mutual respect and a mutual understanding of capabilities, something that had been missing during my first month at Korat. Among the prominent arrivals from Nellis was our old scheduler, Wimpy Peake.

It is an unwritten rule in a fighter squadron that the squadron commander and operations officer play "good cop – bad cop," to keep the organization on track. One of the two is the ramrod, while the other is the father figure. The ramrod beats you into submission, forcing you to do the things you don't want to do, such as pull night mobile or Friday afternoon duty desk. He makes sure that the training takes place, the squadron snack bar is stocked, the paperwork is up to snuff, and the mission is accomplished. You don't have to like him, and he usually projects the image that he doesn't care either way. He's simply there to get the job done.

The father figure shields the organization from abuse from the higher echelons. He goes to bat to keep his people from being overworked and, in the case of combat, from being overexposed to danger without justification. He's the guy who counsels and cajoles, helping you through problems, praising your achievements, and gently correcting your transgressions. You instinctively like him.

Tracy and Loyd weren't like that. There was no bad guy on the team. They didn't lead by intimidation or aggression, but rather through professionalism and charisma. We immediately liked them both. Make no mistake, they weren't coddlers. They were leaders who demanded high standards — the standards that they themselves met and demonstrated on the ground and in the air. The first aircrew meeting after the announcement spelled out the agenda of the new regime.

We were going to be mission effective. We were going to do the job. We were going to take care of our people. We were going to get to the target and come home in formation, doing the job as briefed and without the "every man for himself" scrambling that had often characterized the Route Pack VI missions. We'd shut up on the radio, using hand and aircraft signals rather than radio calls. When the shooting started, everyone knew it, so why garbage up the airwaves with screaming and yelling that did little but point out the obvious? It would become a cliché, but all a good wingman was supposed to say on the radio was "two," "bandits," and "bingo." Acknowledge Lead's direction, call out enemy aircraft, and advise when your fuel is low. Loyd jokingly added, "If you want to say more, it had better be 'Mayday!' and you'd better eject right afterward."

Tactics were going to change from low-altitude run-ins exposed to every peasant with a rifle to a more tailored approach at medium altitude that would provide improved lookout, easier navigation, better target acquisition, and less exposure to small arms. We'd always be in spread formation, line abreast, and with assigned lookout areas of responsibility. All attack profiles would brief a rejoin maneuver coming off the target, so the flight could get back into a mutually supporting formation as quickly as possible. No one would go anywhere alone. If you didn't have a partner to form a two-ship element, you would abort.

Mission accomplishment meant bombs on target. It also meant a prudent evaluation of risk to ensure that returns would be commensurate with the investment. Strafing ten-thousand-dollar trucks was fun, but it wasn't worth risking a fifteen-million-dollar airplane. Armed recce was part of the mission, but trolling for guns wasn't. Loyd was quick to point out that dueling with large caliber guns using our twenty-millimeter cannon was like "pissing in the wind." Silencing a gun was satisfying, but we'd pick our fights. If we found a singleton, we'd be more than happy to put him out of commission, but making multiple strafe passes against a full battery or array of guns was stupid, and we wouldn't be doing it.

Equity in scheduling would be paramount. The whisperings about favoritism and avoidance of high-threat missions by a few would end. Wimpy Peake was taking over the scheduling shop. A new information board would go up behind the ops counter that would list everyone who flew with the squadron, both assigned squadron pilots and attached wing staff members. The board would show individual mission counts by month and for the entire combat tour, with a breakout showing "counters" for one-hundred-mission credit, noncounter combat missions into Laos, and high-threat combat missions into Route Pack VI. You could easily monitor your progress toward the goal as well as ascertain that everyone was carrying an equal share of the load.

We'd get time off that we could use however we wished. Each pilot would accrue one day off for every seven days in a row he worked. You could collect as many days off as you wanted and then go anywhere that was reachable. In one of the strangest convolutions of logic in what was admittedly a strange war, we weren't authorized R&R. Our government had an agreement with the Thais that said we weren't officially conducting combat operations from Thailand. Since we weren't flying combat, we didn't qualify for government-funded rest and recreation. If we could get a hop from a friendly transport crew, we could go anywhere, just as long as we could get back.

The squadron aircraft would be assigned to individual pilots. Each of us would get our own airplane with our name on the canopy rail. We would get to fly our own airplanes whenever they came up for a launch at the same time we were scheduled to fly. We wouldn't have an exclusive ride, but we'd be in our own birds as often as possible. I'd never had an airplane with my name on it. I'd seen photos from World War II and Korea but didn't think such a thing was possible in the modern Air Force. Tracy stressed that having our names on our airplanes was not a decoration, but a responsibility. We were to get out on the flight line, visit our crew chief, and get to know the maintenance side of the operation. These guys worked hard in horrendous heat and humidity to give us safe, mission-ready airplanes. They needed to know that we appreciated their efforts and we were all part of the team.

The new policies made a lot of sense, at least to a new guy like me. Spelling out how we would operate gave everyone an anchor for their operations and clearly indicated that we would get through this together, as a unit. We wouldn't depend on luck, but rather on tactics, skill, common sense, and a respect for each other's capabilities. Knowing that a flight lead wasn't going to endanger me unnecessarily was reassuring. I'd enjoyed flying with Loyd, and it was easy to see that the people arriving in the squadron were cut from the same cloth.

The change wasn't complete, however. In C flight we still had Captain Mitchell as our flight commander. Mitchell had been part of the McConnell group but had arrived at Korat several months after the rest of the squadron because he had been in the Fighter Weapons School at Nellis. When he rejoined the group after graduation, he was nearly thirty missions behind them. He definitely didn't suffer from cowardice or even timidity. He was occasionally aggressive to the point of appearing suicidal. And he topped it off with a clearly manifest disdain for lieutenants. He quite obviously hated us, despite the fact that he had been a lieutenant himself only three or four years earlier. And we returned the favor. We gave him wide berth, hoping to avoid his wrath and stay clear of an impending meltdown. Attracting attention could be dangerous for lieutenants.

Summer was the rainy season in North Vietnam, so the Air Force was scrambling to find an all-weather bombing system to maintain the pressure on the enemy. The latest effort was "Combat Skyspot." The idea was that a ground radar station could direct aircraft to a precise spot in the sky where they would release bombs in level flight from high altitude to hit a designated target. The principle was similar to a radar instrument approach for landing.

Skyspot used a small beacon, about the size of a pack of cigarettes, carried by the lead aircraft to aid the radar controller. High level staff in Saigon decided that a pilot couldn't handle such a complex piece of equipment and fly the airplane, so Skyspot missions typically required rendezvous with a two-seat F-100, an F-4, or even a B-66 to act as pathfinder for the mission.

The concept made a lot of bad assumptions, and Jim Mitchell was determined to make them obvious to everyone. While a precision landing used close-in radar with an aircraft moving into a highly focused radar beam, the Skyspot concept attempted to guide an airplane from one point in space to another, both randomly chosen and often a long, long way from the radar site. Bombs were to be released at fifteen to twenty thousand feet in an area where winds were only roughly known, target location was only approximate, and the vectors on the aircraft at the moment of release could not be predicted. It wasn't your father's Norden bombsight by any stretch of the imagination.

A Skyspot mission into North Vietnam counted the same as a Route Pack VI sortie to a heavily defended bridge. Getting another hash mark on your jungle hat for a level delivery, high-altitude run didn't seem like a bad deal to me at all. Mitchell, however, hated Skyspots only slightly less than he hated lieutenants. If the enemy couldn't shoot at you, you weren't doing your job properly. Given that the bad weather was canceling most Route Pack VI sorties, it was only a matter of time before C flight would be scheduled for a Skyspot.

Under the new administration, we got scheduled by flights. That meant the same group of five or six guys would fly together as often as possible, so Mitchell was leading Bill Ricks, John Russell, and me. Loaded with five Mk-83 1,000-pound bombs, we would join up with an F-100F from Phu Cat, South Vietnam, call sign Misty 31, who would carry the beacon. The target was at the north end of Mu Gia Pass, along the border between North Vietnam and central Laos. We would release on the radar controller's signal from twenty thousand feet. No sweat.

The flight briefing was short and to the point. We'd fly as directed unless the weather in the target area allowed us to see the ground. If we could see the ground, then we would all withhold our bombs when the drop signal was given. Mitchell would have his weapons switches set to release a single bomb that we would score for the radar site, thereby providing them data for their system. The flight would then acquire the target visually and attack it using manual dive bomb and making multiple passes. Afterward, we would explore the road network through Mu Gia Pass for targets of opportunity to strafe. No one pointed out to the flight commander that he had already been shot down once in Mu Gia Pass doing exactly the same thing.

We quickly refueled on Red track then let Brigham coordinate the rendezvous with the F-100. We went through a short series of controlling agencies, each time relaying our mission number, call sign, ordnance load, and remaining fuel endurance, which, after the refueling top-off, was considerable. Cricket handed us off to Panama, who gave us target coordinates, verifying that the prebriefed target was still our primary. Panama then gave us a frequency for Miscue, the radar controller for the drop. Even the mysterious gods who assign call signs seemed to have little faith in the system's accuracy.

It was all easy enough. We paired up on each wing of the pathfinder and simply flew close formation. It was early in the day, so the thunderheads hadn't begun to build, and the bomb-pocked jungle was clear below us. As we started the bomb run we each acknowledged the radar controller's call to check our weapons switches, knowing that we weren't going to drop. As we neared the release point, the radar controller started his countdown, "Prepare to release on my mark. Release in five, four, three, two, one. Mark!"

Mitchell's single bomb came off and disappeared below us. The backseater in the F-100 nearly snapped his neck, checking the formation on both sides of his aircraft and seeing the bombs remaining. Before he could call on the radio about an error, Mitchell preempted him. "Thanks a lot, Misty. Good run, Miscue. Beech flight is going to drop off now. Beech, let's go channel fourteen." We backed off the Hun's wing and eased into route formation and a descending left turn.

As we spiraled down toward Mu Gia Pass, I kept looking through the lead aircraft trying to spot the bomb impact. Nothing. We'd descended from twenty thousand to less than three thousand feet above the jungle canopy when the bomb hit. As we leveled off, a flash in the jungle to our left showed the detonation. We had been remarkably lucky that we hadn't descended into the path of our own falling bomb. The bomb had hit nearly two miles long of the target coordinates. The intended point of impact was easy to see, a bridge, destroyed long ago, across a small river with several fording points graded out of the mud and sand to allow continued truck traffic. The entire area had been bombed repeatedly and the attacks had little apparent effect.

"Okay, Beech. Everyone got the target? Take spacing for a left-hand wheel; we'll be making three passes here. One will be rolling in in twenty seconds." He was handling this target in Mu Gia Pass like a gunnery range in the States. The big difference was that we all knew the pass had lots of guns, and there had even been reports of a possible SAM site. My head was on a swivel, dividing attention between the target, the other aircraft in the flight and checking the ground all around the area for guns. So far I hadn't seen any, but I was still moving my airplane left and right, up and down, in a random, easy jinking sequence and consciously not flying in trail of Russell's airplane.

I set up for "bomb pairs" and punched in the centerline and outboard stations. I dialed in the depression setting for the sight and watched the other airplanes roll in, pull out, and circle the river crossing. Amazingly, nothing was happening beyond the airpower demonstration of four F-105s making multiple bomb runs in a combat zone. We added some new craters to the area, but I strongly suspected that the supplies would flow tonight with hardly a moment's disruption. As I called in for my last run, Mitchell was already descending and heading northbound down the pass searching for trucks.

When the bomb came off, I recovered from my dive until the nose was level with the horizon, then spotted Russell's airplane to the right about a mile ahead. I rolled to set a cutoff angle and let the airspeed build, wondering how long we'd be playing this game. I had about twenty-five hundred pounds of fuel above bingo, so we could be here for fifteen or twenty minutes — a lifetime at low altitude in the pass. I took Russell's right wing, staying about three thousand feet out and pushing line abreast so hard that whenever he turned toward me I was well out in front. I could see Mitch and Ricks ahead and below us, with Mitchell down to around five hundred feet above the road and Bill struggling to avoid the hills and stay out of his way. None of the four of us were as high as a thousand feet and we were well below the crests of the ridges that defined the mountain pass. Looking back I could see occasional flashes from among the trees and red lines of tracers arcing upward and falling behind us. I edged farther forward on Russell.

We were looking for trucks to strafe according to the briefing, but as number four flying at low level in mountainous terrain on a maneuvering leader at nearly five hundred knots, the odds of seeing a truck were somewhere between slim and none. We were three lieutenants accompanying a madman intent on winning the war single-handedly. I tried to position my aircraft to look through my element leader to see the road, but I still had to look for the lead element, watch out for the hillsides, and make sure I kept my airspeed high enough to have maneuvering potential in case of a SAM launch.

Forty miles north of our start point, I saw the nose come up on Mitchell's airplane and breathed a sigh of relief, only to despair moments later when I realized he was simply pulling up to reverse course and retrace our route back down Mu Gia. If any gunners had been waiting to take a shot or been on a coffee break during the first flyby, we were about to give them another chance. But we still didn't see any trucks.

Only two minutes into the rerun, Ricks called bingo. He was down to three thousand pounds of fuel, the prebriefed minimum necessary to depart the target area and return safely to Korat. Thankfully Mitchell responded and started a climb westbound back to home plate. I'd fully expected him to press on at low altitude, still hoping to strafe trucks even though it might mean running out of fuel on the way home.

As we climbed, I cursed this son of a bitch who was hanging us out on a limb. It was one thing to play games with the Skyspot and drop visually. That was getting bombs on a tasked target. It was another to go trolling at low altitude through an area you know is heavily defended on a quest with poor chances for success and even then wouldn't be a good trade if one of us took a hit.

We climbed to thirty-three thousand feet and throttled back to cruise home. I snapped on the autopilot and dropped my oxygen mask to one side of my helmet. I leaned my head back on the headrest and put my arms on the canopy rails. A light press on the rudder pedals was all it took to move in or out to my proper spread position on Russell. Then, sixty miles east of Korat, I saw Lead's airplane rock the wings back and forth — a signal to close up the formation. "Beech, go trail," was the next radio call.

Ricks, Russell, and I sequenced into close trail behind our flight commander. I could tell without looking at the tachometer or fuel flow gauge that he'd pulled the power way back, nearly to idle for a descent into the airfield. I flicked the trim button several times to load the aircraft nose heavy, which would make it easier to stay in position without having to push the stick forward. We were aligned with just nose-tail separation, in idle power, and now going through a series of barrel rolls. I could hear the airflow over the canopy indicating a rise in airspeed, and I could see the Thai landscape ahead of the three aircraft in front of me as we went into a steep dive, then a five-G pull-up into an idle-power loop. I sweated and cursed and fought the airplane, damning my leader and vowing that I wouldn't be thrown out of formation. Then we rolled level, and a quick wing dip signaled us to echelon right for the traffic pattern. We were home.

The 34th Tactical Fighter Squadron arrived from Yokota, Japan. They had been supplying Korat and Tahkli with replacement airplanes and TDY pilots for many months, and now the entire unit relocated to Korat, giving us three full squadrons along with the F-105F Wild Weasel detachment.

The club, which already had tables with red, green, and blue tablecloths, got a new table, this one with a black tablecloth. The bar was more crowded, the mass briefings for Pack VI missions were bigger, and the traffic pattern got a bit busier.

Ray Lewis, who had been flying with us in the 421st, TDY from Yokota, got sent to the 34th, which needed experienced flight leads to help with their local orientation. With the influx of Nellis and USAFE pilots to our squadron, we had plenty of leaders, so Ray got the call. He had spent several short tours at Korat, where he'd been helpful to the lieutenants in the squadron, and he had become known as a steady flight lead who could get you there and back.

Losses had continued through the month of May and into June, but the 421st had been lucky. Tahkli looked snakebit with a string of aircraft going down for various causes ranging from SAMs and guns to engagements with MiGs. It was easy at Korat to think that we were flying smarter and increasing our survivability by not taking unnecessary risks. The Tahkli wing would allege that Korat was weak, and we would respond that they were foolish. Neither was the case. Each wing had tough missions and easy ones, good leaders and bad, aggressive crews and timid ones. It was simply a case of being in the wrong or right place at the wrong or right time.

Ray Lewis wound up in the wrong place at the wrongest of times. He was leading a flight of four against an oil storage area near Kep airfield. It was a tough target with the heaviest of defenses. As he rolled in for his bombing pass, his airplane was hit in the cockpit by 37-mm flak and, as reported by other members of the flight, he died instantly. His plane was seen to continue on the dive-bomb pass without pulling out and then to impact near the target. No chute was seen.[1]

He'd flown with us, and we knew him. He was one of the good guys who spent time with the new pilots, giving them tips on how best to do the job. He was known for his skill and ability in the air. He was also known for Roscoe.

1. Ray Lewis was downed on 20 July 1966.

Roscoe was Ray's dog, a golden, short-haired mix with a lot of Labrador and other breeds, almost all of which were friendly and led the pup to a natural affinity for pilots. According to legend, Ray had brought Roscoe from Yokota on his lap in the cockpit of a 105, but actually, Roscoe had ridden from Japan on the flight deck of a C-130 with an understanding crew who were friends of Ray's.

After we lost Ray, Roscoe slept on the porch of one of the aircrew hootches and would wake up when the morning activity started. The whine of the starter on one of the Datsun trucks meant it was time for Roscoe to start his duty day. He'd wander out from his sleeping place and greet the crews for the first briefing with a tail wag and a nuzzle to a dangling hand that meant he needed his ears scratched. He could apparently count the crews and when a minimum of four had mounted the truck, he would jump in as well to head down to the squadron area for the first briefing.

The dog had the run of the base and could go anywhere he wanted, including the command post and its classified areas. For Pack VI strikes, Roscoe would hang around the flight-planning area until the crews filed into the briefing room. Then he would take his position on one of the four red senior officer chairs at the front of the room. It didn't take long for superstitions to develop around Roscoe's behavior. If Roscoe slept through the briefing, the mission would be an easy one. If he was agitated or walked out midway, things would not go smoothly.

When the day's first briefing was over, Roscoe would typically jump into the truck to accompany the crew to the O Club for breakfast. That usually meant some bacon or sausage, and if the Thai waitresses were in a good mood, possibly a small dish of ice cream. After breakfast the crews would return to the squadron to suit up and go fly, but Roscoe would trot back to the hootch area, where he'd wait for the next crews to rise and take him along for the same sequence of events. On a good day, Roscoe could get three or four breakfasts. When the last one was over, and somehow he knew which flight was last for the morning, Roscoe would then relax in the air-conditioned comfort of the squadron building, waiting for the first crews to return and the lunch cycle to begin.

Roscoe had more than fifty doting masters to care for his every need. The flight surgeons became responsible for his health and well-being, so doctors who had little medical challenge in serving their population of combat pilots with minimal healthcare needs, now were forced to scrounge the clinic library for books on veterinary medicine. The security police were challenged by the Wing Commander to ensure that Roscoe was properly protected, an honor that Roscoe was not always completely comfortable with, particularly when he had his roving eye on one of the semiwild Thai dogs that occasionally wandered onto the base. A split-second decision on whether some barking and growling meant an interloper challenging Roscoe's domain and requiring intervention or whether it was merely an amorous encounter was often required.

Roscoe didn't play favorites. He was the companion of all the pilots in all of the squadrons. He split his time between the tables at dinner and he spent his days in whichever squadron building seemed to need his support. He was colorblind when choosing which truck to ride and he was more than willing to have his back scratched and ears rubbed by any of us. Naturally, we all loved him.

Hate and pride are wonderful substitutes for fear. The new guys in the squadron were easy to work with and we felt like a team. It was a matter of pride to be able to do the job with them. Whether the targets were in the panhandle or the Red River Delta, it was a challenge to fly the best formation position, execute the briefed tactics perfectly, call a visual during the tanker rendezvous first, and perform the wingman's tasks dependably. Leading in combat was a difficult task and being the best wingman in the squadron made that task easier and made survival a lot more likely. All of the lieutenants worked hard at the job and in return, the flight leaders took care of us. Pride in the job drove us. Except when it came to my flight commander, and then it was hate. It worked either way. I seldom felt the fear anymore.

The target was a railyard along the northeast railroad, near Kep. We were loaded with eight 750-pound bombs, six on the centerline and one on each outboard pylon, plus two 450-gallon wing tanks. We would refuel up the Gulf of Tonkin, and a poststrike tanker would give us some gas on the way home. We would cross the panhandle of North Vietnam, tank up, then proceed to a prominent pork-chop-shaped island on the coast near the Chinese border. Mitchell was leading, with Richter on his wing. John Russell was Three, and I was Four. We got our gas and hit the island turn point, descending to coast into North Vietnam on the deck.

Mitchell was one of the few leaders in the squadron who still supported the tactic of low-level run-in to the target. Most had decided that the disadvantages far outweighed any advantage. Enemy radar reached as far as the tanker tracks, so the bad guys knew we were coming. Sure, the low altitude provided shielding from SAM radar, but it also meant you were within range of even the smallest guns. It also made it a whole lot harder to find the targets. Low altitude meant your navigation had to be absolutely perfect, because it was only when you popped up to bombing altitude that you could see to identify your target. A few degrees off on your run-in and you might be too close to drop, you might be so wide that you'd have to float at the apex of your pop exposed to all of the target area guns, or you might simply miss your target entirely.

Let there be no doubt about it, running along on the treetops at 540 knots in a flight of four F-105s loaded with high explosive iron may be the most exciting thing a man can do with his pants on. You've got the most impressive piece of machinery on the planet strapped to your ass, and it responds to your every wish. The throttle controls the beast's heartbeat, and the slightest movement of the stick directs your flight path. You're the Lord of Evil perched on your rocket-powered throne, coming to deliver justice. It's exhilarating and thrilling, frightening and almost orgasmic. But it isn't necessarily tactically sound.

The miles rolled down on the DME and the clock ticked closer to our time-on-target. We skimmed the trees and flowed around the hilltops. Then it was time, and Mitchell called, "Carbon Lead's up . . . ," and the nose of his airplane started to rise with the wings going full white in a flash of condensation from the saturated air. I was spread, line-abreast, about three thousand feet off Russell's left wing, and he was positioned about forty-five hundred feet off Mitchell at the start of the pop-up. We'd briefed to roll in to the right for the attack and come off the target eastbound to get out of the area.

The sky erupted with 37-mm airbursts. White puffballs were everywhere, and more were popping continually. Half a dozen shells burst between me and Russell, and so much flak was going off that I momentarily lost sight of Richter's airplane across the formation. It was like being suddenly immersed in a huge bowl of popcorn, but it wasn't the light and fluffy kind. I heard Karl call his pull up and then Russell was up. I waited a short five seconds, stroked the afterburner, and started up, looking to my right for the target.

Mitchell called, "Carbon's off dry, we're south of the rail-yard. Carbons acknowledge, all off dry." He'd missed the target area, and now we were going to mill around in this flak trap looking for it. Damn him.

"Carbon, let's jettison our tanks and proceed up the rail-road for the target."

I'd just hit the apex and rolled off the attack without committing nose-down for the dive-bomb pass. We were now about twelve thousand feet, and right in the midst of a broken cloud layer. I looked down at the right front console panel and found the inboard jettison button. I punched it in and felt the empty 450s blow. I looked left and right, verifying that the tanks were gone. Then the airplane shuddered violently, the bright yellow master caution light came on, and the blue "MER empty" light flashed. The caution panel light said the stab-aug was off and the squirrelly feel of the stick in my hand verified that. Suddenly the Lord of Evil's empire was crumbling.

Timidly, I eased the stick left and let the nose down, trying to get below the clouds. I wasn't sure what had happened, but whatever it was, it wasn't good. I called, "Carbon Four's got a problem. I think I've been hit. The MER's gone and stab-aug's off. I'm headed outbound." The airplane appeared to be responding, but the lack of stab-aug meant it was fishtailing and very pitch-sensitive. I checked the hydraulic pressure gauges, and when they all showed steady in the green I tried resetting the stab-aug. It worked. The airplane smoothed out and control response felt normal again.

"Roger, Carbon Four, we're off the target and should be in front of you. Say your position." Mitchell had survived and was headed back out. Now the problem was finding the flight and getting safely out of Dodge.

"Carbon Lead, Carbon Four, give me a short hold down for a steer," I called. The DF mode on the radio could give me a bearing pointer to a radio signal. We often used it to help us find tankers or other flights, and now I hoped it would get me back with the rest of Carbon flight. Mitchell counted from one to five, and while he transmitted, the bearing pointer swung up to show him at my one o'clock, somewhere ahead of me.

With the stab-aug back on, I let the airplane down to the treetops, and watched it accelerate to just over seven hundred knots. I didn't much worry about booming the windows out of the enemy's houses, but as long as the airplane was going to fly I was going to make it get me out of bad-guy land as fast as possible. The condensation cloud started at the back of the canopy, and as I went faster it moved forward with the shock wave until the only clear area was straight ahead through the windscreen. It was like a security blanket, and gave a sense, albeit a false one, of being shrouded in invisibility. If I couldn't see outside, maybe they couldn't see in. Suddenly, the dark green of the radar screen flashed white, bloomed into a great milky flare, then it went totally dead. The airplane was still coming apart.

I hit the coast and start a climb to twenty thousand feet over the water, searching frantically for my flight. I have no radar and a sick airplane. My radio is still good, but if it fails I'll be hard pressed to find the poststrike tanker. As I slow to subsonic, the condensation cloud abates and I can see the coastline to my right and dimly make out the built-up area of Haiphong Harbor. There, just to the right and a bit high. There they are. Three airplanes. It's Carbon. I push up the throttle. I close on the airplanes from behind, and then they turn in unison to the west, toward Haiphong. It's only then I can tell that they aren't 105s. They're MiG-21s, and I'm about to rejoin on the guys sent out to kill me.

It's a fighter pilot's dream but with a sick twist. I've got three enemy aircraft in front of me, unaware of my presence, but I've got a badly damaged airplane, I'm approaching minimum fuel, unsure of whether I'll be able to find the tanker, and I'm alone without any members of my flight nearby. The 105 isn't known as the world's greatest dog-fighter and if I open fire on one of these guys I'll have grabbed the proverbial tiger by the tail. Are the MiGs, even now, talking to their radar controller about the stupid American coming up behind them? Are they consciously dragging me closer to the coast where SAMs can shoot and the guns can handle the leftovers? I choose discretion over valor and bank away to the south, straining to look back over my right shoulder to see if the MiGs turn to follow.

I'm not being chased, and in a matter of minutes I can make out the tail-on silhouettes of my flight. I follow the radio channel changes and join up just short of the tanker. Richter has the lowest fuel so he's on the boom first. Mitchell calls for him to take a full internal load because he wants to go truck hunting in Route Pack I before we go home. I curse him one more time.

After Russell tops off I move into precontact position, just below and behind the extended boom of the tanker. I reach down to the center console and pull the handle to open the receptacle. The airplane shudders and Mitchell calls on the radio, "Damn it, Four, you just blew your pylons." I look left and right my wingtips and verify that the outboard pylons, the last remaining bit of hardware suspended from the airplane, are gone. I don't know why, but it is one more symptom of a very sick airplane. I get my gas and drop off the boom, sliding behind Russell's bird and back onto his wing.

"Carbon Lead, Three. Can we go squadron common for a second?" Russell wants to talk to Mitchell. I wonder what he dares to say, and I'm debating whether I should consider mutiny rather than continue to support Mitchell's quest for trucks to strafe. We change frequencies and my dilemma is solved. Russell seems to have read my mind. "Lead, Four's got a really screwed-up airplane. If you want to take Two hunting, I can lead him back to Korat." Common sense momentarily prevails and Mitchell grudgingly approves. John and I drop off his wing and climb for home.

It's only after landing that the mystery of the malfunctions is solved. Hanging from the right wing's inboard station is the remainder of the electrical cannon plug that was part of the fuel tank pylon. When the tanks were jettisoned in the target area, the plug that was supposed to smoothly pull out of the socket like an electrical cord from a wall outlet remained stuck. The remains of the pylon wiring hung from the socket, nearly thirty multicolored wires dangling in segments two to three feet long, tattered from the mach run but still firmly connected. After the pylon came off, the flailing wires were intermittently completing various electrical circuits. When a circuit closed, the MER was jettisoned; when the stab-aug was re-engaged, the radar burned up; when the refueling door was opened, the outboards were blown off.

The crew chief worked at the corroded plug, trying to get the remains of the wiring out without damaging the wing's sheet metal. Trailers with new tanks, new outboard pylons, and a new centerline bomb rack were pulling up in front of the revetment as I gathered my flight gear and headed for the crew truck. Mitchell was trying to kill me, the North Vietnamese were trying to kill me, the damned airplane was trying to kill me. And that didn't even consider the weather and the tanker and the other airplanes flying and fighting the war at the same time. Damn it! They aren't going to succeed. I'm certainly not going to let Mitchell do it, and I'm going to handle the rest.

* * *

A week later Mitchell's tour ended. His last combat mission was unusual because he joined the ranks of the very select few fighter pilots who have shot themselves down.

As a Fighter Weapons School graduate, Mitchell was a natural choice for carrying any exotic weaponry. Despite regular denials in the press, in the middle of 1966 we were deep in a bomb shortage. We didn't have adequate supplies of our favored general-purpose bombs, the M-117 750-pound bomb or the Mk-82 low-drag 500-pounder. To compensate for the shortages and to keep our sortie counts competitive with our opponent, the U.S. Navy, we carried all sorts of strange munitions. There were rockets and finned napalm, mines, and occasionally we were sent on missions into North Vietnam armed only with the Vulcan cannon. Among the strangest loads, however, was the AGM-12C, the Super Bullpup.

The Bullpup was a manually guided missile fired from a fighter at a ground target then flown with a small control-stick down to impact. The original AF version of the missile was in the 750-pound class with roughly 250 pounds of warhead. When the little missile failed to drop reinforced structures like bridges, the engineers built a bigger model with a 1,000-pound warhead. A major difference between the small version and the new, improved model was the method of leaving the launch platform. The little missile fired off a rail just like a Sidewinder. The Super model, with a much larger rocket motor, was programmed to drop off the wing like a bomb, extending a several-foot-long umbilical cord, which when fully extended would trigger the rocket motor. The thinking was that such a large rocket could send an airplane out of control if for some reason the missile got stuck on the rail.

Big or small, the Bullpup was no favorite of the pilots. To guide the missile properly, you had to set up at high altitude and establish a medium-angle dive toward the target. When the missile was fired, the pilot then had to fly his airplane with his right hand and correct the missile track with his left.

Much like walking and chewing gum at the same time, a proper delivery required exceptional coordination. During the delivery, the pilot had to concentrate on the missile's flight to the target, which meant that his airplane had a long, predictable flight path in areas with heavy defenses. With your attention fixed on the missile you couldn't look around for SAMs or guns, and the high altitude meant that you could fire the weapon only in exceptionally good weather.

Mitchell had a two-ship flight, each loaded with a pair of big Bullpups. When he fired the first missile, the forward shackle on the pylon hung up, causing the missile to rotate nose-up when it dropped. When the missile hit the end of the umbilical, the rocket motor fired, but instead of propelling the weapon forward, the missile went upward through the leading edge of his right wing. The missile tore off the leading edge flap, ripped the wing back to the main spar, and destroyed the primary hydraulic lines.

He recovered the airplane and jettisoned tanks and the remaining missile. With the bird still flying he headed for an emergency recovery at the nearest friendly base, which was Nakhon Phanom. Unfortunately, NKP was ill-equipped for receiving an F-105 under even optimum circumstances. The steel-planking runway was way too short for a normal 105 landing, and an emergency touchdown with no flaps would mean a roll-out at nearly two hundred knots. Mitch got lucky as he lowered the landing gear, when the aircraft overboarded the remaining hydraulic fluid and it became unflyable. He bailed out on five mile final and was picked up almost immediately by the base rescue helicopter.

This was Mitchell's ninety-ninth North Vietnam mission and his second bailout; the wing commander declared Mitch's helicopter ride as his hundredth mission. He left several days later. I don't recall wishing him good-bye.

CHAPTER 12

The Thunder Rolls

You can't simply have a bombing campaign and say, "We're bombing North Vietnam." You've got to have a code name. Of course, a code name implies that the operation is a secret. Nobody knows what you are doing except the select few insiders who are making the decisions. In the case of bombing North Vietnam, the code name was Rolling Thunder, and it wasn't a secret from anybody.

All you had to do was pick up *Time* magazine with a picture of Korean War ace Jim Kasler on the cover, labeled as "The World's Greatest Fighter Pilot." Inside you could read the air order of battle in Thailand, a summary of typical targeting, a profile of the Thunderchief and Phantom, and a bio of Kasler's accomplishments in the last bout of Asian unpleasantness fifteen years earlier. What made it funny was that every tactical aviator who had ever strapped on a jet considered that title his and his alone. The American public was, I suppose, expected to assume we were serious about the war if we were unleashing the trophy holder in this event.

Or you could find the depressing issue of *Newsweek* that declared an F-105 pilot was shot down once every sixty-five missions. *Newsweek* offered a detailed summary of the incredible defensive array that the North Vietnamese had assembled and went on to label Pack VI the "most heavily defended area in the history of aerial warfare." The statistics showed that it was virtually impossible to beat the odds and fly the tour without getting shot down.

Despite the daily reports of losses in the U.S. newspapers, the front-page features in the weeklies, and the nightly din-

nertime reports from the TV talking heads, the military's official position was that we weren't conducting combat operations from Thailand. We were required to carry on the
charade of ignorance even when we were among our own
leadership. If we were hit on a mission and struggling home
with a wounded airplane, we were forbidden to report "battle
damage" over the radio. The required terminology was
"mishap," as though we'd experienced some sort of minor
mid-air accident during a training sortie or possibly an over-
G during a range mission pullout. No one could ever explain
why the term "battle damage" would compromise our secret
presence, but the daily radio chatter about SAMs, MiGs,
flak, and bomb-dropping wouldn't.

Since we weren't flying combat we didn't get R&R. We
could get "permissive TDY." In the military everyone has to
be accounted for and particularly when outside of the United
States, they must have some official status. Permissive TDY
meant we were authorized to be away from our duty station,
but it gave no priority when it came to travel. When we got
time off, we went to the squadron's admin section and told
Sergeant Morgan where we might try to go. He typed up a letter stating that we were authorized to be away from our duty
station and the commander signed it. There was no fund citation and no money was allocated for our travel or expenses.

Getting away from Korat was never a problem. You could
always get a hop out on a C-130 or some other aircraft that
had dropped a load of supplies and was heading home
empty. If your ambition was simply to lounge around a
swimming pool, drink cold beer, and maybe chase a stewardess, the preferred destination was Bangkok. A new hotel
had just opened, the Siam Intercontinental, and it quickly became a fighter pilot favorite. It didn't hurt that the hotel was
also the turnaround residence for Pan-American aircrews
flying from the States. A four-hour taxi ride from Korat City
to Bangkok in an air-conditioned Mercedes cost ten bucks a
head and was ready to leave whenever you were.

If you had a few days you could stretch as far as you dared.
Sergeant Morgan's letter would simply list any place you

thought you might go. Typically, we considered Japan, Okinawa, the Philippines, Bangkok, Hong Kong, and even Hawaii as reachable. The hops out were never a problem. It was the return trip that was a challenge and stories of strange occurrences abounded.

Rumor held that the CIA had posted agents in air terminals in all the likely places we might show up. When we couldn't get transportation the normal way, the spooks would step in and help us out. The theory was that since F-105 pilots were in such short supply and since we would wind up stranded around Asia with our unfunded permissive TDY letters, we would need help getting back to our bases. To get home, all you had to do was attract some attention in an airlift terminal. That wasn't too difficult for a typical fighter pilot, particularly one who had been unwinding a bit after several weeks of combat. I didn't know if the tales were true, but I was about to find out.

My roommate, Bill Ricks, and I had gotten up to twenty-five missions, and it seemed only natural that we go traveling together. When a ferry flight opportunity came along to deliver an airplane to Yokota, Bill jumped at the chance, and I agreed to catch a hop out and meet up with him in Tokyo. Although Bill was a strict Mormon, married and the father of two, we were the same age, we had been through a lot together, and I was pretty sure we'd have a good time. Bill looked like he might be ready for a drink.

Our plan worked perfectly. Bill took a 105 and I found a C-124 heading from Korat to Tachikawa Air Base, Japan. We rendezvoused at the Tachi BOQ and then headed into downtown Tokyo to see the sights. We attempted to get quarters at the U.S. military hotel but got turned away because it was reserved for troops on R&R from Vietnam. It didn't matter to us; we simply hopped a cab and rode up the hill to the Tokyo Hilton.

We had three great days, eating sukiyaki and Kobe beef, touring temples and palaces and even seeing a Japanese burlesque show that proved beyond any doubt that slapstick humor could cross cultural lines even if you don't speak the language. I enjoyed seeing a modern Asian capital, and Bill got to experience his first hangover. All went well until it came time to return to Korat. We checked out of the Hilton and took a taxi to Tachikawa's air terminal. There, Ricks and I stood in line waiting to check in with a rosy-cheeked young airman wearing a name tag that announced he was a "Customer Service Representative of the Military Airlift Command." It seemed only slightly oxymoronic to link the job title with a command that was notorious for passenger abuse.

Bill had temporary duty orders with a fund citation for travel back to Thailand. I had the simple two-paragraph letter from my squadron commander authorizing me to go anywhere in Asia. Bill immediately got booked on a contract airline flight to Don Muang airport at Bangkok. I got a quizzical look from the two-striper.

"Sir, I'm afraid that you aren't qualified to travel on jet aircraft." My jaw dropped.

"What? I'm standing here in a flight suit, wearing wings and with a letter from a tactical fighter squadron, and I'm not qualified to travel on jets? What the hell do you mean?" I had instantly lost any pretense of civility. You simply don't tell a fighter pilot that he can't fly jets.

"I mean you aren't authorized to travel on jets. You can only travel on organizational aircraft," was the stammered reply.

"What the hell is an 'organizational aircraft'?"

"Those are the in-theater C-130s assigned here."

"Okay, put me on one of those," I replied.

"I'm sorry, sir, but all seats on C-130s are reserved for combat troops returning to Vietnam. And all flights to Thailand go to Vietnam first, so there are no available seats for Thailand passengers."

"So, you're saying that I can't fly on jets, but only on organizational aircraft, but I can't fly on those either? Well, what can I fly on?"

"I'm sorry, but you can't fly on anything we have here," he replied with a smirk.

That's when I made some rather intemperate comments about the young man's mother, father, and what he could do with his customer service name tag. I turned away from the counter and stormed off, headed for the BOQ where I was going to be spending the night and pondering alternatives to get back to the squadron.

It was only natural to cross the street from the Q to the Officers' Club, not only for some sustenance but to figure out a plan. All fighter pilots know that olives and gin contain all of the necessary nutrients to maintain life and promote wisdom. It looked as though I was in a survival situation and a proper infusion of alcohol might help. The bartender made a passable martini, and I was on my second one when the public address speaker crackled and announced, "Lieutenant Rasimus, you have a call on line three. Lieutenant Rasimus, you have a call. Please pick up any white phone."

I headed down the hall wondering if I'd heard a mispronunciation of someone else's name. No one could possibly know of my whereabouts. Since leaving the terminal I'd seen no one and talked to no one except the BOQ desk clerk. Ricks was already on board his airliner, so it couldn't have been him. I picked up the phone and identified myself.

The disembodied voice on the line offered no identification but simply wanted to know if I was trying to go to Korat. I admitted that I needed a ride. That's all it took. "You've been designated a diplomatic courier. Report to hangar three at oh-six-hundred tomorrow and ask for Mister Jones. Good-bye." The connection was broken before I could ask any questions.

I wasn't sure what had just happened. The conversation had been short and to the point, but I didn't know what had triggered it. Who was looking out for me? Who was watching? I returned to the bar and scribbled the instructions down on a cocktail napkin so I wouldn't forget. Then I went through another martini and a steak dinner. A few after-dinner cognacs and some story swapping with the crew of a C-124 at the bar left me ready for bed about midnight. I set the alarm and made sure my bag was packed except for my Dopp kit, which I left out for a morning shave and shower.

Mister Jones was waiting near the door of the hangar when I showed up a few minutes before six. He handed me a web belt with a canvas holster attached and a rusty Webley revolver. I didn't know that the U.S. military had such weapons, but before I could comment, Jones pointed to a pallet being picked up by a forklift. "That's eighteen hundred pounds of classified confidential paperwork. You're to accompany the pallet to Kadena. When you get there someone will give you further instructions. Sign here." He pushed a clipboard into my hand.

The forklift dropped the pallet onto the elevator of a C-124 sitting right outside the hangar door. I went up the steps to the cargo deck. The crew was my drinking buddies from the night before. They pushed me up the ladder to the cockpit and after exchanging pleasantries pointed out that the flight deck had four bunks and I was welcome to whichever one I wanted. I could only assume that their hangovers were as bad as mine, so I gladly accepted the rack time and marveled at their ability to get up and fly this morning. Four hours of droning propellers lullabied me all the way to touchdown in Okinawa. As we taxied to our parking space I collected my B-4 bag, my flight cap, and the rusty Webley. I considered strapping the holster on and doing my best John Wayne but figured that the out-of-date equipment would make me look more like a rank-and-file foot soldier from the Gunga Din era, so I carried the belt and holstered gun in one hand and dragged my bag with the other.

A blue sedan was waiting just off the wingtip with a security-police sergeant standing by the door. He saluted me and simultaneously extended a clipboard. "Sign here, Lieutenant, and I'll relieve you of the classified. Then jump in and the driver here will take you to your transport. There's a tanker cranking up just down the ramp, and they're holding for you, sir."

As promised, the KC-135's engines were already running when we drove up. The tanker crew chief grabbed my bag from the trunk and led me to the ladder. Four airliner-style seats were bolted to the flat floor halfway down the fuselage; otherwise the interior was totally empty. The chief motioned me to one of the seats then returned to the cockpit to resume his regular duties. I sat alone in the cavernous cabin listening as the engines spooled up and we rolled out. Soon we were airborne and heading toward the Gulf of Tonkin to rendezvous with a pair of F-4Cs en route from Clark in the Philippines to Cam Ranh Bay in South Vietnam. We passed some gas to the fighters, and I got a boomer's view of a refueling. Then it was on to Korat.

The tanker wasn't based at Korat; he wasn't even going to refuel there. He simply dropped me off and, without shutting down the engines, taxied back to the runway and departed for Don Muang, where he would be based for the next two weeks. I was just priority cargo. Bill Ricks had gotten back only a few hours earlier than I did.

Tales of my odyssey took a backseat at the squadron dinner table to talk about the new emphasis of Rolling Thunder that had been unveiled while Bill and I were sightseeing in Tokyo. Since my arrival in early May, the pattern had been one of three or four major targets per month in Pack VI. Bridges, railyards, or supply areas would be pulled from the list of JCS-approved targets and strike packages would attack them until destroyed. Usually this meant several days of large strike forces then a reversion to the routine road cuts and interdiction missions in the lower packages. If the target was hit quickly, then we had several days of easier missions. If the target survived, it meant days of going into the meatgrinder until the job got done. The more periods of respite you got, the more likely you were to survive.

At the end of May we had conducted a huge strike on Yen Bai. For nearly three hours, more than one hundred airplanes had bombed the town's barracks, marshaling yards, and transportation points. Tahkli had lost two airplanes, but Korat came through unscathed. Then most of June had reverted to the pattern. One or two major targets per week, tasked until hit, and then routine interdiction.

But that wasn't the "rolling" of Rolling Thunder. "Rolling" meant that we would gradually increase pressure on the North Vietnamese to achieve our national political objectives. We'd start on the edges and roll slowly into the heart of the country, making it hurt a little more each week until they finally capitulated. In the process we would gain the support of lesser nations around the world, which would applaud our restraint, and we would assuage any Soviet or Chinese fears that we were bent on imperialist conquest that might endanger their sovereignty. Little by little we would tighten the grip, until, like a submission hold in wrestling, the North Vietnamese would cry, "Uncle." We would force the North to stop supporting the Viet Cong insurgency, we would demonstrate our political, moral, and military superiority to the rest of the world, and we would succeed without causing a nuclear war. When you write the policy in a paragraph it sounds ridiculous, but if you write a whole book espousing it as a theory of postnuclear international diplomacy, you're liable to get a White House fellowship.

It was time to start rolling again, and those of us at the cutting edge of the national-policy sword would be doing the thundering. But the focus had shifted. Now the campaign was going to deny the enemy their fuel. While Ricks and I had been playing tourist during the last two days of June, the Air Force and the Navy had unleashed massive raids on POL supplies — petroleum, oil, and lubricants. Our forces had conducted coordinated attacks on virtually all of the major storage, processing, and shipment areas in the Red River Delta. In two days of bombing, more than 60 percent of all the fuel and oil in the north had been destroyed and more than 85 percent of the storage capacity. From now on, every day we would target POL supplies in Pack VI. If the weather was good, we would be going downtown.

The crews were surprisingly enthusiastic. The targets had been something tangible, and the results were immediate. Poststrike reconnaissance photos showed huge columns of smoke rising from badly damaged tank farms and processing areas. The next day's edition of the *Stars and Stripes* featured the photos on the front page, and the newest issue of *Time* magazine displayed the flaming wreckage of the Hanoi tank farm in vivid color on the cover. The guys had the distinct impression that we were stepping up our efforts and intended to win the war, which created a palpable difference in everyone's attitude. Attacking in large, coordinated waves seemed more professional, more satisfying, more military than nibbling in puny two-ship flights at suspected storage areas and dirt road intersections. There was certainly a lot more adrenaline involved.

Our confidence in the new Weasels was also rising. The 105Fs had much better gear than the old Huns, and the June trips to Hanoi showcased their capability. When the SAM radars came on the air, the Weasel knew it and advised the strike force. When the SAM was getting ready to fire, the Weasel could identify the activity and warn you. When there was a launch, the Weasel could call it almost before the smoke left the ground. Shrikes appeared to threaten the sites, and the Weasel's warnings were timely and appeared reliable. Almost all of our aircraft now had the APR-25/26 radar warning gear installed, and we all felt that knowing what types of radar were looking at us and when gave us more of the big picture.

For the 421st, there was special excitement. Our new squadron commander, Major Tracy, had been flying with a Weasel flight supporting the Hanoi POL raid when they were attacked by MiG-17s. The MiGs had slashed through the flight and Tracy had taken a hit that penetrated the cockpit and destroyed part of his instrument panel. He'd had his hand knocked from the throttle and most of the left side of the cockpit mangled. Despite the damage, he'd been able to reverse on the MiG and bring his gun to bear. The last anyone saw of the MiG was as he rolled inverted, flaming and disappeared into a low cloud deck. The kill hadn't been confirmed yet, but few doubted that the boss would get the credit.[1]

The daily schedule pattern was changed. Now, each day started with a predawn mass briefing for a Hanoi-area target.

1. Maj. Fred Tracy received credit for downing a MiG-17 on 29 June 1966 after unspecified ground operatives discovered wreckage at the coordinates of the claim.

A second strike package for the afternoon would start the preparation cycle about ten o'clock in the morning. Each group would typically consist of four strike flights with spares and one or two SAM-suppression Weasel flights. To ensure that flights would be used regardless of the weather conditions, each flight had a primary target in Pack VI, a secondary target in the panhandle or Pack V, and a tertiary backup working in Laos — a noncounter mission. The sequence of events would start with max tension as you assembled, prepared maps, took the group briefing on sequencing, weather, defenses, and target then went to the club for breakfast. At some point during the hour or so after the mass brief, the field phone in the O Club dining room would chirp and the command post would tell us with code words whether we were going to the primary or not. The later the call, the higher the tension level. Once you knew whether you were going downtown or to a secondary target, things seemed to stabilize and you began operating with a professional level of confidence. Indecision and confusion could kill you. When the word came and defined the day's mission, you could then get down to business.

The experienced flight leads in the squadron looked out for the lieutenants, and we responded by supporting our leaders. They got us to the tankers, found the targets, handled the navigation, and made the decisions. When the weather was marginal we knew they would get us around or through the mess, and they wouldn't hang us out unnecessarily. Our job was to fly wing, stay in position where they could see us, keep our mouths shut unless we had something important to say, and put bombs on target. They had experience and judgment. We had the skills of youth — fast reflexes, good vision, and the flexibility to adjust to changing situations. Most important, we had confidence in each other.

As we increased the number of missions into the Red River Delta, losses increased. The 105 Weasels took the hardest hit as they struggled to develop tactics to support the strike force. They would always be first into the target area and last out. To do their job they had to go deep into SAM territory and always position themselves between the threat and the friendly fighters. When SAM radar came up, rather than duck into ground clutter, the Weasel had to dance with the devil, feinting and thrusting to keep the radar on the air until he could fire a Shrike or acquire the missile site visually. Exposure was the name of the game if SAMs were going to be killed, and it cost dearly. In the first month after their arrival, five of the six Weasels at Tahkli were lost. Only one of the Korat birds went down. By the end of July, the single remaining Weasel crew at Tahkli was sent to Korat. The surviving half-dozen Weasels from our base would fly the SAM suppression mission for the entire theater.

The Weasels weren't the only ones climbing a learning curve. The SAM site operators were learning as well. While our guys learned how to interpret the flashing lights and beeping signals of the RHAW gear, the SA-2 crews were finding new ways to operate. We found out that the classic sequence of radar events that led to a launch wasn't always necessary. Typically, detection of a target gave a slow pulse frequency radar indication. When the SAM site began to concentrate on you, the pulse frequency increased and a second light showed on the display panel. When data were being loaded on the missile, an "activity" light came on and when guidance commands started, a "launch" light and tone told you to start getting concerned about evasion. Somehow the whole sequence seemed to be wired directly into your heart rate and respiration. As the radar intensity ratcheted higher your body functions increased, and with the launch light an instant flood of sweat drenched your back and rolled down your forehead into your eyes.

The Weasel could launch a Shrike and the SAM site would often turn off their radar. That didn't necessarily mean that they were unable to fire. The air defense crews learned through practice that they could input data to their missile from early warning radar sites so that they could minimize their electronic signals until just prior to launch. Earlier it had just been a theory, now we saw them practicing the technique and getting better at it every day. We got less warning or the SAM sites became less vulnerable to Shrikes. The Weasels still took a toll and through the months following the Hanoi oil raids, they claimed lots of site kills. Somehow, regardless of how many sites we killed, we always had more sites to deal with the next day.

JCS didn't have enough POL targets to keep the force busy, so they expanded the list to include bridges, storage areas, military assembly areas, and railroads. The bridges at Bac Giang and Bac Ninh were regulars, along with industrial facilities around Thai Nguyen. Oil storage and processing facilities at Phu Tho, Viet Tri, Phuc Yen, and Kep showed up routinely on the daily frag. Most of us kept a list of familiar targets and turn points in our distribution boxes in the secure planning area at the command post. North Vietnam isn't a very big country, particularly when you are traveling at five or six hundred knots, so there weren't many alternate ways in and out of the regular target areas.

The only variation on each Pack VI target was how we would refuel. The shortest and most common route took us over Laos and the Black River and then turned eastbound at the Red to the target area. Occasionally we would use the over-water route with refueling over the gulf. And when Seventh Air Force really wanted to get our hearts racing, we would go in one way and out the other — in by land and out by sea or vice-versa. No one liked that alternative because it required you to transit heavily defended areas that you wouldn't normally want to visit, it took a lot of fuel, and you weren't always sure what the weather would be like on the other side.

The nightly rains ended about two in the morning giving an hour for the latest plague to emerge from the jungle. Baht bugs had been replaced by tiny, half-dollar-sized green frogs that were everywhere underfoot when you came out of the hootch at three to find a truck assembling a flight for the ride down to the command post. They cheeped with tiny little voices and leaped, apparently without looking beforehand, to bump into the legs of your flying suit leaving little damp spots just above boot level.

Our target for the day was the bridge at Bac Ninh on the northeast railroad. The tankers were in the gulf both coming and going which wasn't bad news at all for that target area. Ingress would be along the mountainous coast, and the only heavy defenses were along the railroad itself and in the flatlands where the narrow valley that harbored the rail line opened up on the delta. I was flying wing on Major Loyd, with the new assistant operations officer, Maj. Ken Frank, flying Three, and Karl Richter as Four. The load was five Mk-83 low-drag bombs. The rain of the night before hinted that the monsoon was overhead and the only weather factor would be local. The target area several hundred miles north of us would be reasonably clear.

As the gear and flaps were coming up, the weak howling of an emergency beeper on guard played as background to the routine radio chatter of takeoff, departure control, and contact with Invert for flight following to the Brown Anchor tanker track north of Danang. We climbed to eighteen thousand feet and went to tactical spread. Loyd asked Invert if they were getting a beeper and the depressing reply was that it had been a bad morning already. The first strike package, primarily out of Tahkli, but with support from other bases, had five airplanes down. Before Loyd could ask about rescue efforts, Invert advised that all five were down in the flats over the Red and only one had a pending rescue effort ongoing.

Single-seat airplanes leave you alone with your thoughts. The airplanes have an intercom system, but its primary function is for communication with ground personnel, who plug into a jack in the wheel well during engine start and preflight checks. At some point after leaving pilot training where intercoms are your link with the instructor, most guys choose to turn the system off after the crew chief disconnects. There's no reason to hear the feedback of your own breathing, and it's simply one more noise to obstruct something important like a radio call or a RHAW gear warning tone. So you cruise, bomb-laden and on autopilot, across Laos and the panhandle to the deep blue water of the Gulf of Tonkin, arms draped on the canopy rails looking left and right, watching the scenery and thinking. The beepers come and go in the background, and each time you hear it you wonder if you should shut off guard channel or if it will go away in a minute or two. You wonder who is down and how it happened. Are they alive or dead? Inevitably, you wonder what others would think if it were your beacon. Would they be cruising comfortably in the morning sun, or would they be doing something for you? What could you be doing now? Nothing. You're too far away. You've got a target to go to. There's a tanker coming up, and you're just a wingman. You've got a job to do.

We switch channels and talk to Panama, the radar control site on Monkey Mountain near Danang. They turn us north and point us at Brown Anchor 31, the lead tanker in a cell of four. Brown 31 is eighty miles north of us and heading our way. We'll pass left shoulder to left shoulder if we continue, but we'll be doing a fighter turn-on rendezvous, meaning that at around twenty-five miles we'll start a left turn to fall into trail behind the tanker. Panama gives us azimuth and distance calls as we close. I'm flying wing and focusing my search with the radar, trying to find the tanker before anyone else in the flight does. I check the radar antenna and slowly spin the antenna tilt knob through level flight to just slightly nose high. There's a blip, ten left at thirty-five. Panama calls, "Parrot flight, you've got Brown 31 bearing three-five-zero at thirty-four miles from your position."

Loyd's looking. I've got a sun glint off a wing. I call, "Parrot Two's got visual, left eleven at thirty."

Panama verifies, "Parrot, that's your tanker."

Loyd glances my way momentarily then back at the spot I've indicated on the horizon. "Parrot's judy," he calls, indicating we'll complete the rendezvous ourselves without any more help from Panama. We hold steady for a count of five then enter a smooth left turn, sliding into refueling position just behind the tanker. As we head southbound down the gulf, we start taking gas. Just before I turn my radar to standby, I watch the whole show of following flights appear as blips across my scope. We're all going to targets along the northeast railroad, with several flights heading to the Bac Ninh bridge and others hitting various choke points along the line. Time on target is spread out over half an hour, and each flight has its own tactical authority.

We get our gas and drop off the tanker at the north end of the track. The howling of the emergency beeper has stopped, and I don't know whether that means the poor guy has been captured, the battery has gone dead, or he's evading and simply turned it off to save power. I hope it's the latter, but deep inside I suspect the worst. No one gets picked up out of Pack VI.

As we cruise up the Gulf at twenty thousand feet I sweep the coastline ahead with my radar, painting the map of the landfall ahead of us and the easy-to-find, pork-chop-shaped island that sits on our nose. We've got a good plan. We'll turn inbound at the south tip of the island, a prominent point that's easy to find visually or if the weather had been bad, on our radar. The North Vietnamese know that we use the island for navigation, so they will undoubtedly welcome us with a barrage of 37- and 57-mm flak. It's always too low and always bursts behind us, but one of these days they're bound to get lucky.

Rather than head straight for the target, we're going to angle north, working our way along the twenty-mile buffer zone with the China border. That will keep us clear of SAM sites along the usual route to Kep and the railroad. When we get to the rail line, we'll turn southbound and head for the bridge along the west side of the narrow valley, so that we can attack and be headed outbound to the east when we get to Bac Ninh. We'll spend most of the ingress at four to six thousand feet above the ground then pop up to about twelve thousand for our dive-bomb pass. With only scattered midlevel clouds, navigation should be easy in the clear morning air.

We descend and turn left at the coast. I've got the Doppler set to the coordinates of the intersection of the railroad and the buffer zone. The flight is spread and nearly line abreast, almost a mile wide and humping over the dark green jungle at 540 knots. It's nine miles a minute, an easy number to handle for mental math to judge time to the target. Once we get close, we'll push up to 600 knots airspeed, which will give us plenty of energy for the pop-up. On our way out our speed won't matter; we'll just want to get back into formation to watch for SAMs and MiGs. The APR-25/26 isn't showing much activity this far north of the populated delta area, only an occasional chirp of a Spoon Rest or Bar Lock early warning radar. No Fan Songs or Fire Cans yet. That will come soon enough.

The white puffy clouds and the dark blue morning sky contrast with the deep emerald green of the jungle hills. Gray karst formations rise out of the foliage creating a beautiful landscape below us. The airplanes ride smoothly and for a moment the sheer exhilaration is enough to blank out the fact that this is war, we are deep in enemy territory and in a moment all hell is going to break loose. We're going to rain death and destruction down on an enemy who is going to be trying extremely hard to stop us. Two minutes to the turn point.

There it is. The railroad is in sight in a narrow cut in the mountains barely three miles wide. Now the turn down to Bac Ninh. Wait. What's that? We're over the tracks, and below us is a rail siding; no, it's two sidings along the main line. A small railyard, right here at the buffer zone. And there are two trains filling the tracks. A small station house sits on the east side and in an instant I picture tired engineers who've parked their trains, knowing even better than the pilots overhead that the rules of engagement call this a buffer zone. They're probably in the station house talking over a cup of coffee about the night's run into or out of Hanoi with their freight of war materials. I call, "Parrot Two has a pair of trains on the tracks right below us," not sure what we are going to do about it.

Loyd doesn't hesitate for a second. "Roger, tally-ho. Coming left. We'll roll in to the north and off right outbound. One'll be up in ten." Shit hot. We're going to hit something real. I'm on the inside of the turn, and I start to slide behind Lead as he comes around. I watch the AB light on his plane and the nose come up. I cut the corner and pass behind his flight path then throw the throttle outboard and feel the nozzles open then the push as the burner lights.

The bang of the afterburners has caught the trainmen's attention. Guns around the railyard start to flash and puffs of 37 mm begin to appear low and to my left as I hit twelve thousand feet and roll inverted to pull down on the target. They're shooting at Three and Four. I've got the trains under the pipper, and I can see Loyd's bombs going off already. He's hit near the north end of the trains, so I adjust toward the center of the string of boxcars. A huge plume of white smoke erupts as one of the engineers has apparently thrown full throttle to his locomotive, but he's already trying to drag derailed wreckage down broken tracks. I feel the jolts of the bombs coming off as I mash on the pickle button and I'm already pulling off and looking for my lead's aircraft. He's in a hard right turn coming to one o'clock and climbing. I set my cutoff and look back over my right shoulder to see Three and Four just coming off the target.

Loyd keeps his rejoin turn going until he's parallel to the railroad southbound then reverses to head out. We're back into our spread and clear of the flak in less than a minute. As we're on our way outbound, a strange notion enters my head. This is fun. It's a rush, a thrill, a challenge to do something that most people can't even conceive of and couldn't do even if they wanted to. Parrot flight is roaring across the countryside, headed for the coast, and it suddenly occurs to me that what we're doing is a lot like stealing hubcaps.

When I was growing up in Chicago the guys in the neighborhood would occasionally decide that we needed to steal some hubcaps. We would talk about what style was particularly cool and make a choice between Lincoln spinners or Plymouth cones or maybe even some aftermarket custom jobs like chrome Moons. Then we'd scout the neighborhood streets until we found a likely target. Four guys would approach the car late at night and then, one to a wheel, crouch down to pop off the cap. Invariably as we were pulling the caps off someone would drop one, and it would rotate on the ground making a huge noise and alerting the car owner, usually a big, burly, blue-collar kind of guy in a sleeveless undershirt with a can of beer in his hand. He'd turn on the porch light and scream out, "Hey, what youse guys doing dere?" We would take off running, and maybe he would chase us.

We didn't need the hubcaps; we wanted the chase, the adrenaline rush of tweaking some poor working stiff's nose and getting a chase. Now we're a whole lot faster, and what we're doing is in the name of national policy, but each morning we decide what kind of hubcaps we're going to steal for the day. Then we plan our strategy and sneak into the neighborhood, sometimes at low altitude, sometimes by a circuitous routing. Then we grab the prize and run away. If we get chased a bit that's so much the better, as long as we don't get caught. We wind up with a huge rush and a release that leaves us chattering and swaggering for hours afterward. Then we sleep, and the next morning we do it again. Some are convinced it's patriotism, doing your part for the security of the free world, but henceforth I'll always recognize it as stealing hubcaps.

At the coast we head south to the poststrike tanker then back across the North Vietnam panhandle and back to Korat. Even after landing we're feeling pumped about our strike results and eager to get to debrief. The cold command post air-conditioning does little to quell our enthusiasm, until the tech sergeant intel debriefer raises an eyebrow at our strike report. He excuses himself and charges down the hall, returning in less than a minute with the chief of intel, Lieutenant Colonel Winter. "What'd you guys do?" he asks.

We recount our ingress plan and our luck at finding the trains. We describe our attack and each of us confirms an estimate that at least three-quarters of our bombs hit the trains or the tracks. We're fairly certain we didn't get either of the engines but we estimate at least forty boxcars destroyed and all of the tracks cut. We point out on the map where the attack took place. The white-haired intel officer shakes his head and grimly points out that it looks as though we've struck in the China buffer zone. "It looks like you've busted the ROE," he announces.

"What does that mean?" Loyd inquires. "We're authorized to maneuver in the buffer zone, aren't we?"

"Sure," replies Winter, "but you aren't supposed to strike targets in the zone. It's a sanctuary to make sure that we don't inadvertently drop anything in China."

"Yeah, but isn't it clear that they're using the ROE to protect their trains and where we struck is definitely in North Vietnam?" Richter wants to know.

"Doesn't matter. You can't drop in the buffer." Winter suggests we take a look at our flight data again. "What did you use to establish the coordinates you gave us? How did you determine the location of the drop?"

I volunteer that I was using my Doppler coordinates for the intersection of the railroad and the buffer zone. It looked to me like we were two miles north of the intersection when we hit the tracks. Ken Frank says he was trying to use Red Crown TACAN, a navigation station on a destroyer in the Gulf. The signal was intermittent that far inland, and he wasn't too sure of the radial and distance. Richter thinks his Doppler might have shown us right at the intersection. Loyd looks at each of us then turns to Winter. "I think our initial plot might have been a bit off. Let me see that map again. Sure, here we are, right near this peak and just past this little village. That's right. Here's where the siding is. It's about two miles south of the buffer zone. Don't you agree?" He polls the members of the flight. We all nod enthusiastically.

The senior intel officer has seen this before. He eases into the hint of a smile and says, "I thought so. Nice job, guys." He initials the report and returns to his office.

Whiplash was a quick reaction alert force. Each day the wing at Korat was required to ready a four-ship flight to respond to an emergency. It might be to help a downed crew rescue effort or it could be in support of ground forces in Laos. The responsibility to man the force rotated between the three squadrons. Usually the command post would try to get you launched, so it meant you would fly but it didn't always ensure a counter. Most crews didn't like the tasking because it meant you had to brief early in the morning then stay together with the other members of the flight for most of the day. The flight lead carried a small handheld FM radio and had to advise the command post of the flight's whereabouts at all times. The birds were preflighted at the beginning of the alert period and readied for engine start. Response time was fifteen minutes from notification until rolling out.

Wimpy Peake, Joe Vojir, Bill Ricks, and I got Whiplash duty. Wimpy liked to take the tasking himself because he could work on the next day's schedule and clear up paperwork while still getting to fly missions. We had the afternoon period from noon until dark, so we briefed about ten-thirty then preflighted the airplanes, which were parked side-by-side at the far east end of the ramp. We were loaded with six cans of finned napalm each. Call sign was Whiplash Bravo, indicating we were the second Whiplash flight of the day after the morning alert birds had flown.

We had almost abandoned hope of flying by three-thirty in the afternoon when the command post phone behind the duty desk rasped. The regular schedule had already launched, so it could only mean Whiplash was going. Behind the desk Wayne Spelius was scribbling the details on a notepad as the rest of us grabbed our gear and headed for the door. Wimpy took the note and briefed us in the crew van as we rode out to the airplanes. We were going up to northern Laos to contact a forward air controller (FAC), call sign Butterfly 44. We had lat/long for the contact point as well as a TACAN cut off channel 36 in the Plain of Jars in the highlands of the Barrel Roll area.

The crew chiefs were standing by at the foot of the ladders as we bounced out of the truck and ran to the planes. They followed us up to the cockpits and helped us get strapped in then pulled the ladders and stood by for engine start. Wimpy waved a run-up signal and all four carts fired simultaneously, covering the ramp with black, eye-watering smoke. Barely three minutes later he made his taxi call to the tower, and we were rolling out.

The weather was mostly broken clouds, and the scramble to get things in the cockpit working left me puffing, but we were able to get leveled off at twenty thousand and spread out. I checked my Doppler position against the Udorn TACAN information and did a quick update to make the numbers for bearing and distance agree. The radar was on eighty-mile scope, and all I had to do was watch the landscape go by. I wondered what Butterfly 44 was doing.

Across the Mekong along the north border of Thailand, we changed channels to Cricket and asked for words for Whiplash Bravo. They confirmed that we were still to rendezvous with the FAC in northern Laos. We switched to the FAC frequency, and Wimpy called him when we were 120 miles out. We didn't get an answer. The miles rolled down and Wimpy kept calling Butterfly 44. No response. Then, at just 40 miles short of the contact area, we got a weak, out-of-breath response. "Hello, Whiplash. Hello, Whiplash. This is Butterfly 44. Do you copy?"

"Roger, Butterfly. We've got four nickels for you with twenty-four cans of nape and twenty mike-mike. We'll play for about twenty minutes and we're now about 40 miles out."

"Thanks, Whiplash, copy your numbers. I'm on the ground now refueling. I'm standing on the wing pumping gas in the airplane, but I should be airborne in about three more minutes. The target isn't very far away." If I was stealing hubcaps, this guy was a full-fledged car thief. He's on the ground in the midst of heavily contested Indian country, pumping his own gas, and he doesn't seem overly concerned.

Wimpy advises that we'll set up an orbit at the contact point and wait for Butterfly's instructions. We descend to fourteen thousand feet and work our way around the puffy cumulus clouds. It may be difficult to work here. A lot will depend on where the target is.

"Whiplash, Butterfly 44's on the roll. Be with you in a minute. Are you ready for a briefing?" He's panting and breathless from the exertion of refueling, and now he's taking off from the dirt strip.

"Roger, Butterfly. Go ahead."

"Okay, Whiplash. We've got a valley three miles north of my base with an estimated fifteen hundred Pathet Lao regulars. The valley is about four miles long by two miles wide and I've got about two hundred Royal Laotians on the hilltops to the south. I need you to put your napalm in the valley and we'll try to spread it around. Can you give me multiple passes dropping pairs?"

"We'll be happy to do that, Butterfly," is Wimpy's reply. I revise my estimate of Butterfly 44. He's not stealing cars or hubcaps. He's running an entire Mafia. He's the lone round-eye in the midst of an Asian civil war and apparently loving every minute of it.

"Whiplash, Butterfly 44 has you in sight. If you check your ten o'clock low, you should be able to pick me up. I've got a white Pilatus Porter, and I'm level at six thousand feet in a left-hand orbit. Defenses in this area are small arms and automatic weapons with reported 23 and 37 millimeter coming out of the valley earlier today. I'd like you to work the valley from east to west and come off south. The friendlies are on the hilltops to the south. Call visual on me."

"Okay, Butterfly, Whiplash Lead has you in sight. Whiplash acknowledge visual."

We call the FAC in sight in order, "Two ... Three ... Four." In a left-hand wheel we trail around the circle waiting for the controller to mark the target.

"Whiplash, I'm afraid I can't mark for you. The ROE don't allow me to carry ordnance. But if you've got me in sight, I'll point out the target area with my left wingtip. Call the target area, and call in from the east." The white airplane stands out against the dark jungle, flying a tiny circle in a clearing among the clouds. He banks and his wingtip indicates an area of trees. "Got it?" he queries.

"Roger, Butterfly. Whiplash Lead's in from the east."

"Cleared hot, Whiplash. I'm holding off to the north."

Wimpy rolls in and I can see the shiny aluminum napalm cans leave his airplane. The fins keep them aerodynamically straight so they don't tumble and smear, but the fireball in the jungle is still impressive. "Nice hit, Lead. Two put yours just west of Lead's smoke. Three, step it further west, and Four, finish off the end of the valley. Two's cleared hot."

I roll in and drop. "Okay, Whiplash, you're cleared flight lead discretion for multiple attacks. Keep working the valley, and stay clear of the ridge to the south." Butterfly lets us run our own pattern.

We circle, dropping the napalm and coating the valley floor with fire. As Wimpy calls in for his third pass, he reminds Butterfly 44 that we've still got some playtime and we can strafe. Butterfly approves, so we circle around and drop down to strafe the valley. The twinkle of the incendiary rounds shows the pattern of the guns as we come around again and again. The cordite smell of the gun fills the cockpit, tickles my nose and makes my eyes sting. As I pull off the target area I look to my left, and I can see the outline of people on the top of the ridgeline. They're waving and jumping up and down. It's the small contingent of the Royal Laotian army who've been watching our air show. They know now that they won't have to enter the valley today and won't have to fight a force many times larger than their own.

Joe Vojir calls bingo and Wimpy turns off the target into a gentle climb, heading for home. Butterfly 44 comes on the radio, "Thanks a lot guys. I've got you on the target at 16:40, off at 17:12 with 100 percent of ordnance on target. I'll forward some BDA when our guys walk through there tomorrow, but right now all I can say is thank you. You've saved the fort for another night."

I can't imagine his situation. I can't conceive being in the jungle with a tiny airplane and a hugely outnumbered ground force. I can't believe that he lives there and controls an air war in which he isn't allowed to shoot back. As I cruise back to my safe air base with my air-conditioned room, white sheets, hot shower, and cold beer at the Officers' Club, I wonder what kind of a man is this. What could I possibly have to complain about? The mission hasn't been a counter, but I'm feeling damn good about it.

The club is crowded when we get there, with the squadron dining tables half filled and the bar lined with fighter pilots in sweaty flight suits. The nonrated officers don't spend much time here, except for meals at their small tables. We elbow our way in for a cold beer and the latest news on what other flights have done during the day. As usual since the increased frequency of Pack VI strikes, there's news of a loss. We ask for a name, but none of us recognize it. We grab a second beer and head for dinner. The special is rib-eye steak, and regardless of how you ask for it the Thai waitress smilingly returns with it well done. For dessert we have hot apple pie. You can have it with ice cream, but most of us know that the cook will put the ice cream on the pie before it is heated, resulting in a soupy mess. I wonder if Butterfly 44 has had apple pie recently. Probably not.

After dinner we head back to our rooms one by one. We figured out early in the tour that heavy drinking can't be a regular event for most of us. Almost everyone starts out with a few nights of partying and songfests, but the first time you have to strap on an airplane with a pounding hangover you learn the lesson. You need to be clear-headed to get the job done. Whether you're a wingman or a leader, others depend on you, so you have a drink or two and then try to sleep. Maybe you write a letter or read a few pages of a book. Some don shorts and running shoes and jog around the hootch area in the summer evening twilight. A few new guys stay behind at the bar for some courage drinking and a few celebrate an event, a birthday or a successful mission or a tribute to a fallen buddy, but for most of us it's bedtime. I hope Butterfly 44 has a good night. I hope he has many good nights. He earns them.

CHAPTER 13

Bailouts and Bootleg Counters

The squadron buildings on the quadrangle at Korat had been built in a hurry, with little concern for amenities like indoor plumbing or windows. While the problem of latrine facilities was handled by the central building on the quad, the place where Andrew Jackson's statue would stand on a municipal square, the case of windows was more complex. When the power from the diesel generators two blocks away would occasionally go off, the building would be plunged into darkness that was scarcely lessened by opening the three small access doors. Major Tracy decided he absolutely had to have a window in his office.

Fighter squadrons are veritable warehouses of hidden talents. Mention a project in a squadron, any kind of a project, and you are certain to find someone with the skills to accomplish the job. It may be not what you expected, but something will happen. Want a window, Boss? No sweat, we'll have it done by tomorrow. We don't need no steenkin' work orders.

Ed Harvey headed over to the command post and scrounged some tools. Kenny Hallmark and Karl Richter wangled a cache of lumber from the supply yard to frame the window. The only problem was glass. There was none to be found and before the first cut was made in the office wall it looked as though the project would founder. That's when Sergeant Morgan proved his worth yet again. He'd just built new scheduling boards and had several desktop-sized sheets of Plexiglas left over. The problem was solved. We'd build a plastic window.

About four hours of sawing, measuring, hammering, and swearing later, the boss had a window behind his desk. He walked in, sat down, put his feet up on the desk, and leaned back in his chair. Looking out he could see the departure end of Runway 24. He pronounced it a job well done.

Less than a week later the boss was churning out some paperwork when the bang of the afterburners from the ten o'clock flight prompted him to raise his head and look out his window. No fighter pilot can resist watching airplanes for very long, and Fred Tracy was no exception. The airplanes, one by one, passed into his view. The gear was coming up and the afterburner blazing. One, then Two, fifteen seconds later Three, then Four. But something was unusual. The blazing tail of four extended all the way up the fuselage ahead of the rudder and slab. Four was level, then sinking slightly. Suddenly, the canopy came off the airplane, then the ejection seat blasted clear. The airplane continued sinking until it impacted less than half a mile from the departure end of the runway. Joe Vojir swung once then landed in the tall jungle grass just off the overrun. The view of the fireball through the new Plexiglas window was spectacular.

Vojir was uninjured beyond a bit of stiffness from the jolt of ejecting. That night at the dinner table he recounted that his only real fear came after he hit the ground. As he lay in the jungle grass he heard a loud hissing by his right shoulder. He'd heard tales of the infamous banded krait, a "two-stepper" snake that was so poisonous that when bitten you only lived for two more steps. He froze, waiting for the sting of fangs and wondering if someone would come to his aid before he was bitten. Only when he realized that the hiss was coming from the automatically activated bailout bottle of high-pressure oxygen in his parachute backpack did he relax.

The loss of Joe Vojir's aircraft at the airfield was fortunate. There had been numerous accounts of airplanes being "hit" when no ground fire was observed. The explanation had always been that a lucky shot had been the cause of loss. Wreckage was never recovered, but the sequence of events was always the same. Cruising along, suddenly there is an engine fire light followed shortly thereafter by hydraulic failure and loss of control. Pilots seldom reported structural damage beforehand, and the only indication of a problem was the fire light. The wreckage from Joe's airplane would disclose another way that the 105 could kill you.

Modern jet engines consist of a compressor section, a combustion chamber area, and a turbine in the exhaust stream. The Pratt & Whitney J-75 that powered the Thunderchief had fifteen stages of compressor, row after row of bladed wheels, each succeeding wheel with smaller blades to increase the pressure of air as it moved from the front of the engine to the combustion area. The compressor was driven by a turbine section consisting of three bladed wheels spun by the high-speed exhaust from the main engine section. The turbine assembly was built up of individual blades fitted to a ratchetlike axle assembly, commonly referred to as a "Christmas tree." The wreckage of Joe's airplane revealed that the Christmas tree had fractured, sending turbine blades flying out from the rapidly spinning engine shaft. Throwing one or two blades unbalanced the turbine wheels and almost immediately threw the rest of the blades, creating a huge buzz saw that destroyed the aft section of the airplane, rupturing fuel tanks, cutting hydraulic lines, and severing flight controls.

The cause was heat stress fatigue resulting from running the engines at high throttle settings for extended periods of time. The solution was to inspect engines more frequently and to establish new criteria for calculating time on an engine before major overhaul. Rather than simply total the flying hours, maintenance crews multiplied them by a factor based on the types of missions the airplane had flown. Combat missions accumulated time on the engines more quickly than noncombat flying. Laos and Pack I missions multiplied flying time by 1.5 while Pack VI missions multiplied by 5. Engines would be changed much more frequently. The solution made sense, but it didn't come in time to save the life of Buzz Bullock in the 34th, who died when his engine blew up during takeoff roll and his survival gear prematurely opened

his lapbelt during ejection. It was also too late for Dain Mil-
liman in the 469th, who died when his burning airplane
crashed on the Korat runway after the engine exploded at
liftoff.

Bill Loyd's lessons about rescue were always in the backs of
our minds. Losses occurred every day and hope of rescue
was an important aspect of going to battle. You could run
only so far on professionalism or patriotism, and the adrenaline rush of stealing the fat guy's hubcaps only came on the
outbound leg of the mission. It took more than that to go to
the briefing each morning and sit in a room with twenty-five
or thirty guys, knowing that one or more of you probably
wouldn't be back that night. Rescue was critical, and we
were all ready, willing, and able to support any effort to get
one of our guys back.

Kenny Hallmark had been shot down and picked up. He'd
been forced to bail out at a higher speed than he wanted and
suffered some wind-blast flailing. The ejection left him with
a badly sprained knee and two horrific shiners. In the mornings Ken would hobble down to the squadron on crutches to
see what work he could do around the building then spend
most of the afternoon on a cot in front of his hootch reading
magazines. He'd get a couple of weeks of rehab then return
to the flying schedule.

When we participated in a rescue effort we got an occasional bonus. All commanders agreed that mission counters
were based not necessarily on the number of flights, but on
entries into North Vietnam. What was meant was that if you
were required to exit North Vietnam, tap a tanker for gas,
and then re-enter to support a rescue operation, you could get
another counter. Multiple trips into NVN on a single flight
could result in multiple counters, which would speed up the
process of amassing one hundred missions.

Maj. Ken Frank was one of the most eager to volunteer for
rescues. The merest hint of a "Mayday" or the first squawk
of an emergency beeper would have Ken switching to the

nearest controlling agency channel to offer his flight for duty capping a rescue force, escorting a Jolly Green, or delivering ordnance to help protect a downed crewman. Ken's eagerness resulted in a bit of embarrassment, however, on the day Wayne Spelius set the record for fastest rescue recovery.

Wayne Spelius had been in my pilot training class at Williams AFB, and we'd checked out in the 105 together at Nellis. He was a tall, extremely skinny guy with a dry sense of humor that took a little getting used to. He had beaten me out in pilot training with a strong academic performance, and after a whole year indicating a preference for B-52s, he had decided he'd really like to fly a 105. Had I missed getting my Thunderchief slot, I'd have never forgiven him. It had all worked out in the long run, though, and now we were both in the same squadron and had become friends. At Korat he'd picked up a nickname based on his long, gangly arms and legs. He was "Spider" Spelius.

Frank and Spider were on a two-ship armed recce mission in Pack I. They hadn't yet found something to expend their ordnance on when the radio blared out the emergency call, "Mayday. Mayday. Mayday. Pistol Two is hit. I've got a fire light and I'm heading feet wet. I'm going down, position is just north of Dong Hoi."

It didn't take Frank but a split second to flip his UHF radio over to guard channel and respond, "Roger, Pistol. We've got a pair of 105s approximately your position, and we'll be with you shortly. Let's go to Cricket." He switched to the airborne command post to offer his flight for rescue.

"Cricket, Cricket, this is Pistol. Understand Pistol Two is . . . Uhh, standby please." The lights went on suddenly. Frank and Spelius were Pistol flight. He turned, straining left and right, looking for his wingman. He tried to recall the last time he'd checked for him. Spider was the distressed pilot. It was his own wingie that was in trouble.

"Cricket, Pistol. My wingman just called Mayday, and we're separated. Can we get some rescue help moving toward the Dong Hoi area? I'll be on-scene command until you get things organized." He bent the airplane around in a hard turn and headed toward the bomb-cratered Dong Hoi runway, scanning the area with his radar.

"Pistol Lead, this is Pistol Two on guard. I'm eastbound, just passing the coast and climbing through ten thousand. I've got a fire light and have lost utility hydraulic. I don't know how long this thing will hold together." And just when Spider seemed to have his situation under relative control — "I've just had an explosion. I'm getting out." He ejected.

Less than a minute elapsed before Spider's commentary resumed. "Mayday, Mayday. Pistol Two is going down about five miles off the coast abeam Dong Hoi."

The reply was almost instantaneous. "Pistol Two, this is King One-Six. I'm near your position; say your situation."

"Roger, King One-Six, this is Pistol Two. I've bailed out and am descending. I'm in the chute using my survival radio now. Are you an Albatross?"

"That's affirmative, Pistol; King is an SA-16 Albatross. Say your position."

"Roger King, check your right two o'clock and slightly high. I'm just off your right wing now." In a remarkable coincidence, the rescue flying boat was patrolling right at the position that Spider chose to eject.

King orbited Wayne as he descended slowly in his parachute then set up to land on the water just prior to his touchdown. As the parachute collapsed around his splashdown, the flying boat taxied carefully up to him and pulled him out after less than two minutes in the water. Spelius set a recovery record and got to spend a night at Danang buying drinks for the rescue guys. Ken Frank didn't get an extra counter that day, but he did get plenty of teasing about knowing his call sign and watching his wingman.

My gear is getting way too heavy. I've added a second survival radio and a spare battery to my vest. That makes two radios, an emergency beeper, and a battery, along with the radio in the seat kit and the beeper in the parachute. The logic is impeccable. Radio communication is absolutely essential to a successful rescue. You must talk to your rescuers. You can lose your seat kit during bailout or during descent or during a run for cover when you hit the ground. That means a radio in your vest. You might break an antenna or have a circuit failure. That means a second radio in your vest. You might have a dead battery and the jungle simply has no charger stations. That means a spare battery . . . or maybe two. The radios aren't to be questioned.

But I've got too much weight on my shoulders and too many hard lumps prodding me in the stomach, the waist, the chest, the arms. I've got to get rid of something. Maybe the guns. Do I really need two guns? The .38 Smith is fine, but six rounds won't last very long in a firefight. The Beretta on my G-suit isn't very heavy and the ammo is a bit lighter than the .38 Special stuff. The idea of having a weapon in hand while reloading is comforting. I'm not sure if I could really fight my way out of a ground situation, but giving up a gun is probably not a good idea. The guns stay.

What's to lose? What should I remove from my gear? I grab my vest and G-suit during the afternoon and take them down the hall into an empty briefing room. I unload the pockets and spread all of the equipment on the table. In a matter of minutes, I'm joined by Richter and Hallmark. When I explain what I'm doing they get their gear, and now we've got bits and pieces of survival equipment spread over tables, chairs, and floor. We discuss and evaluate each item. We begin to reload our vests, starting with the essentials and discarding anything we deem unnecessary.

The radios, batteries, guns, and ammo are first. Then come the flares. The Mk-6 day/night tubes stay firmly taped to the G-suit. We discuss the rocket-jet pen flares for a few seconds then insert them into the vest's flat inner pocket. The silver foil space blanket generates a lot of discussion because none of us figures we'll ever use a blanket to sleep in the hot and steamy jungle. Then we talk about signaling with the silver side or collecting water, or using it to shield from snakes and spiders and crawly things. The blanket stays.

The first-aid kit doesn't generate a challenge. Gotta have a supply of medicine, some bandages, and antiseptic. No questions asked. Ditto for the compass, the hunting knife, the wire saw — no real weight or size involved there. The mirror is a keeper. Signal with it, maybe even look around corners. Probably won't need to shave. What about the fishing kit? Never can tell, could get hungry. Water bottles in the G-suit pockets? All the survival books say drink the water right away after landing to deter shock and dehydration. Maybe I can dump the sawed off fourteen-inch machete I've got on my G-suit thigh opposite the Beretta. Nope. Might need to hack through the jungle.

The whole exercise lasts about an hour. When we've finished, the only item lying on the table is the plastic police whistle. It's less than half an ounce. But it's something. Chuck it.

Three days later I'm climbing out from Pack II after dropping on a suspected truck park, listening to the end game of a rescue in progress. We can hear the helicopter talking to the survivor on the radio. Apparently a PJ has gone down the hoist cable into the jungle and is trying to locate the pilot, who can't move because of a leg injury. The PJ can't find him. The Jolly Green asks the pilot to blow his whistle to provide a signal to the rescuer. After landing I find myself in the life-support shop standing next to Ken Hallmark as Sergeant Leonard asks him why he needs another whistle. There appears to be a rash of misplaced whistles and a heavy run on replacements. My gear doesn't seem quite as heavy anymore. You never can tell when you might need a plastic whistle.

Not all rescues had happy endings. It was only a few days later that Ken Frank and I participated in a more complex scenario. We were flying a two-ship, call sign Pine, headed for the Cape Mui Ron ferry in Pack I on armed recce. We had just crossed the Mekong eastbound across Laos when we began to hear radio calls on a rescue in progress. Fresno 01, an F-104 from Udorn was down and a flight of four A-1 Sandys was overhead trying to establish contact before bringing the Jolly Green in for pickup.

We cruised inbound, line abreast, listening to the dialog and getting the picture of what was going on. I switched my nav control to DF so that each time the lead A-1 made a radio call, my bearing pointer showed his position. We had plenty of fuel and a full load of ordnance, so if we were needed, we'd be immediately available. The 104 had been shot down along the coastal flatlands southeast of Dong Hoi. The A-1s had relieved the 104 wingman, who had started the rescue effort but didn't have enough fuel to remain on scene for more than a few minutes. The Sandys were calling on the radio to establish contact with the survivor, but they weren't getting any answer.

"Fresno Lead, Fresno Lead, this is Sandy Three-One on guard. If you read me come up voice or beeper. Fresno Lead, come up voice or beeper." The A-1 was quartering back and forth over the area, trying to find the downed pilot. The calls droned on seeking some signal from the survivor to pinpoint his position, but things didn't sound good.

"Fresno, Fresno, Sandy Three-One on guard. If you read come up voice. Fresno, Sandy Three-One, give me a flash, give me smoke. Fresno, this is Sandy, come up voice." The calls went on without results, and then things went from bad to worse. "Fresno Lead this is Sandy Three-One. Fresno, Sandy Thr . . ." The transmission ended abruptly in mid-word. A scream on the radio told the world that the situation had changed.

"Mayday. Mayday. This is Sandy Three-Three. I'm hit. I'm on fire. Mayday. I'm burning. My wing is on fire. Mayday. This is Sandy Three-Three." An old and very sick fighter pilot joke flashed through my mind as we waited for Sandy 33 to end his radio call. The story involved a panic-stricken pilot screaming his last words on the radio and asking what can be done. A senior, grizzled flight lead replies, "Shut up and die like a man." The terror in the voice of the rescue pilot was very apparent and there was no doubt that if I had been sitting in a burning airplane fueled by 130 octane aviation gas, I'd be just as scared.

Ken Frank thought he heard a break in the transmission, and I could hear him call, "Sandy Three-Three, Pine. Say your position," but the squeal in the radio told me that Sandy was still transmitting and had only taken a breath. Sandy 33 continued to transmit, screaming of fire and begging for help, but in the process blocking the radio and preventing anyone from helping him or Sandy 31. Major Frank and I were about forty miles west of Dong Hoi and descending gradually into the search area. The DF bearing pointer showed Sandy 33 passing north of our position, headed outbound toward Nakhon Phanom.

Then he paused. I heard the voice of Ralph Beardsley, one of the experienced captains from my squadron. Ralph was inbound with another flight and had been monitoring the events just as we had. "Sandy Three-Three, this is Elm. Are you bailing out?"

A few seconds elapsed and then a calmer Sandy 33 replied, "No, Elm. It appears to be holding together. I'm climbing out passing eight thousand, and the fire appears to have blown out."

"Roger, Sandy Three-Three. I think I've got you in sight. I'm coming up on your right; say your airspeed. I'll join up and check you over." I wasn't sure how fast an A-1 could go, but I knew very well how slow a bomb-laden 105 could fly and I sincerely doubted that this proposal would work out well.

Sandy 33 called, "One forty" and within seconds we heard Ralph admitting that he'd have to try something a bit different. Even with gear and flaps down, Beardsley would have a tough time getting much under one eighty.

Ken Frank and I had reached the coast and switched to rescue secondary frequency to find out what had happened to

Sandy 31. Ken called, "Any Sandy, this is Pine. What's your status? Sandy, Sandy, this is Pine."

It didn't take more than one call to get a response from a clearly shaken Sandy 32. He was now leading Sandy 34 and holding in an orbit just offshore. He briefed us on what he knew but wasn't sure exactly what had happened. They had been quartering the search area, trying to establish contact with Fresno Lead. He had been spread wide on his leader when suddenly Sandy 33 had called on his VHF radio that he'd taken a hit and was switching to guard channel. Sandy 32 had looked around trying to acquire 33 to render assistance and when he looked back for his leader, he was nowhere to be found. Apparently, Sandy 31 had been hit at the same time and was now down as well.

Sandy 32 wanted to search the area for his leader but wasn't sure if he could survive back over the beach. Frank suggested that our 105s might be able to make a few passes over the area at a more survivable speed. We got no arguments over the proposal.

We rolled into a descent and headed for Sandy 31's last known position. The land was dead flat, rice paddies and narrow canals lined with low bushes. We rolled down the countryside at two hundred feet and just a shade over five hundred knots. I stayed line abreast on my leader and planned ahead for reversals at the end of each pass so I wouldn't get spit out of formation. We were in our third pass over the area when we caught a small tendril of smoke coming up out of the corner of a rice paddy. We pulled up into a whifferdill and crossturned back over the area to check out the smoke. We saw a black smudge on the ground, nearly symmetrical, indicating that the A-1 had hit almost perfectly flat. Nothing remained to indicate that the wreckage had ever been an airplane except the large rotary engine block.

Nothing was ever found of Fresno Lead. The F-104 pilot was captured by the North Vietnamese and died in captivity. Sandy 31 had apparently died instantly when 37-mm guns hit his aircraft. Sandy 33 was successfully escorted back to base, but when he lowered his landing gear for an approach, he discovered that the wing fire had burned away most of the right main gear assembly. He bailed out and was recovered. It was just another day in paradise.[1]

I wasn't about to go through the CIA hassle again for a few days of relaxation. Making scenes in air terminals and herding pallets of paperwork around the Far East armed with a weapon that had been discarded by Lawrence of Arabia was not my idea of a great way to spend a vacation. When the next opportunity came to get away from Korat for a couple of days, Bangkok was at the top of my list of choices. Bill Ricks and I coordinated our time off, and when Bill Loyd said it was okay we headed for Korat City, where we found a Thai driver with an air-conditioned Mercedes sedan who would drive us to Bangkok for ten bucks apiece. It was a booming business for the fast-talking taxi entrepreneur, who coordinated a small fleet of cars catering to the needs of the fighter pilots from the base. We told him where we wanted to go and when we would be coming back, and we conducted the proper amount of Asian haggling before agreeing to the price that we all knew we would pay regardless. Ten bucks each. Three passengers. Leave right now. Me, Ricks, and Loyd.

We were new at this, so we could be excused for making a few mistakes. The driver we'd been assigned spoke little more than pidgin English, but that was a whole lot more than our command of Thai. We had the basic "sawadee," which serves much like the Hawaiian "aloha," an all-purpose hello, good-bye, and how-are-ya? We could say thank you, "kup koon," and even glorify it by adding "mak" at the end, which made the phrase, thank you, very much. After that, we were pretty much stumped, resorting to lots of hand signals, facial

1. Fresno 01 was downed on 1 September 1966. From the 435th TFS, deployed to Udorn RTAB, the pilot was Maj. Norman Schmidt. The A-1 Sandy 31 was flown by Maj. H. C. Nichols, and Sandy 33 was flown by Capt. A. L. Minnick.

expressions, and the really lame practice of pronouncing good things as "number one" and bad things as "number ten." We could perform a passable "wai," the respectful bow with hands folded as if in prayer, and even knew that how high one held one's hands during this maneuver indicated the level of respect. Never touch a Thai above the shoulders, never point the sole of your shoe at someone, even if sitting with your legs crossed in a chair, and never, under any circumstances, do anything that might be construed as disrespect to the King and the royal family, Yul Brynner notwithstanding.

Before we'd cleared the outskirts of Korat City, the driver turned to us in the backseat and said, "You want drinkee?" Obviously he had hauled a lot of fighter pilots back and forth from Bangkok. With little discussion the three of us responded simultaneously with an unqualified yes. He pulled over to a roadside stand adjacent to a gas station. From a small pushcart and several Coleman ice chests, a tiny, wizened old woman was running a full-blown restaurant operation. Spaced around her cart were four folding card tables, each with a complement of rickety chairs. Her cart held a fly-specked glass case that proudly displayed bowls of ingredients for her meal menu. Next to a stack of chipped dinner plates, a single gas burner held a greasy blackened wok. We didn't see any sign of running water or any indication of how she would clean used utensils and dinnerware before using them again. In several of the chairs sat Thai men engaged in animated conversation and smoking their after-lunch cigarettes. The warm greeting from the old lady to the taxi driver suggested that either he was a regular customer or they were related.

With the driver negotiating to get us a much higher price than a local would pay, Loyd and I bought two beers each. Ricks, still grappling with his Mormon background, opted for a Coke, recognizable by the familiar bottle shape rather than the Thai script labeling. The beers were Singha, a somewhat bitter ale that when ice cold was very good, but when warmed to room temperature developed the distinct aroma of monkey piss. The bottles held half a liter rather than twelve ounces, so we felt adequately prepared for the trip. Fortunately, the beer was nearly frozen.

The trip provided us a better view of the countryside than we could get from the cockpit of a speeding jet. The road from Korat to the capital, known as the Friendship Highway, had been built by the Americans primarily for the purpose of moving jet fuel and other supplies from the ports south of Bangkok to the air bases up-country. Tanker trucks streamed continually up and down the road, dwarfing the few passenger vehicles driven by Thais. Each truck reflected the Thai owner's personality, with gaudy decorative lights and silver metal trim adorning the fenders, hood, and the driver's open-air cab. Most of the trucks held as many as five men in the cab, possibly because the driver was trying to make a few bucks by hauling passengers or was carrying relief drivers for long trips. Within the cab there was invariably an eight-by-ten color photograph of the King in a gold filigree frame, often with red velvet drapery surrounding the portrait and small votive candles burning on each side. The advisability of carrying burning candles on a jet fuel transporter had apparently not been discussed when the contract was let.

The countryside was beautiful. Tall, graceful trees surrounded rice fields where young boys and girls, usually barefoot and clad only in wrap-around sarongs, guided huge water buffalo pulling plows or carts. We passed villages, each with a central Buddhist temple or wat, easily recognized by its orange tile roof and gilded upturned eaves. Rows of stores in each town bustled with people engaged in tailoring, blacksmithing, auto repair, or agricultural commerce. Almost all shops had several chairs on the walkway in front for customers and merchants to sit, sipping tea and listening to the radio, or watching a small black and white television. We enjoyed our beers and watched the panorama drift by.

In the towns we saw school-aged children in what looked like a national uniform of white shirt and blue shorts or skirt, with a small backpack of schoolbooks. With their rice bowls in hand, teenaged Buddhist monks in bright saffron robes trudged in single file, living a life totally dependent on the people's charity. On one hillside we passed a huge statue of the Buddha, easily one hundred feet high, carved from white stone. The scene displayed a tranquil and simple rural existence. Certainly not a life filled with America's late twentieth-century amenities, but a life that the Thai people most assuredly valued.

As we approached Bangkok, the two-lane highway expanded to four, then six, then eight lanes of bumper-to-bumper traffic. Swarms of two-cycle motor scooters danced in and out between the cars emitting blue clouds of eye-watering exhaust. The smell of the klongs, the exhaust from the gridlocked vehicles, and the aroma of a million cooking fires preparing the evening meal in open-windowed houses on stilts along the many canals managed to penetrate the taxi's air-conditioned environment. We made our way to our destination, the newly opened Siam Intercontinental Hotel, accompanied by lots of fist shaking and what was either Thai cursing or praying by our driver. Somehow, we arrived safely.

The hotel was impressive. A huge, stylized pagoda roof covered the central reception area, and two long wings of deluxe rooms encircled an incredible swimming pool and garden area. From glass windows next to the reception desk, we could see groups of young men lying around the pool basking in the sun. They were obviously other tactical aviators from the other Thailand bases, collected here for the same reasons we were. We were back in civilization and, barring a taxi disaster, there was a good chance that we would live through the next four days. It was a wonderful feeling.

Ricks and I played tourist for a bit, checking out the Emerald Buddha, the Reclining Buddha, the TV-watching Buddha, the Grocery Shopping Buddha and at least a half dozen other occupation-specific renditions of the revered philosopher. We hit a few jewelry shops and quickly learned that quality star sapphires don't come cheap, even if you are buying them in the country of origin. Cheap jewelry is the only thing that comes cheap. A stop at a small printer's stall got me a hundred business cards, printed on one side with my name and occupation as "Fighter Pilot." A list of qualifications described me as "coup-qualified," "mercenary — foreign & domestic," "world traveler," and "ruler of the skies." On the back was the marginally blasphemous quotation, "Yea though I walk through the valley of the shadow of death I shall fear no evil, for I am the meanest son-of-a-bitch in the valley."

We still had plenty of time to hang around the pool during the day and hang around the bar at night. We made the mandatory pilgrimage to Nick's Number One Steakhouse for the French onion soup and Kobe beef filets that were famous throughout the region. Nick, a Hungarian expatriate, had made a fine business catering to European diplomats and businessmen passing through Bangkok over the years. Now, with thousands of Americans seeking relief from participation in the war, Nick's business was really booming. The cheese-encrusted soup, the incredibly tender rare beef, a martini, and a bottle of Bordeaux were welcome changes from the abused dining fare of the Korat club. We shook Nick's hand, complimented his food, and extravagantly tipped his charming and beautiful daughter, who had served us.

Two guys from the 469th, who were staying at the hotel, and I headed down to Pat Pong Road, Bangkok's adult entertainment center. Here, jammed shoulder to shoulder for more than a mile, were gaudy neon bars, strip joints, massage parlors, and discos. The culture was more Las Vegas or North Beach than Asian, but reflected how Thai business practicality satisfied the free market demand for sex. Beautiful young girls and beautiful young boys impersonating girls were on display dancing on tables, tending bar, and sipping champagne cocktails with young GIs who were eager to spend their next month's paycheck for a little bit of silicone-enhanced companionship. There was money to be made and a bit of exhibitionism and prostitution was hardly new to the back streets of Bangkok.

We routed our way through one of the larger massage parlors, where we selected a masseuse from a bull-pen room filled with giggling Thai girls gossiping behind one-way glass. We stood in a darkened area, inspecting the girls, commenting on legs, breasts, butts, and smiles. Each girl wore a standard pink uniform and each had a clearly visible red tag with a number pinned to the right shoulder. When we found one we liked, we told the proprietor the number. The mama-san called the girl from the bull pen, gave her a basket with soap and towels, then directed her to lead us down a dim hallway to a bathing room.

Communicating with sign language mostly, my girl directed me to disrobe, pointing at a pair of hooks on the back of the door for clothing then at a large square tub that she began filling with water. As I slipped out of my shirt and trousers, she unbuttoned her pink dress and let it drop to the floor. She stood there in white bra and panties, waving impatiently for me to get out of my Jockey shorts and get into the tub.

It beat the hell out of the shower in the Korat hootch, which was usually cold. The water was wonderfully warm, and the Thai girl wouldn't let me do anything for myself. She laughed and sang softly to herself as she proceeded to lather a small sponge and wash me from head to toe. Using a small wooden bucket, she rinsed the suds away then motioned me to stand so that she could dry me with several large towels. Another wave directed me to the padded massage table in the center of the room. She spread more dry towels then directed me to lay facedown on the table.

The massage was incredible. Starting at my fingers, working her way up my arms to my shoulders, she slowly worked each muscle, kneading, stroking, and squeezing softly. Each arm got the treatment, then my feet, and up each leg. My back, shoulders, and butt, all got prodded, poked, and rubbed. Then it was flip over and get the same treatment on chest, thighs, waist, and the rather insistent erection that had developed. By the time the treatment was over, no stiff muscles remained. Relaxation was total.

When the four days were over, exactly as agreed upon, the dark gray Mercedes appeared at the hotel door, ready to return us to Korat and the war. The driver had brought along a cooler of Singha and Cokes on ice for our return trip. Four hours later we were back on base, out of our civilian clothes, and back in our faded cotton flying suits, hovering near the Officers' Club door waiting for the posting of next day's schedule. Just like slipping on the uniform and hash-marked jungle hat, the pressure and tension eased firmly back upon our shoulders. We were back at war.

As we approached the end of the summer, the daily routine of Pack VI briefing and flying became less and less remarkable. With more than sixty missions, I was comfortable in almost any situation and confident that I could get in and out of virtually any target area. My new flight commander, Maj. Bob Dundas, was one of the high-time 105 pilots from Germany. He was quiet, calm, and a real pro. Each flight in the squadron now had a Major flight commander and all of them were solid, trustworthy leaders who knew their way around. In addition to Dundas, we had Bob Phillips, Dan MacIntosh, Wimpy Peake, Ralph Beardsley, John Malone, and Chuck Franklin. I was beginning to think about life after Korat. Maybe it was possible.

The idea of a hundred-mission tour seemed pretty good from the point of view of a young lieutenant, but it was creating problems for the Air Force. In their attempt to create an equitable policy for what was apparently going to become a protracted war, the personnel folks acted like politicians running for office. They promised things that might get them elected but which weren't the best choices for fighting the war.

First, they declared that there would be no involuntary second combat tours until everyone on active duty had flown his first tour. On the surface that sounded good because it meant that there would be no shirking and guys who had done their duty wouldn't be funneled back into the war again and again until they were inevitably lost. The problem was that only certain kinds of flying jobs were useful in Vietnam. While the USAF had more than twenty-five thousand active duty pilots, only a small percentage of those pilots did the kind of job that was applicable to the war. Pilots flying transports, strategic bombers, and training aircraft just weren't useful in the combat zone, where we needed fighter pilots and forward air controllers. No problem, the personnel weenies decided, we'll just rule that all pilots are created equal. While fighter pilots scoffed, the heavy drivers and training commandos said, "See? We've always told you so."

Training in the F-105 had taken me almost nine months. Each of the nine graduates right out of undergraduate pilot training (UPT) had received 120 hours of flying to master a very complex aircraft. A new class started every six weeks at Nellis, alternating between the two squadrons. Nine pilots every six weeks and reassignment of existing F-105 pilots to combat units meant that we would run out of qualified pilots in fairly short order. The solution was the "universally assignable pilot."

Rather than nine new graduates who had fought for the assignment and graduated at the top of their pilot training class, the Air Force increased the class size to sixteen. They discontinued the "long course" for new fighter pilots and devised a short course of sixty hours over four months for older pilots. Now the training system would graduate twice as many 105 pilots twice as often — pilots with half the hours in the 105, but who were "experienced." It didn't matter that the hundreds or even thousands of hours of experience involved driving straight and level in a C-124 cargo plane or was limited to less than two Gs in a B-52. It didn't matter that the pilot had spent the last ten years in a staff job. Pilots who hadn't been upside down in an aircraft or flown formation since they'd pinned on their wings were now becoming instant fighter pilots. A pilot was a pilot. Anybody with wings could become a fighter pilot. With enough bananas, you could teach a monkey to fly. They were all just meat for the grinder.

They weren't all bad. The first groups of retreads were mostly volunteers. They came from SAC, MAC, and training command. Some had been in fighters long ago and some had never flown a small jet since graduation from UPT. They wanted to fly the 105, though, and that was in their favor. But wishing doesn't always make it so, and some of them had little talent for the job. A few went down the path that I had managed to avoid and quit before flying their first combat mission. One major with more than fifteen years of flying, mostly in air defense interceptors, arrived at Korat and promptly declared he had back problems that prevented him from flying in ejection-seat aircraft. His creative excuse may have served to rationalize his decision not to fly, but none of us believed him. He ate his meals alone for the two weeks it took to get him off the base.

Because they were senior, the retreads presented a problem for scheduling. They had little fighter experience but higher military rank. Though they were still having problems flying formation and refueling, they couldn't be held as wingmen indefinitely. Majors and senior captains needed to become element and flight leads. They would become flight commanders on the ground, so they needed to be leaders in the air as well. A partial solution was to route many into wing staff positions in the command post, frag shop, and operations. They would fly as attached crewmembers in the squadrons rather than be assigned. Their lack of tactical background meant they could screw up management decisions then come down to the squadron and get in the way while flying.

Some, however, were eager and aggressive. They had, for one reason or another, been routed into heavies or training assignments early in their careers and now had an opportunity to get into tactical fighters. They worked hard at learning the business and didn't gripe about not being immediately thrust into leadership roles. They acknowledged that they were still learning how to employ the 105 and accepted that they would gain responsibility as they demonstrated the ability to handle it. Like "Dirty Harry" Callahan, they were men who knew their limitations. These pilots fit into the 421st and joined the team.

We got guys like Ken Whittemore, who'd been a B-52 pilot, and Bob Loken, who came out of B-47s. There were Frank Reamer and Harry Mattoon, who had been doing pilot training. And there was Burris Begley, who'd been in F-86s long ago but had spent the last ten years pushing a desk as an Air National Guard adviser.

The influx of senior people inevitably led to an attempt at empire-building. Lieutenants typically don't worry about much except their primary job, which for us was flying combat and staying alive. Captains and majors, however, needed visibility if they were going to be promoted and advance their careers. The war was too young for most of us to appreciate that if we survived the tour we would have a significant promotion credential. The captains and majors needed an additional duty. They needed a job that would show their potential and that might also aid them in staying alive. There were way too many midlevel managers coming through the pipeline for the available squadron commander, ops officer, and even flight commander positions. They needed to create some opportunities and maybe even build in some life insurance.

Major Loyd was sitting behind the ops desk late in the afternoon. The last missions of the day had launched, Wimpy was building the next day's schedule, and Loyd had told the lieutenant duty officer to take the afternoon off. Two majors walked in and asked Bill if they could speak to the operations officer. Their new stiff jungle boots, patch-adorned flying suits, and failure to recognize Loyd as the ops officer marked them as very new arrivals, new to Korat, and new to the F-105.

Loyd didn't rise to greet them. He remained seated with his feet on the desk, twirling his handlebar mustache. They introduced themselves and confirmed the obvious. They had just come out of training and were assigned to the wing. Both had been in SAC and had run stan-eval or training pro-

grams for bomber crews. They were going to establish a
wing training program in which they would be responsible
for documenting the qualifications of various categories of
pilots. They would certify flight and element leads, instructor pilots, and other, yet to be determined, skill levels. Of
course, in doing this very important job, they would have to
fly check rides as flight examiners, and that would mean they
could only do their job flying missions to Pack I. No, they
wouldn't be able to give check rides on Pack VI missions.
Much too complicated, what with the defenses and all. And
of course noncounter missions in Laos wouldn't be suffi-
ciently challenging to evaluate other pilots properly.

Loyd looked at them contemptuously. They pointed past
him at the mission count board behind his chair. "How many
of those pilots are in training?" they wanted to know.

Now he stood. "You sniveling piece of crap. You come in
here, without a single combat sortie, and want to know who
is in training? You want to scrounge a tour's worth of easy
counters and avoid going downtown? Who the hell do you
think you are? Look at that board. Look at it! The average
man on that board has more than sixty missions. They've all
been to Hanoi ten or fifteen times. They're all flight leads.
There's nobody in training here. We're a combat squadron,
and we're all qualified. Now get your sorry ass out of here."

They left. That was the end of the training shop proposal
as far as our operations were concerned. The two would
eventually be assigned to other squadrons. I'm certain they
asked the deputy commander for operations to assign them
somewhere other than the 421st. Watching them work for
Bill might have made for some interesting times. Major
Tracy came out of his office, looked around, and quietly
asked, "What's all the commotion?"

"Nothing. Just some guys looking for a job," Loyd answered.

It had been a trying day. The weather was lousy all over Vietnam, from the Chinese border to the southern tip of military
region IV, well south of Saigon. A tropical storm was

swirling in the Gulf of Tonkin and targets were socked in everywhere. Despite the pressure to get the missions off, most of us knew that we wouldn't be doing much. A slip of briefing times had been announced the night before in the hope that a few hours delay would allow the morning sunshine to burn off some of the cloud cover and possibly dissipate the storm. We'd briefed at ten in the morning then been put on a weather hold, waiting for an RF-4C from Udorn to make a run across the Red River Delta to see what it looked like.

We got a go to launch to the tankers at about one-thirty. It was pouring rain as we preflighted, hump-backed in ponchos covering our parachutes and trying to keep just a little bit dry. Crew chiefs were soaked, and opening the canopies for just the few seconds needed to climb the ladders and position our gear was more than enough to soak the seat cushions and drip water over all of the electronics on the flat consoles. There were going to be plenty of radio and nav gear failures when we got airborne.

We rolled down the runway and managed to rejoin under the clouds, then climbed out, bouncing along in tight formation trying to stay close enough to see the lead aircraft in the murky weather. It was virtually impossible to get the air-conditioning adjusted and stay in position. For a moment freezing cold air was blasting against my wet flight suit, then a frantic grab at the temperature rheostat and back to the throttle to fight back into position. Now it's too hot, and the sweat is rolling down my nose into my mask, where my breathing is making a gurgling sound from the moisture pooled above the intake valve. Another grab at the knob, and once again it's too cold, and the condensation clouds coming from the nozzles threaten to fog my flight instruments. Then we're out of the weather and on top in bright sunlight. We move out to tactical spread and continue on to the tanker.

Refueling is routine, and we get words from Cricket that we should try to find some open space to dump our bombs on Ban Karai Pass or anywhere in the clear in Pack I. We drop off the tanker and head east, moving between towers of cumulus and hoping to find a break in the weather, but it's solid beneath us as far as the eye can see in all directions. My radar tells me we're over the panhandle of North Vietnam, and the coast is about forty miles ahead. It's a counter. We've flown into the Route Pack, now the question is what are we going to do?

Lead rocks his wings, and we close up to fingertip formation, four airplanes with virtually overlapped wings as we descend into the weather. We're over the Gulf now, so we don't need to worry about mountains. We've got a reasonable altimeter setting, and I've got a feeling that we're going to feel our way down to the water. It's possible that my leader is going to try to use the terrain avoidance setting of the radar to get us down as low as possible. It was designed for low-level nuclear runs but could be used as a rough guide to get down to about five hundred feet over the Gulf. There's no telling if the system has been maintained or exercised since the aircraft has been at Korat. I've got a momentary image of four airplanes smoothly flying into the water in perfect formation, but I trust my leader not to screw up.

We're in a lazy bank, about 20 degrees and very smooth as we turn through north to head back into land. The descent is passing three thousand feet on the altimeter, and I can see the outline of the coastal radar return out of the corner of my eye. There isn't much turbulence in the rain clouds, but they are thick enough that it's getting quite dark. Hanging on the wing is a challenge. Passing one thousand now and we're wings-level headed toward the beach. Eight hundred feet and I can see a bit of water below us. Now we're level at four hundred feet, doing 450 knots and headed for the bright yellow sand of the coastline about two miles ahead. "Green 'em up," Lead calls. "Release on my call."

There's a slight rise to the ceiling as we get closer to the land. We ease up slightly and it's now apparent that we're going to dump the bombs as soon as we get over land. There isn't enough space to get dive-bomb altitude and the weather won't allow us to search for targets. Formation release is the only alternative. The radar image of the coast looks like we must be near the Quang Khe ferry, so there's a good chance that our bombs could upset roads, fords, ferries, or lighters in the area. The cursor shows us tracking toward the south bank of the inlet. We might even get lucky and hit a tactical bicycle or elephant. We pickle as soon as we get over land, dropping in near level flight from a loose route formation. I see Lead motion upward with his thumb, and we close up to tight formation again to climb straight ahead into the murk. I glance nervously at the RHAW scope, hoping the miserable weather has given the Vietnamese radar operators a reason to take the day off. The scope stays dark. The buzzes and beeps that would indicate a defensive reaction stay silent.

Back at Korat we finish the paperwork and debrief, thankful that the day is over and we're back on solid ground. Another mark goes on the hatband and we all jump into the squadron trucks to head for the club and a cold beer. Riding down the flight line road, past the control tower, we see the normally empty maintenance ramp filled with F-4s. Apparently we've got visitors.

The club is packed when we arrive. The Phantom squadrons from Danang have been flushed out to inland bases in anticipation of high winds and violent weather from the tropical storm swirling in the Gulf. We've got two dozen F-4s spending the night and maybe longer with us. The crews have gotten to the bar ahead of us and staked out the best seats. The Phantom guys are very clearly segregated. Frontseaters are older, generally captains and above. Backseat pilots are all lieutenants, and we see a number of familiar faces, guys from our pilot training classes. Backseaters drink with backseaters, and frontseaters drink with frontseaters. Our older guys merge with the F-4 nose gunners, while the 105 lieutenants naturally link up with the GIBs, the "guys in back."

Introductions are made so that we all get to know each other. I introduce guys from my class at Willy; Richter names the guys from Craig; Kenny Hallmark points out his buddies from Laughlin. We get immediately to the beer drinking and the inevitable arguments about aircraft superiority. Friendly arguments go on about radars and MiG kills, bomb accuracy and load capacity, and, of course, the superiority of single-seat fighter pilots over all others that walk this earth. Throughout the discussion the Danang folks repeatedly ask about "that little red-headed guy."

They know he's a 105 driver from Korat, but they don't have a name. They want to see him and "talk" to him. Apparently he diverted to Danang a couple of weeks ago and made quite an impression. He was short, cocky, and pugnacious. He walked into their bar and immediately took over. He was knocking people off barstools and announcing that he was from the Air Force Inspector General's Office, come to ensure compliance with the recently announced rule that T-shirts should not show in the neck opening of flying suits. He would approach a likely victim and without warning reach out and grab the exposed collar of a T-shirt then pull forward, ripping the shirt and often a handful of chest hair out of the front of the guy's flying suit. He had broken glasses, ripped flying suits, bought drinks, led songs, told stories, insulted mothers, and generally been a one-man party. After about the fourth or fifth T-shirt ripping, the Phantom squadron had banded together, grabbed the culprit, ripped his flying suit off and thrown him naked out the front door of the Danang club. Now, they wished to revisit old times and remake the acquaintance.

I looked at Richter, who looked at John Russell, who glanced over at Nels Running, who jabbed Pete Foley in the ribs. They had to be describing Glen Nix. He was short, red-haired, and definitely a suspect. We were familiar with the T-shirt trick and knew full well that Glen liked to stir up the bar. Nix had diverted into Danang with an aircraft problem a few weeks earlier and had spent the night. It had to be him. Instinctively, we knew that we didn't want to identify him or even acknowledge that we knew such a person. Coyly we suggested that maybe the guy came from Tahkli or possibly even from Kadena. It might not be a Korat pilot at all. Alas, it was too late. Nix walked in the front door.

He scanned the room and headed for the bar. He was flying with the 13th Squadron on this TDY, so he elbowed his way between a couple of guys from the group and yelled for the bartender to pour him a Crown Royal on the rocks. He knew a couple of the F-4 frontseaters and waved a greeting, too busy to note the quietly gathering circle of lieutenants closing in behind him. At about the time the bartender placed the glass in front of Glen, two of the GIBs flanked him and placed their arms around his shoulders. Simultaneously, the largest of the lieutenants, an ex–football lineman, grabbed him around the waist and in a remarkably choreographed effort two others fastened to his legs. The glass dropped and broke as they pulled Nix backward off the barstool. In a flash, they ripped the sleeves from his flight suit, tore the legs upward from the lower zippers, and as though it had been presegmented, the flight suit came off in one big sage-green sheet. They carried the squirming, struggling, swearing redhead to the patio door, which several of the visitors were holding open. With little fanfare they swung Nix twice and on the third swing tossed him out into the flower bed wearing nothing but his boots and white government-issue boxer shorts. The 105 pilots laughed and the Phantom Phlyers applauded as he stood up, shook off the dirt, and with his dignity bruised, but still intact, Nix returned to the bar, picked up the barstool, and ordered another whisky.

The party went on for several hours, ending in a songfest, with an underwear-clad Nix in the front row of the tenor section. Justice had been meted out. The F-4 guys had gotten their satisfaction, the F-105 troops had a laugh, and Glen knew he deserved it. Life was good.

CHAPTER 14

Of MiGs and Mustaches

I had been visiting my airplane about twice a week. She was 62-4334, my personal airplane, with my name on the left canopy rail and that of the crew chief, Tech. Sgt. Jack Church, on the right. It was one of the newer airplanes off the assembly line, produced in fiscal year 1962 as indicated by the serial number prefix. The airplane had a personality with certain consistencies that regular flying had disclosed. New or old, dented or polished, it made little difference to a young fighter pilot. She was mine. The stab-aug system was just a bit squirrelly. Nothing that couldn't be controlled, in fact nothing that could be found and corrected on the ground. It just gave a little nudge to the rudder pedals every once in a while. Cruise along, straight and level, and then the bird would give a little hip flip. I'd write it up after the flight and the next time I'd check, the write-up would be cleared as "ops checked. OK." I didn't mind because the rest of the aircraft systems were nearly perfect. The Doppler nav, in particular, was accurate to an unheard-of degree. If I updated off a TACAN station after takeoff, the coordinates displayed were always right. If the bearing pointer said a particular target was on the nose, I could follow the arrow and get there. If the distance to go wound down to zero, I had arrived overhead at the destination.

The assistant crew chief was a two-stripe airman named Baker who loved to be a part of the flying operation. If Sergeant Church wasn't around, he referred to 334 as "his" airplane. When Church was in the revetment, then it became "our" bird. During one of my visits he asked me if I had a

name for the airplane. He'd learned that he could paint a
name on the left nose gear door if the pilot agreed, and he
wanted 334 to be one of the first on the line with an identity.
I hadn't thought about a name before, so I wasn't ready. We
talked for a while about the 105 and nicknames that I had,
searching for something that might be appropriate. The only
thing I answered to was "Raz," but that didn't seem to suggest anything. I wasn't quite up to challenging fate with an
aggressive moniker like War Wagon, nor did I feel that anything on the order of Glamorous Glennis or Diamond Lil in a
Betty Grable – style pose would work.

Then I mentioned that an old friend who I'd grown up with
in Chicago had been writing me letters. He had just graduated from college and recently finished Officer Training
School with an Air Force commission and was ready to start
pilot training. Because he was following in my footsteps he
had begun addressing me as "Batman" and signing his letters
"Robin" or "Boy Wonder." Baker said that would work.
How would I like 334 to be the "Bat Bird"? I thought it
seemed reasonable.

The next time I came down the flight line, Baker had done
his work. There, on the nose gear door, was the name "Bat
Bird" in a spooky, quaking script. But, there was more, lots
more. The side of the nose, just below the gun-bay door, displayed a large, dark red, almost burgundy moon nearly three
feet in diameter. Silhouetted on the blood-dark moon was a
black bat with wings spread, glowing yellow eyes, and a
fiery yellow afterburner from the tail. The large radar reflec-
tor mounted on the aircraft nose gear was still bright red, like
the reflectors on all of the other airplanes in the squadron,
but the Bat Bird's now had a white diamond in the center
with the bat silhouette proudly displayed. Each 450-gallon
wing tank had a red moon on the nose with yet another afterburning bat profile. I liked it, but Sergeant Church wasn't
sure it was all right. I assured him that if there were any problems, I'd accept full responsibility. Church walked away,
shaking his head over what had happened to his airplane.
Baker was thrilled.

* * *

We got a call from the command post about two in the afternoon. Wimpy Peake had been on a road recce in Pack V north of Dien Bien Phu that morning and had reported seeing a road grader on the highway. Could we generate a four-ship add-on to go hunting for the grader? Major Tracy looked around the squadron and said no problem. He grabbed me for wing, Maj. Ken Whittemore as Three and Joe Vojir as Four. Maintenance loaded up four airplanes with six Mk-82s each and the command post found a tanker on Blue track that could pass six thousand pounds to each of us. We briefed and headed up to Pack V, looking for a road grader. I was flying the Bat Bird.

The weather was remarkably good for a summer afternoon, with unlimited visibility and only light scattered puffies to break up the view. We dropped off the tanker and went into a tactical spread. I cranked the coordinates of Dien Bien Phu in my Doppler and then set a second lat/long destination as the point where the road to China intersected with the buffer zone. The two destinations defined the section of road we were supposed to be searching. Working that far north meant we'd have to be careful not to drop in the Chinese buffer zone. I wondered if the grader had moved back into the sanctuary in the afternoon to protect it from strikes such as ours. Tracy had briefed that we'd start at the north end of the road and work our way back south to the infamous valley where the French had met their final defeat back in 1954.

Tracy headed straight toward the buffer zone. The element was stacked high and abeam as we cruised at eighteen thousand feet. I thought we'd descend to a reasonable recce altitude as we approached the road but we stayed at eighteen. I switched the Doppler to the north coordinates and watched the mileage roll down to zero then start increasing as we continued northward. I could see the narrow valley and the white line of the road beneath us. We were in the buffer zone and headed north. The mileage hit twenty, then twenty-five, and still increasing. We crossed the China border and still Tracy

gave no indication that he was about to turn. At thirty miles
from the buffer line, I made a brief radio call. "Bronco Lead,
Two. Check nav." I doubted that he was depending solely on
Doppler for orientation, but if so, I wanted the boss to know
that I had a reliable system. The reply was a terse, "Roger."

The only sound from the RHAW was an occasional beep
from an early warning radar. No SAMs were around. No
guns. We were now at seventy-five miles north of the buffer
zone line and at least fifty miles into China. This was way out
on a limb. No rescue was going to come here for us, and any
targets we found for our Mk-82s would certainly create an
international incident. The only good thing was that we were
too far inland for Red Crown to monitor our position, and it
was too late in the day for the College Eye EC-121 to be flying overland to see what we were up to. I certainly didn't
know what we were doing. My head was on a swivel as I
tried to search for enemy aircraft. I wished I hadn't cut my
map off at the border of North Vietnam because I desperately wanted to know where the nearest Chinese airfields
were. Then Major Whittemore called, "Bronco, Three confirms Two. Check nav." Now at ninety miles north of the
buffer I had an ally, someone else who knew where we were
and was worried about it. Without a comment Tracy called a
crossturn, and we reversed course and headed out.

We dropped down, found our road segment, and looked
for the road grader. The flight essed back and forth over the
two-lane dirt highway watching for trucks or construction
equipment. At the south end of the road we overflew Dien
Bien Phu, the tiny valley battleground of that pivotal, bloody
siege where Vo Nguyen Giap had demonstrated the fine art
of guerrilla warfare to the French Foreign Legion. Several
cemeteries were visible on the south and east sides of the
valley with literally hundreds of neatly aligned white grave
markers, row upon row of Legionnaires who never went
home. We found no trucks or bulldozers and finally dropped
our bombs on a choke point along the road north of the town.
Defenses were light.

It was dark when we got back to Korat, and for the first

time since training at Nellis I had to scramble around the cockpit to find light switches to illuminate the instruments and control my exterior lights as we approached the airfield. Regardless of the darkness we flew a four-ship down initial and landed from an overhead pattern. When we got on the crew van to head for debrief, I didn't mention the navigational "error" until Whittemore asked me what I had seen. I mentioned that 334 had a very reliable Doppler, and I had been pretty sure of my position throughout.

Tracy just barely cracked a smile. "You guys are right," he admitted. "You knew exactly where we were, but I've got one MiG now. How am I ever going to get another one if we don't go where they are?"

Tracy wasn't Mitchell. He didn't have the frightening disregard for his own life that would drag us all into unnecessary danger. Tracy was the squadron commander, and we trusted him. He was mature, steady, and reliable. He wasn't known for hanging his wingmen out, yet we'd just gone MiG hunting deep into China without a prebriefing and certainly under conditions such that if we had gotten into an air battle, the outcome would have to have been hidden or denied. Was killing a MiG, particularly a MiG from a nation not actively involved in the war, worth this kind of risk? Were MiG kills that couldn't be acknowledged really MiG kills at all?

Had Chinese MiGs come up, we would have had to jettison our bombs. Dropping in China was definitely bad. We didn't have Sidewinders or missile armament for air-to-air battle, only our guns. The F-105 was fast, but most of the books told us it wasn't a good idea to fight a turning engagement with the MiG-17, -19, or -21. Each of them could beat us in turn rate and turn radius. We only got MiG kills with a bit of luck and by capitalizing on the enemy's errors. If they overshot and blundered out in front of us, we could hose them down, but whenever the 'Chief entered a turning and burning engagement with the small, agile MiG, it was likely to lose. I left the debrief wondering what I had seen and what it meant.

*   *   *

Near the end of the summer John Casper came to the squadron. He was among the last of the long-course lieutenants to graduate from Nellis and had been twelve weeks behind Richter, Ricks, and me in the Cobras. John was a most unlikely-looking fighter pilot, a bit on the chubby side with a boyish grin and an ambling gait that put him between Oliver Hardy and Huckleberry Hound. He was always ready for a beer or a joke and got along with everybody.

Casper jumped into the war with both feet. He flew the schedule and stayed around the squadron soaking up information from guys with a lot more missions. Evenings, he'd be at the club, hanging around the bar, sipping a beer, and filling the air with clouds of noxious smoke from the big green cigar he puffed. The House of Windsor Palmas were almost a part of John's uniform. He smoked just one a day, but he usually carried one in his hand unlit so it became a kind of trademark. The 'gars weren't available at the BX, so John had them shipped from home. When he ran out, the whole squadron worried about when the mail from the States would bring his replacements, and we shared his joy when a "box of greenies" showed up at the post office parcel window. John would usually celebrate the arrival at the club that night by offering everyone around him a cigar. Even those who didn't smoke would accept and fire up a stogie. The stories would flow freely and the bar would fill with a nearly impenetrable fog. It never occurred to us that we were encouraging the next shortage when we so eagerly accepted his handouts and joined in creating the stench.

It seemed that John had only been with us a few days, but it was actually nearly three weeks when we got the news at lunch that he'd been shot down on the morning mission in Mu Gia Pass. It was his tenth counter. He'd been on a two-ship, bombing a well-abused creek crossing, moving the dirt around and probably not doing much to slow the flow of war materials southward. A wall of 37 mm had come up, and John had come off the target with the airplane on fire. He'd pulled off and made it several miles away before the airplane went uncontrollable and he ejected. The good news was that other flights were in the area, and they had already established radio contact with John on the ground. The Sandys and Jolly Green were inbound, and it looked good to get John out.

John was back by dinnertime. He was logged into the base clinic for the evening to get a checkout for aches, pains, and bruises, but the flight surgeons released him within hours when they couldn't find a thing wrong and his incessant demands for a beer and a cigar became intolerable. John showed up at the club just as most of us were getting ready to head for the hootches to get some sleep, but it was a time for a celebration, so we raised some glasses to John and his rescuers. Then we hoisted one or two more with the quiet prayer of thanks that it wasn't us and a fervent hope that we would be so lucky when our time came. The beers led to a songfest and each of us vied to remember the raunchiest, most obscenity-laden ballads, rounds, and ditties. Older pilots reworked songs from the Korean War to reflect local names and places, while younger guys embellished songs they had learned in pilot training or in college. Maj. Rock Campbell, a classic Irish tenor in the 34th Squadron came over and stood us all up in a chorus line then directed us in a Gilbert and Sullivan–style operetta recreating a poor individual's experience in shaving with a rusty razor. Cigars fumed, whiskey flowed, and the voices got louder but no more tuneful. It all sounded pretty good to us, and who else counted? It was foolishness of the highest order but seemed perfectly appropriate to the celebration. It could have gone on all night, but common sense finally prevailed when Major Loyd closed the party with an order that everyone on the next day's schedule had better get to bed. He told Casper to see him in his office at nine the next morning.

The morning light revealed a slightly hungover and decidedly shaken John Casper. The adrenaline rush of the shootdown and rescue had fully abated, and now it had sunk in that he had been inches from death or imprisonment. Loyd looked at John and understood the situation. He congratulated John on his good fortune but then stressed how important it was after being thrown from a horse to get back on.

John was going to continue to fly and do his job. Neither John nor Loyd had suggested that John quit. John simply needed to understand that he was a valuable commodity and needed to help the squadron. He would have the day off to relax and lay around, but tomorrow he would be on the schedule again. "Oh, and one last thing . . ." Loyd twirled the end of his handlebar mustache. "John, grow a mustache."

"But Boss, I'm blonde and I don't have much of a beard. I can't grow a mustache." Casper pleaded, "I'll look like a fool with a couple of scraggly little hairs on my lip."

"Doesn't matter, Lieutenant. That's an order. It's for your own good. A mustache makes you bulletproof. Look at all the mustaches in this squadron. You don't see those people getting shot down. I want you to report to me before flying tomorrow and show me that you haven't shaved your upper lip." Loyd had spoken.

Loyd's mustache was incredibly black and with a bit of wax at the ends, and trained by constant twirling, it had grown to almost a full ram's-horn curl on each side. Other mustaches didn't have the substance or style his had, but each reflected a bit of the owner's personality. Wimpy chose, for some perverse reason, to grow a small, Hercule Poirot version. His was slightly less wide than his mouth, but had a tight little twist at each tip that stuck straight forward like the horns of a tiny cow. Bob Loken's 'stache was reminiscent of Groucho Marx's greasepaint model. Bob had an exceptionally tall upper lip area, so his mustache seemed incredibly deep, yet it never seemed to mature. Four inches wide and almost two inches high, Loken's mustache boasted amazing area but never seemed to intensify beyond an apparent four-day growth. It didn't matter. If there were any truth to the notion that mustaches made you bulletproof, we weren't going to be without one. We weren't about to press our luck.

My mustache was doing quite well. It would never have the breadth of Bill Loyd's, but it no longer looked like sprigs of weeds sprouting on a well-worn path. It had filled in and I was now cultivating the tips, hoping to get a reasonable-looking curl at the ends. Nervous twisting of those tips often left the corners of my mouth raw and irritated, and it was distinctly possible that the continual tugging and twirling wore off the new growth faster than it was being produced. With more than sixty hash marks around the band of my jungle hat and a decided fade to my flying suits from hand washing and sun drying, the mustache gave me a look of confidence and experience that readily belied any apprehension I might have still had. It was not an uncommon occurrence to have non-rated captains and majors salute 105-flying lieutenants as we conducted routine business around the base. The cliché has always been that respect is earned, and there was little doubt among any who knew what we were doing that we should be shown respect. The salute from higher-ranking officers was an honor that was deeply appreciated.

Maj. Bob Phillips was leading on a day I gave my mustache an exceptional challenge. We were the third flight in a string of four attacking the railroad bridge at Bac Giang yet one more time. Ken Whittemore was flying element Lead, with Bill Ricks on his wing. I was Two. The route was over water to the pork-chop island then in along the east-west mountain ridge with a final run across twenty-five miles of flatland to the railroad. Defenses were as good as they get: loads of guns, lots of overlapping SAM sites, and a target just ten miles off the end of the runway at Kep. We carried five Mk-83s — three on the centerline MER and one on each outboard, plus 450-gallon inboard tanks.

We hit the coast and descended to low altitude to use the mountain ridge as a shield against the SAM sites that lined the coast from the port at Cam Pha all the way to Haiphong. I was on the left wing in our usual spread. The sky was bright blue with just scattered altocumulus and although it was afternoon, the view into the sun was excellent. As we roared over the treetops we would occasionally rise above the ridge and the RHAW would light up with triple-A and SAM warnings. The center of the vector scope displayed an angry blob of radar signals, so many that it was virtually impossible to distinguish any single threat as worse than any other. The continual buzzing and beeping of the audio played as background to the radio calls. The yellow ACTIVITY warning light came on within five miles after we crossed over land and simply stayed on, indicating that SAM guidance signals would accompany us all the way to the target.

Whenever I could, I checked outside the flight to my left, looking for threats along the ridge top. Each time I looked over my shoulder, I saw vestiges of bright orange smoke. SAMs were being fired from the other side of the ridge at us, at the flights minutes ahead or in anticipation of meeting the flight coming behind. The bright orange from the booster's nitric acid oxidizer stayed long after the missile had gone on its course, and unless you could actually see the site, you simply took it as yet more pollution from the battle. We didn't see any missiles, but that didn't mean they weren't there. Some had undoubtedly impacted the ridge as our intermittent radar return was gained and then lost again.

The radio chatter was more intense than usual. The flights ahead had already hit the flats and as I strained to look forward, maintain my formation position, and avoid the ground, I heard the Weasel call a SAM launch. It was a damn credible warning considering the RHAW indications and the amount of booster smoke I'd already seen. A bright flash on the horizon in front of us meant a SAM detonation and then a huge fireball erupted indicating a hit. The flare almost immediately broke into two descending arcs of flame as the aircraft came apart. There was no radio call, and there was no emergency beeper. Whoever had been hit had been killed instantly. Phillips called us to "Green 'em up," and I busied myself with weapons switches. I'd been preset all the way from the coast and all I needed to do was flip the master arm switch and confirm my sight setting. Three green station-selector lights blinked at me, and the red rings of the gun sight filled the combining glass.

We were nearly to the end of the ridge and the calls from the flights ahead indicated that they were being engaged by MiGs. I strained to see ahead of us, and then, just to the left of the nose, well above the horizon, I saw a pair of tiny sil-

houettes. They arced gracefully upward, and in a remarkably
tight reversal, changed course back downward. The incredible turn told me immediately that I wasn't looking at F-105s.
I could just barely make out the planform in the turn —
swept wings angled sharply back from a stubby nose. I knew
my aircraft — I'd been building model airplanes since the
fourth grade. They were Sabres, F-86s. Of course.

But are there Sabres in Southeast Asia? Sure, the Aussies
have been flying Sabres down south. Yeah, they're Australian Mark 6s. In the time expansion of combat, the whole
analysis seemed to take minutes. In actuality it couldn't have
been more than three seconds from sighting to planform
view to postulating an identification hypothesis to discarding
a bullshit impossibility and realizing what they were. MiGs!
They were MiG-17s. Two of them, and they were the attack-
ers that the flights ahead had called. I mashed on the mike
button. "Lead, we've got MiGs."

The feedback in my headset told me that I'd forgotten my
call sign, I hadn't said where the MiGs were, and the frightened soprano of my voice was downright embarrassing. I re-
grouped, took a deep breath, called on a more profundo
basso and tried again, "Elm Lead, this is Two. We've got a
pair of MiGs, left eleven, slightly high at ten miles." Much
better.

Bob Phillips was calm. "Elm, let's jettison our tanks. Set
up guns."

I flashed back to the tank jettison fiasco two months earlier
then reached down and blew the 450s away. I scanned the
area again and tried to retain a visual on the MiGs. That's
when we got a surprise, but Elm flight wasn't alone in being
surprised.

We had reached the end of the ridgeline and were just entering the flatlands when a MiG-17 popped up from low altitude and with an incredible amount of airspeed into the
midst of Elm flight. The radar controllers for the tiny fighter
had apparently vectored him parallel to our track on the opposite side of the ridge intending to have him hit us at the end
of the hills, unseen and with at least one and possibly two

good gun targets before we could react defensively. It was a great plan, but he screwed up. He was just a bit too fast and just a bit too early.

Now we were a five-ship: four F-105s in tactical spread and a MiG-17 level and line abreast between Lead and Three. I could see the tiny white helmet in the MiG's bubble canopy turning frantically left and right as the driver tried to figure out what had happened. What I had just seen the MiGs in front of us do in terms of turn ability told me that we were no match for the little interceptor in maneuvering. We could go a hell of a lot faster, a whole lot further, and we had a quantum advantage in technology, but we didn't have his turn rate and radius. Something was going to happen pretty quick now. I called, "Elm, we've got a MiG in the middle."

I saw Phillips's head snap right to see the enemy airplane. He'd been setting up an attack on the aircraft ahead of us, as well as trying to see the other 105 flights and find the target. If it wasn't task saturation, it was close. Now, the situation demanded something different. "Elm, let's jettison the bombs, AB now, in-place left."

It sounded like a good plan to me. Jettison the bombs meant we wouldn't get to the target, but the first two flights of the day already had done that. It also meant we had some improved maneuver potential. The in-place turn meant we would all do a simultaneous 180-degree turn, reversing course and rolling out back in our tactical spread. AB, of course, meant let's get on our horses and ride.

I hadn't yet had time to reset to guns, so I pickled off the bombs into the hillside. I already had the throttle against the full military power stop, so it only took a flick of the wrist to go outboard for afterburner. The turn was into my side of the formation, so I had my tail covered by the other three 105s. Nothing could go wrong from here, but it did.

Burner lights required three things to happen in sequence. The tail cone speed brakes would open slightly, then the engine afterburner nozzle would open, and finally the fuel control would dump JP-4 into the burner section along with an extra dose of fuel at the top of the main engine combustion section to create a "hot streak" in the exhaust to light off the AB. If the nozzles didn't open, the fuel wouldn't flow. The nozzle opened, but the burner still didn't light. I felt the characteristic loss of thrust as the relaxed nozzle reduced the engine pressure, but I didn't get the reassuring kick in the pants of an AB light.

Now there were four F-105s being chased by the MiG-17 with one of them a whole lot slower than the other three. I had started on the inside of the turn, and when it was completed I was at least a mile behind the other aircraft, all trucking along at six hundred knots while I lost altitude and tried to keep enough airspeed to preserve some maneuvering capability. I pulled the throttle back inboard, felt the nozzles respond, and then slammed the throttle back out to the AB position. I got a light.

I strained to see behind me in my left turn, then looked over my upper shoulder, back to where I could just see the tip of my own rudder. There, barely five hundred feet off my right wingtip, was the MiG-17. He wasn't tiny anymore. He was huge, and he was shooting. The 37-mm cannon in his nose didn't fire anywhere near as fast as my own Vulcan, but with a projectile twice as large, he wouldn't have to hit me more than once or twice. The muzzle blast from his gun was incredible. A huge red flame, cycling just faster than once a second, marked each round. The flash would sprout forward then, before the flame burned out, wrap backward over his nose. I wondered how he could see past the fireworks display, but I supposed his view was a lot more comfortable than mine.

I looked back forward and saw I had 450 knots, and now that the AB was cooking I needed to do something pretty quick. The MiG and I were waltzing at less than a thousand feet and coming up on the ridge that clearly marked the way back to the Gulf. This might just be the time for one of Tom Gibbs's special, last-ditch, always works, high-G barrel rolls. I left the burner in, and since I was already on the edge of the buffet I increased the pull and fed in all the top rudder I could. The airplane seemed to scream in protest as the nose came up and we flat-plated over the top of the roll. The -17 probably had never seen the entire top of a 105 before, particularly one that was so close. He went flying underneath as I pitched back into his attack, inverted and desperately trying to avoid a midair. Then, with the roll only half completed, I neutralized the rudder and eased the stick forward until I was light in the seat. With all of the big Pratt & Whitney's push working on a zero-G airplane, I rolled upright and headed to the weeds. It didn't take longer than an average lifetime for the airspeed to hit the mach and the MiG to disappear in my rearview mirror.

The rest of Elm flight looked pretty good as I caught up with them. While we headed to the poststrike tanker I tried to erase the image of the flashing nose of the MiG. It would stick with me for a long time. I didn't know whether it was skill, luck, or a mustache that had kept me from taking a hit, but I was glad to be alive. I silently thanked God, Republic, Pratt & Whitney, Bob Phillips, Bill Loyd, Tom Gibbs, and whoever invented the high-G barrel roll.

John Casper kept flying and started growing his mustache. It was, as he predicted, a disgusting little wispy worm on his upper lip. Charlie Chan in those old 1940s movies sported a more luxuriant growth. It didn't matter: An order is an order, and bulletproof is a good thing. Missions gradually added up until John had twenty-five counters and was scheduled for some time off.

We were gathered around a table at the club when Casper announced that he would be heading for Bangkok the following morning for four days of lying in the sun around the Siam Intercontinental pool. Silent alarms went off in several heads at once. This could be a problem.

"John, you're entering a very dangerous situation here. You'll be at the Siam, and you know, of course, that the Pan Am crews lay over there, so you'll be seeing a lot of round-eye stewardesses, won't you?" I asked him. John nodded agreement that he did have some aspirations in that direction.

Richter jumped in. "Right, and you're going to try to get lucky aren't you?"

"You'll find some cutie, and she's going to laugh at the mustache for sure." I continued. "You're going to be tempted to shave it off just for a roll in the hay. And that's a very dangerous thing to do. Why do you have that mustache, John?"

"Because it makes me bulletproof," he immediately replied although there was ample evidence that he was in a state of conflict. If there were to be a list of priorities at that moment, getting laid in Bangkok seemed more pressing than superstitious defense mechanisms.

"Right!" Richter said. "So, we're your friends aren't we? We want you to be bulletproof, don't we? We're concerned about your well-being, not some stewardess. You've got to swear to us that you'll return with your mustache intact."

"What? You want me to swear?" Casper could see where this was going. He was pretty certain that the scenario we had laid out was exactly what was going to happen. A scraggly mustache at Korat was one thing, but lying around the pool sipping tall rum drinks with tiny bamboo umbrellas and talking up a couple of cute American girls was an entirely different story. He hesitated. We pressed. He gave in. He swore to return with his mustache.

Four days later, Casper appeared at the bar around dinnertime. The mustache was intact. He came up to the squadron dining table and looked at several of us seated there. "You bastards," he started out. "I swore, so I did what I promised. But you guys will never know the cost. There were all kinds of stews there, and I looked like a fool with this scrawny 'stache. They giggled and pointed and wouldn't even talk to me. Well, I did what I said I would, but I don't have to keep it now. I'm shaving it off tonight." He headed for the door amidst a chorus of protests.

Morning dawned on a clean-shaven John Casper. He appeared for the mass briefing on a strike package to a target near Kep. We all noticed his absent mustache, but no one commented. The mission would be tough enough that we had plenty on our minds.

All went well until coming off the target, when everyone on the primary strike frequency heard Casper's voice calling that he'd been hit. He was headed for the coast with his airplane on fire. His element lead was on his wing trying to provide support and advising him of what his airplane looked like externally. The bird was trailing smoke and descending. John reported a flameout. Airstarts weren't working, and he was getting lower and lower with nearly ten miles left to go before he was clear of land. John Malone was on his wing calling out altitudes. When he got down to one thousand feet, Malone called to bail out.

Down to eight hundred feet and Malone watched Casper's helmet brace up against the ejection seat headrest. Then a jerking motion as John pulled on the ejection handle. Nothing happened. The airplanes had been undergoing a modification to change the ejection seats from a ballistic cannon shell to a smoother and more powerful rocket motor. The old seat would have jettisoned the canopy when the handles were raised, then ejected when the trigger was squeezed. The new seat did nothing but arm itself when the handles came up. When the trigger was squeezed with the new rocket mod, the canopy would come off and, with a short three-tenths of a second delay, the seat rocketpack would fire. Casper must have one of the new seats. Then Malone watched with horror as the ejection seat fired through the canopy. The shards of canopy Plexiglas burst into a cloud around the seat, which tumbled upward trailing bright orange flame from the back. At the apex of the seat's flight Malone watched Casper's now limp body fall from the seat as the parachute started to open. The thrust of the seat's ballistic charge had the chair and John still moving forward and up, so the chute opened below him. The sudden tug of the opening chute pulled John back down, and he fell through the partially open canopy. Pilot, parachute, ejection seat, and the crashing airplane all hit the water simultaneously. The last thing Malone saw as his own airplane hurtled onward was the splash of several impacts. Survival seemed impossible.

It was less than a minute before the tiny voice came up on guard channel. Casper was alive! He was in the water and alive. He had his radio out and was already climbing into his deployed life raft. It wasn't a perfect situation, though. The low flyby of a burning Thunderchief had alerted the coastal fishermen, and John was only a few hundred yards offshore among the coastal islands. He saw several boats pushing off the beach and raising sail, heading out to retrieve him.

If one listened really hard, one could almost hear the bugles and hoof beats of the 7th Cavalry coming to the rescue. It wasn't John Wayne or Randolph Scott, however; it was our arch rival, the United States Navy. The carrier on Yankee Station regularly launched A-1s to patrol along the coast for rescue duty, even during USAF strikes. A pair of Spads was coming in from the east, guns blazing, driving the boats back to shore. Casper paddled his raft as quickly as he could away from land, while the Navy A-1s made pass after pass over his position. Casper rowing frantically with his arms, headed eastbound, screaming breathlessly to come and get him, while the Navy rescuers flew tight circles shooting over his head, driving the junks back to the west. In less than twenty minutes a Sea King helicopter appeared and pulled John out of his raft to safety.

John spent the night on the carrier and found out that regulations regarding alcohol aboard ships were not very tightly enforced. Two days later a Navy mail shuttle delivered John to Danang, where he caught a T-39 back to Korat. He'd been shot down twice in twenty-six missions and was now the first person to be successfully rescued twice from North Vietnam. His war was officially over. Any doubts that anyone in the squadron might have had regarding the effectiveness of mustaches was firmly dispelled. No one was going to be doing any shaving of the upper lip anytime soon. There would be a lot of mustaches around the bar at the Siam Intercontinental, and if the Pan Am stews wanted to talk to fighter pilots they would have to deal with it.

CHAPTER 15

Hits and Misses

Roscoe lifted his head and pawed twice at his left ear. He slipped his front paws off the wing commander's red leather chair and eased himself down onto the floor in front of the briefer's podium. When he shook vigorously his collar rattled, attracting everyone's undivided attention. The intel officer momentarily paused and watched as Roscoe strolled slowly out of the main briefing room. All eyes followed the dog. We might as well watch Roscoe; the graphic on the main screen of the target for the day showed little more than the black-and-white, eight-by-ten photos that we'd found in our map package. And they didn't show much.

The target photo displayed a vertical view of jungle, nothing but treetops cut only by a single-lane dirt road that slashed from the top right to the lower left corner of the picture. Near the bottom third of the photo a second road intersected at a right angle. That was it, just a T-intersection of dirt road in deep jungle. Two white lines on a featureless black background. The coordinates and the accompanying map indicated that the location was less than five miles from Kep airfield, but there were no landmarks of any prominence to help us find the intersection. A white rectangle outlined the desired area of bomb impact, but, of course, that wouldn't be there when we were looking for the target. The target itself was described as "approximately fifty barrels of suspected POL." The pilots had all agreed in the planning room that we must have indeed been winning the war if we were sending sixteen bombers, four SAM-suppression aircraft, eight MiGCAP, two stand-off jammers, and eight tankers for fifty barrels of something buried at a jungle inter-section. The briefing officer seemed a bit embarrassed by the target and waited somewhat apprehensively for questions from the aircrews. It wasn't his fault, so we didn't harass him. Credit for targeting rightfully belonged in Washington.

The weather was forecast to be marginal, with lots of cu-mulus buildup over land. There was every expectation that we wouldn't get into the target area, so the briefing carefully pointed out the requirement to not, under any circumstances engage in armed reconnaissance in the Navy's section of Pack VI. The Navy had graciously authorized two alternate targets for use if we were unable to get to our primary. We could drop on a dirt road intersection along the coast, where two trails from nowhere crossed on their way to oblivion. Or, if we wished, we could jettison on a supply point located in the foothills about five miles inland. No evidence indicated that supplies were there now or had been there at any time in the past. Each of us dutifully recorded the coordinates of the approved alternates and drew little black triangles on our maps.

Bill Loyd was leading Musket flight with me on his wing. Karl Richter was leading the element with Joe Vojir flying Four. We were loaded with two 3,000-pounders each. The flight was the second of four flights, each with five-minute spacing on the target. We'd refuel up the Gulf and coast in at the pork chop, then down the ridge. It was the same as we'd done a dozen times already. Loyd briefed the details and what he expected from each of us in the target area. When he asked if anyone had anything else, Richter pulled a folder out of his flight publication bag. He'd been doing some re-search in the command post, and he'd found something of interest.

"Okay, I know we've got to hit the primary, that's the job. But if we can't get in because of the weather, I've got a bet-ter alternate than the dumping grounds the Navy gave us. I found this, just a few miles south of our coast-in point. It's right on the edge of the water, so if the buildups are blocking us, we can hit it easily." Richter flipped an intel photo onto the briefing table. We all leaned forward to get a look. Loyd turned the picture to face him but left it on the table.

Karl continued. "There's an oil storage tank that's listed as one thousand metric tons, at the south end of the railyard at Cam Pha. The photo shows it as white, but the date on the picture says it's more than a year old, so it might have been camo'd by now. What do you think, Boss? Isn't this a bit better than fifty barrels?"

Loyd examined the photo carefully. Compliance with the rules of engagement was always a question. This wasn't close to the China border buffer, it wasn't in the proscribed areas around central Hanoi or Haiphong, and it wasn't a MiG base or a SAM site under construction. It was clearly a military target. It had value, it could be reached easily, and it didn't appear to endanger third-party nations engaged in safely providing aid and comfort to our enemy. It seemed like a viable option. He nodded slowly and told us to mark down the coordinates and indicate the area on our maps. He was going to check with the command post, and if we needed the target he would delay a final decision until we got to that point. He clearly wasn't overcome with the enthusiasm that Karl had for the off-track excursion.

We grabbed our gear and headed for the airplanes. The nightly rains had eased off late in the summer, and the tiny frogs had been replaced with a plague of bright green, three-inch-long flying grasshoppers. They weren't as ugly as the baht bugs nor did they squish underfoot like the frogs. They were hardly noticeable, jumping out of your path with a loud whir of their wings and staying pretty much in damp grassy areas. Things went well until the point after takeoff when, with gear and flaps up, and still in afterburner, I engaged the air-conditioning and two of the huge hoppers who had spent the night in the relative coolness of the ventilation ducts on each side of my head were blown past my helmet and into the area on either side of the gun-sight combining glass. The flying green objects took my mind off of completing my rejoin as I started swatting around the cockpit with my rolled-up map. If there was one thing that could distract from the task at hand, it was stuff flying around in your cockpit.

By the time we dropped off the tanker at 20 degrees north in the Gulf of Tonkin, we could see that we wouldn't get to the fifty barrels today. The sky was clear over the dark blue waters, but dark clouds towered from the hilltops to well over thirty thousand feet almost everywhere over the land. Musket flight would take a look and try to weave a course between the buildups, but entering SAM territory was foolish if you couldn't see the ground and a reasonable distance around your aircraft. Defense against SAMs required early acquisition of the missile and the ability to maneuver against it. The missile could see through clouds, but we couldn't. The rules were simple. You don't fly over a solid undercast. You don't fly in the clouds in SAM areas. You don't fly immediately under an overcast, and you don't fly if you can't see a SAM far enough away to maneuver against it. If the clouds were heavy, we weren't going to get in.

When we got to the coast, the clouds were still a significant obstacle. We feinted slightly right of track, but the corridor quickly closed ahead of us. The RHAW beeped intermittently with GCI radar pings and only occasionally popped up a vector toward a weak Fire Can. We headed back to the coast and tried another route but had no luck. Two other flights had already declared weather aborts and radioed that they were dropping on the Navy alternate. It was crunch time.

"Musket, green 'em up for Karl's target." Loyd had decided it was a good idea. We turned south along the coast at ten thousand feet. The flight wheeled southbound, staying just along the waterfront. Dark gray limestone karst popped through the jungle on our right and left, some formations on the mainland and some on the string of coastal islands. I flipped the nav switch to the second destination I had set, the railyard at Cam Pha. The vector scope began to light up with greater insistence. The buzzing of multiple Fire Cans provided background in my headset to the radio calls of the other flights coming off the jettison targets and heading toward the poststrike tankers. A single Fan Song indicated a SAM site showing interest in our passage off to the right of my nose.

A small town appeared ahead of us, nestled along the coastal foothills. Rather than the usual thatch-roofed hootches of a mountain village it had a more regular, industrial-style architecture. The railyard appeared clearly, six or eight parallel sets of tracks in a yard more than a mile long, with ore cars from the nearby coal mines on several sidings. Two huge gantries straddled railroad cars, capable of lifting and dumping full loads of coal from mine hoppers into trucks. At the southwest corner of the yard was the oil storage tank, surrounded on three sides by dark green trees. Along the south end of the yard, a coastal waterway allowed for ship access.

"Musket's got the target, low on our left. I'm up and rolling in left in ten. I'll be off left and hold the turn 'til everyone's aboard." I slid across behind Loyd's airplane to take spacing and watched Richter pull further right to establish his own run. The afterburner blazed on Musket Lead as he pulled up slightly and rolled into the bomb run. I stroked the burner and check-turned into the target to set up about 20 degrees off Loyd's run-in. The RHAW buzzing was continuous now and black clouds of 85 mm were popping where Lead had just been. The bursts tracked his dive down then back up, following through into the pullout. Black dots enunciated where Musket Lead had been and gone.

I pointed the airplane at the ground and checked my dive angle. I was at about 35 degrees with the pipper in the middle of the tracks with three thousand feet to go until release altitude. I could let the sight drift up to the tank and should be right at 30 degrees when I get to thirty-five hundred feet on the altimeter. The guns were alive now. Everything that wasn't railyard was muzzle flashes. I was stunned to see red footballs coming past the canopy. Glowing red and looking like passes from Joe Namath, the 85 mm shells in flight were passing my right wingtip and over my canopy, closer than I ever thought possible. I left the AB cooking and pressed the attack as Loyd's bombs went off short of the tank. I'd never considered the possibility that one could see bullets in the air, but if the bullets were four inches in diameter and the perspective was one of head-on closure, then it was definitely possible. They were big, they were red, they were close, and they were undoubtedly deadly.

The combination of steep and fast meant that my two bombs went just long of the target, hitting the water's edge. Richter and Vojir were in their dive behind me, and I hoped they would do better. I jinked hard right as soon as the nose of my aircraft came level with the horizon, trying to avoid the cloud of 37-mm puffballs ahead of my flight path. Loyd's airplane was coming left about two miles ahead of me, covered in the white vapor that indicated he was pulling hard and going fast. I rolled back left to get some cutoff, still in afterburner and scrambling for altitude to get clear of the small guns. I heard Karl call off the target, then "Lead in sight." Vojir's call came just a few seconds later. A quick glance back over my left wing showed clouds of bomb smoke covering the entire south half of the railyard, and the two mist shrouded 105s arcing across the turn to close back into tactical.

It took mere seconds to get clear of the target area and out of gun range. No wonder the Navy guarded targets like that so jealously. One could come in off the water, run the short gauntlet of target defenses, and get safely back out to sea in short order. Even if you were hit, it wouldn't take long to get to an area where pickup was possible. Would I trade? No, not in a million years. If the hubcaps were too easy to get, it wasn't worth the effort.

Back at Korat the adrenaline rush was still strong as we hopped in the crew van. Our little red Datsuns had been replaced by more traditional blue American-made vehicles. The squadron commander had a Ford sedan and the aircrews had two blue step-van delivery-style trucks that made getting in and out easier when loaded down with flying gear. The vans were large enough to carry several flights to and from the flight line together. The other strike flights didn't seem particularly thrilled with their weather aborts and jettison on the alternates, but Musket flight was still chattering. Vojir was talking about the tracks that had been ripped up, while Karl was already planning for the next opportunity to get his own personal oil storage tank. Loyd looked at me and asked, "How fast were you going coming off the target, Raz? Man, they were really tracking you."

I hadn't really thought about it at the time but decided it was pretty damned fast. "About 750, I think," was my reply.

"Damn it, if you ever take a hit at that speed, you won't stand a chance of getting out of the airplane. What the hell were you doing?"

"I dunno, Boss. I had lots of cutoff and all that speed, but I wasn't gaining on you. How fast were you going?" Loyd grinned, knowing that he'd been found out. A bit of big-bore gunfire can do that to a guy.

The debrief went well, until we got to the part about the target. In seconds a scowling Lieutenant Colonel Winter was back in our debriefing cubicle staring straight at Loyd. "What the hell did you do this time?" was his question.

We recounted the mission, described the target, and gave our interpretation of the ROE that had made it all possible. Richter kept stressing the difference between a thousand tons of oil and fifty buried barrels. Winter shook his head, frustrated with the difficulty of controlling headstrong pilots. The part we had overlooked, he explained patiently, was the paragraph prohibiting attacks on JCS targets that had not been previously struck. The Cam Pha oil storage tank was a target on the Joint Chiefs list, and it wasn't supposed to be destroyed until, somewhere between the croissants and the orange juice at a Tuesday morning strategy meeting, President Johnson and Secretary McNamara decided it was time. "Now," Winter finished, "you guys stay here until I can figure out how to handle this. You four are not to leave the command post until I personally clear you. You can't go to lunch, can't go to the squadron and, under no circumstances are you to talk to anyone else without my approval. Got that?" When we nodded our understanding, he stormed off.

For the next two hours we waited. We strolled through the planning area. We looked at books we had seldom seen, describing new weaponry under development and new electronic countermeasures that might help to defeat enemy defenses. We examined in detail the black-and-white before and after photos of target damage. We paged through the ROE books, hoping to convince anyone observing that we were serious about complying with the detailed and continuously changing rules that seemed to serve no purpose other than to favor the enemy and endanger the good guys.

As the time slowly passed, apprehension was beginning to set in. What did they do to people who violated the ROE? We searched the dog-eared pages for some clues about penalties. Would we get a trial by a jury of our peers? There's no way that other pilots would convict us for hitting a real target rather than dumping bombs on a jungle intersection. Were there different categories of violations, the bureaucratic equivalent of felonies and misdemeanors? Were we facing fines or prison terms? Would they throw us out of the Air Force or, maybe worse, ground us and make us finish the war pushing paper and seeking ROE violations committed by other pilots, caught doing their best to hurt the enemy? The fertile minds of lieutenants weighed the options, while Loyd quietly sipped a cup of coffee.

Winter returned at last. "Okay, you guys are off the hook. Here's what we've got. The rule specifies that unstruck JCS targets are prohibited. Cam Pha has never been on an approved target list. The JCS hasn't released it yet. But here's where we hauled your asses out of the fire. It seems that about four months ago a Navy A-4 took a hit on a target further inland. On his way out he dropped the two 250-pound bombs that he still had on his bird in the Cam Pha area. As far as I can tell, that makes it 'previously struck.' At least that's the way we're going to report it."

We shook our heads, marveling at the convoluted workings of the process. One by one we thanked Colonel Winter for his help and solemnly promised to be more careful in the future. Loyd shook his hand, and we headed out the command post door.

Does a condemned man sleep the night before his execution? Is it necessary for him to show up well rested for the ceremony? Sleep was becoming a problem. The daily pattern required a three or four o'clock get-up to make a predawn strike-package briefing three hours before takeoff. Preflight and taxi were in the morning twilight and during the joinups out of traffic we were always looking into the sun, which was just peeping over the horizon. After refueling, the morning time-on-target was always between eight and nine. That allowed a couple of hours for the aircraft to return, refuel, and reload, and then to assemble an afternoon package. Two attacks per day didn't allow much flexibility in the time intervals.

When it all went on schedule, we recovered back at Korat with debriefs finished in time for lunch. If you played your cards right, you could head back to the room and catch a two- or three-hour nap. Once the schedule was posted at five or six in the evening for the next day's sorties, it got difficult to sleep. If that little Roman numeral at the end of the briefing time and call-sign line was a six, the tension made rest impossible. Somehow, each day, there was a short interval when the adrenaline from the morning flight abated, and sleep was feasible. The mind tricked the body into believing that the threat was over. If you thought about it a bit, you would surely realize that you'd be part of the big go the next day, regardless of what time it was, but if it hadn't shown up on paper yet, then maybe it wouldn't happen.

The schedule was delivered to the O Club bulletin board just as John Russell and I were walking in the door for dinner. In the morning I was flying Four on John's wing in a flight with Ralph Beardsley and Bob Loken, one of the new guys recently arrived from the retread course. Briefing was at nine o'clock, so we were on the day's second strike. The Roman numeral was, of course, a six. We would learn the details on targets, routes, and tankers in the morning. With the threat more than twelve hours away, maybe I could sleep.

Several of us hung around after dinner, sipping on a beer and talking about follow-on assignments, making the big assumption that there was life after Korat. We were reaching a mission count that required each of us to submit an assignment preference form to personnel and the promise was that folks with hundred-mission credit were going to get a high priority. Richter had made up his mind that he would apply for a second tour and become the first to reach an almost magical two hundred missions. Two lieutenants from Tahkli had gone beyond one hundred back in May, but they had only received approval for twenty mission increments. Lucky Eckman had been shot down during the big Yen Bai raid and demonstrated the appropriateness of his nickname by being picked up within an hour. Bill Ardern, Lucky's classmate from the academy, had decided that he was pushing his luck too far, so he opted to end his combat flying. Lucky and Bill both returned to the States. Karl was going to request approval for a full tour. He was even planning beyond two hundred missions for a move to a South Vietnam base where he could get a local checkout in an F-100 or other aircraft to fly a tour of close air support. He expressed a patriotic need to defeat Communism, but it was also clear that he was hooked on the rush of stealing hubcaps.

My roommate, Bill Ricks, had taken a few days off and gone to Kadena to check out the opportunities for assignment to one of the local squadrons. I had the room to myself, and when I slid into the sheets I thought that maybe I'd have a quiet night. My thoughts, however, wouldn't let me sleep. I was dozing and waking, each time falling into a dream that had me hit in the target area. There was no resolution to the scenario, merely a cloudy, dark, flak-filled sky and the pressure of the mission. I wasn't killed or captured. I didn't recover successfully or crash. I simply woke with a start then rolled over again to try to sleep.

The sound was something like a love-starved cat on a

moonlit night, serenading the lady cats in the neighborhood. It was a cross between a wail and a whine, mostly high-pitched but occasionally dipping into lower registers, becoming a melody almost, but not quite. I looked at the clock and saw that it was only ten-thirty. I closed my eyes again, and the sound returned. The squealing was coming from the room next door. I sat up in bed and listened to be sure. It was definitely coming from Doc Goldman's room.

As the squadron flight surgeon, Ron Goldman lived in the 421st hootch area. A few days earlier we'd had a vacancy in the C flight hootch, so the Doc had moved in. Flight commanders and above had their own rooms, but lieutenants and junior captains shared. Goldman had little in common with the pilots, and although we liked him we felt more comfortable rooming with another guy doing the same job as we were. The irregular hours of briefings and returns to the room would also have interfered with Doc's routine office hour requirements, so he lived alone.

I got out of bed and went next door. I was amazed when he answered my pounding wearing his bathrobe and holding a violin. On the floor in the center of his room stood a music stand, illuminated by a small light clipped onto the open songbook. A straight-backed chair faced the music stand, and an open violin case rested nearby on the bed. I smothered a laugh, and with patently mock belligerence asked, "What the hell is going on?"

"I was just practicing," he replied. "Did it disturb you?"

"Listen, Doc, I've got a Pack VI go in the morning, and I really need to get some sleep. Could you maybe schedule your practices over lunch rather than the middle of the god-damned night?"

"Gosh, I'm sorry. I didn't realize it was that loud. Are you having trouble sleeping?" The doctor mode kicked in and replaced the struggling musician. "If you want, I can give you something to help you get some rest."

When we had reported to Nellis for training, the hospital had given each incoming pilot a small package with three pills. One was for sleep, one was a stimulant, and one was a strong analgesic for pain relief. They were a "stop" pill, a "go" pill, and a "no sweat" pill. We were instructed to take one a day for three days and record any effects. I hadn't noticed any effect from any of them. I had a few of each in my survival gear and had heard of some guys taking a few with them on R&R trips. I had never considered any aids to sleep other than an after-dinner drink or three, so I expressed my skepticism that the standard sleeping pill would work.

Goldman nodded in understanding but said he had something more effective than what was usually prescribed. He reassured me that it wouldn't leave me hung over or groggy in the morning. I admitted that I could sure use a good night's sleep. I took the small white tablet he handed me and headed to the central sitting area to get a cold glass of water from the refrigerator. I returned to bed.

I pulled the sheets up and closed my eyes. I glanced at the clock. It took about ten minutes. I felt my lower legs go numb. Insensitivity slowly crawled up from my lower extremities. My hands tingled for a few seconds then disappeared. Like some ethereal quicksand, the unconsciousness crept from the outer tips of my body toward the core. I knew that if the hootch suddenly caught fire I could not rise from the bed. As the numbness closed on my brain, I cursed Goldman. I slept.

The alarm jolted me awake. I couldn't tell how long it had been ringing, but knew instinctively that it had been buzzing for a while. It was seven o'clock, so I hadn't overslept. As promised, I wasn't hung over or groggy, but the terror of the creeping numbness from the night before made me vow never again to take any of the doc's little white pills. The next time his violin practice disturbed me I would simply go next door and crush his fiddle into tiny toothpicks, shove his bow up his ass, and bend his music stand into coat hangers. The satisfaction would most assuredly guarantee me a good, undisturbed night's rest.

I showered and shrugged my way into a clean flying suit. I pushed the polished jungle boots aside and dug out my now well-worn leather flying boots. It was superstition, I knew, but I wore only leather boots to Pack VI. My rationale was that I didn't want to be stuck in jail for years with cloth boots, but I knew that didn't make sense. There was no evidence that the North Vietnamese would allow anyone to keep their boots anyway. Still, the leather boots were part of my high-threat-mission ritual. I headed to the club for breakfast.

The briefing was standard. The target was a POL trans-shipment point just off the northwest end of the runway at Phuc Yen airfield. Phuc Yen was the largest of the MiG bases located just a few miles north of the Red River, where it passed through Hanoi. It remained proscribed in the ROE. We'd face the usual array of defenses and the added complication of possible heavy afternoon thunderstorm buildups. Four flights of 105s would attack the same target in five-minute trail along with a Weasel flight of an F-105F and three single-seat Ds. Refueling was scheduled for ingress only. We were Sixgun flight, last ones on the target.

Ralph Beardsley was one of the younger flight leads in the squadron's group of experienced F-105 pilots. He was smooth and confident, with a flair for tactics. He seemed always to have a plan to minimize exposure and maximize the probability of survival in the target area. The plans didn't need to be particularly complex, in fact the simpler the better. The most important thing was to vary what happened in those few terror-filled seconds from popup to getaway. Different dive angles, different run-in headings, and a saturation of the enemy's defenses in a short period of time could make a big difference, but stringing out the attack and flying the same flight path in sequence was a recipe for disaster. Being last on the target could mean the enemy was alerted to us, or it could mean they would all have their heads down when we finally arrived.

We planned to approach from the north along the eastern slope of the prominent ridgeline that pointed toward Hanoi from just west of Thai Nguyen. The ridge had become a favorite navigation aid for attacks into the area of the capital because of its prominence as a landmark as well as its ability to shield against radar detection. The rough terrain held few roads and virtually no villages. Moving heavy guns or the large transporters of SAMs and radars onto the ridge was almost impossible. The regular passage of F-105s had scattered fuel tanks and bomb suspension gear along the ridge, as well as, unfortunately, the wreckage of a number of aircraft. On our maps the ridge had a Vietnamese name, but we had begun to call it Thud Ridge. We had bought it for a heavy price, but now we owned it. It was our safe haven, an island of dubious security surrounded on all sides by threats.

At the southern tip of the ridge we would split into two elements, with each pair angling away from the straight line run-in to the target. At six miles from the target, the element leads would pop up to twelve thousand feet and roll-in to their dive-bomb pass. The wingmen would continue ten seconds further and start their pull up. According to the plan, all four airplanes would come from different attack headings, creating a pincer attack with the wingmen only seconds behind the leaders. Egress would have us returning the way we had come, back to the safety of the ridge.

The weather was every bit as bad as the weather-guesser had promised. From tanker drop-off all the way to the Red River crossing point just north of Yen Bai, we maneuvered through black corridors of storm clouds. When we could see the ground, it was in deep shadow with the mists of heavy rains descending from the bottoms of murky buildups. We had about ten-miles visibility as we crossed the Red, descending to just skim the top of the ridge. An easy turn pointed us toward the target and our airspeed built up to 540 knots. The bomb-laden airplanes were rock-steady, rolling like Cadillacs on a wide-open Western highway. Beardsley called for tank jettison forty miles north of the target.

The first flight had made it through the weather but had gotten disoriented and apparently missed the ridgeline and then missed the target. The second and third flights had aborted prior to the Red River, unable to find a passage through the weather. Sixgun was going to get there. We heard the clearly recognizable southern drawl of Pappy Robinson, the Weasel, as he directed his flight against an array of electronic threats. It seemed that Pappy never paid much attention to his call sign and simply depended on voice recognition to manage the battle. Everyone knew what he sounded like and had confidence in his capabilities. The deep voice with the Virginia accent was like a familiar old uncle visiting at Christmas and telling of his adventures. He'd lived through a lot and his stories were exciting. Today he was calling lots of SAM radar activity, but he followed each advisory with a reassuring, "Steady, boys. No launches."

Disco, the EC-121, orbiting more than one hundred miles away, was not so reassuring. With little regard for necessary radio communications in the battle area, Disco would regularly overpower the primary strike frequency with loud, often irrelevant warnings of SAM launches or MiG flights on guard channel. As far as we could tell, the SAM warnings came from Disco's monitoring of a wide range of frequencies. When they heard a SAM sighting from a flight, they would broadcast a SAM warning on guard. Disco didn't seem to register the fact that the threatened flight had already called the SAM and that a SAM that had already either hit or missed its target didn't threaten the other flights airborne. Disco's job was to call SAM warnings, regardless of how extraneous they might be. "Disco on guard. SAM, SAM. 19 degrees, 35 minutes north, 105 degrees, 55 minutes east. Time 12:15. Disco out." It was a long way from where Sixgun was. Probably a Navy strike somewhere south of us.

"Sixgun split." Russell veered toward me, and I kept spacing as we moved to bracket the target. "Sixgun Lead is up," signaled that Beardsley had started his pop.

Russell called his pop and I glanced down at the sweep-second hand of the clock to start timing my ten-second spacing. I'm scanning the dark landscape to my right, trying to find the target area. Time's up, I light the AB and start a smooth four-G pull to 30 degrees nose high. I'm watching the altimeter tape slide through the thousands of feet and wondering if I'll have enough room under the cloud layer to hit my apex. The guns are active and I can see the end of the Phuc Yen runway below. Lead's bombs start to detonate and

Pappy Robinson's voice is in the background calling, "Launch, launch. Take it down."

I'm in the clouds, rolling inverted and pulling back down. I've got the target area and keep the pull going until I'm established in my dive. I roll back to upright, check my dive angle, and ease the throttle out of the AB detent but keep it pushed to the front stop as the airspeed builds back toward five hundred. Then it's pickle and come hard right. I don't do much of a pullout, trying to get back into the comfort of ground clutter and maximum speed back to the ridge. The SAMs are airborne, just off my nose, climbing on an orange column of smoke that's much brighter than anything else I can see. There are two of them, almost in a formation, leveling out and remaining stationary along the right edge of the canopy bow. They've started to descend and the smoke trail shows their trajectory exactly. I check my altimeter and see I'm passing through fifteen hundred feet, less than one thousand above the ground. The SAMs are still arcing downward and Pappy's voice is again calling, "This is a valid launch, Sixgun. Heads up over there." Don't I know it. It's two against one, and I'm the meat in the SAM sandwich.

I'm getting down really low when the lead of the two missiles seems to level off. Either I've blanked the radar site's view of my aircraft, or the missile has stopped receiving command guidance. It passes ahead of me and slightly high. The second missile looks as though it will pass behind, but just to make sure I turn into the attack. The missile detonates just past my tail. I reverse my turn back to the left and can pick up a single 105 already hugging the ridge. I close on the friendly airplane, but I'm not quite ready to start climbing. It's Russell's bird, so we're back together outbound. I've got time to glance at the radar, but there's too much ground clutter to let me find the lead element. I assume that John's got a visual or is going to cut them off at the north end of the ridge when we turn back west.

We're climbing through ten thousand feet in the clear area near Yen Bai, about five miles in trail with the lead element when the stick pulses in my hand. Nothing more, just a flutter on my fingertips, then a more aggressive thump. The stick vibrates then thumps again. Now I can feel the aircraft wanting to porpoise just a bit with stick inputs. The master caution light comes on and I check the panel to find the stab-aug-off caution light illuminated. Checking the autopilot and stab-aug control panel confirms the caution light. The engage buttons are popped. I glance down at the hydraulic gauges on the lower right corner of the instrument panel. Utility pressure and primary flight control two are rock steady at three thousand psi, but the P-1 gauge is fluctuating wildly between zero and one thousand. Nothing signals trouble in a 105 more than hydraulic pressure loss. Not fire, not electrical, nothing.

I close the gap between my aircraft and Russell's then call on the radio, "Sixgun Three, Four's just lost P-1 hydraulic. Stab-aug is off too." I watch Russell's helmet snap right to look at my aircraft. He rocks his wings to signal me to come closer. When I've closed to within fifty feet, he points forward then raises four fingers indicating he wants me to take the lead so that he can fly formation around my aircraft and look me over. I nod assent and look forward, continuing on course and climbing into the clear as we proceed out of North Vietnam and into Laos.

John moves his aircraft around mine in a smooth pattern, rising high on my left wing, then low, sliding below and behind my tail then moving forward onto the right wing, checking first low then high. He moves line-abreast on the right wing, then taps his helmet and holds up two fingers. He wants me to go to channel two on the radio. I nod.

"Sixgun Three, check."

I acknowledge, "Sixgun Four."

"Roger, Raz. You've got a couple of holes in your right wing," he reports. I turn to the right and lean forward, straining to see what can be seen. Russell continues, "It looks like one hole in the bottom of the wing on the outboard gear door and then about three tears across the top of the wing. Probably took a 37 into the bottom that blew up in the wheel well and then opened up the top. You got any other problems but the hydraulics?"

"So far, all I've got is the stab-aug out and P-1 gone to zero. The other hydraulics are steady, and nothing else seems to be affected. The airplane's a little squirrelly, but that's not a major concern."

"Okay, then let's plan on putting it into Udorn. That's the first friendly base on the way home. We'll declare an emergency when we contact Cricket. That all right with you?" I nod. "Sixgun Three, let's go back strike primary." We change channels and continue outbound. We're level in the clear at twenty-five thousand.

"Sixgun Lead, Three."

"Roger Three, Sixgun Lead," Beardsley responds.

"Sixgun Three and Four are holding hands about ten miles in trail with you, on top. Four's taken a hit and I suggest I escort him into Udorn if that's okay with you." Russell briefly outlines the plan and Sixgun Lead approves. We continue southbound.

We report our "mishap" to Cricket, then contact Udorn Approach. The airplane is flyable with no stab-aug, but feels a bit uncomfortable with an almost continual snaking back and forth. Roll is almost normal, but pitch requires a constant awareness to avoid over-controlling. I'll fly the lead on the recovery so that John can watch the airplane for any warning signs that problems might get worse. Udorn directs our descent to a precision approach, straight-in to the field, landing runway three-zero. The weather is good in Thailand and won't be a factor.

As we cross the Mekong just west of Vientiane, I'm beginning to feel more comfortable with friendly territory beneath me. The Udorn controller directs us onto a downwind leg then turns us onto base. I firmly move the gear handle down, then watch as the three position indicators move from up, to barber-pole in-transit indication, then flash two green and one red. The nose and left main gear read down and locked, but the right gear indicates unsafe. I ask John if he can see more damage in the wheel well and to advise me what position the gear is in. He reports that it looks normal, but there are several lose wires dangling. The main strut is down and the bracing shackle looks like it is properly extended. Udorn Approach advises we'll be turning to final in thirty seconds. I report the unsafe gear and advise that I'll be trying to stop straight ahead on the runway. Udorn tells me that crash equipment is in place.

I lower the flaps to full and ease into the turn, trying to keep the airplane from gyrating too badly. I can see the runway ahead. We're stabilized on final, about twenty knots fast, with Russell on my right wing. I'll land and Russell will execute a low approach and head back to Korat. Things are looking good, then Udorn Approach calls, "Sixgun Four, this is Udorn Approach. Landing clearance is canceled. Go around to the east side of the runway, climb, and maintain three thousand five hundred, heading three one zero degrees. Acknowledge."

"Uhhh, Udorn, this is Sixgun Four. Are you still aware that we're emergency aircraft with mishap damage?"

"Roger, Sixgun. Udorn has home-based traffic landing opposite direction, a flight of two local F-104s. Call level three thousand five hundred."

"Udorn, Sixgun Four. Are the 104s in an emergency situation?" I push the throttles forward and ease the nose up, hoping that the controller may change his mind but knowing that he won't. I raise the flaps to half, but there's no way I'm going to try raising the gear, which may not respond, or if it does come up may not come back down again for the next approach. I glance over at John, who simply shrugs his shoulders in disbelief.

"Negative, Sixgun. The 104s have priority for a formation low approach. Wing policy gives priority to locally stationed aircraft."

We come around again, this time there's no interruption, and I approach the overrun wondering if I can respond quickly enough if the right main gear collapses on touchdown. John's tight on my wing, watching the landing gear, the holes in my wing, and ready to let me know if there are leaks or fires or anything else. I'm planning to try to keep the wing up on landing and get into burner before disaster strikes. I'm slowing and easing the bird onto the runway as softly as I can. A slight jolt indicates touchdown and then roll-out. The right main holds. John's airplane surges ahead of me as he retracts his gear and accelerates down the side of the runway. I pull the drag chute handle and feel the reassuring deceleration. I watch John climb out at the departure end with a wing rock wishing me luck.

At the end of the runway, emergency vehicles surround the airplane. Gear downlock pins are inserted and the fire chief gives me a smile and a thumbs up signal. He points to a blue truck with a large "Follow-Me" sign on the back. We taxi slowly down the semicircular taxiway to an open-sided maintenance hangar. The truck leads me in and a crew chief signals that chocks are in, and I'm cleared for engine shutdown.

I can barely get my personal gear clear of the airplane before a small army of maintainers push yellow platforms around the battle-scarred wing. A fuel truck has pulled up in front of the bird and a sheet-metal worker is kneeling on the right wing hacking away at the turned-up metal around the holes. A station wagon driven by a lieutenant from the command post is waiting for me. I'm whisked away to a debrief of my part of the mission, and within less than twenty minutes I'm back in the station wagon heading for a C-47 parked in front of the control tower. The Gooney Bird has the right engine running and the door open, waiting. The staff sergeant flight mechanic grabs my parachute and survival vest from the back of the vehicle and leads me to the airplane. I'm the lone passenger, seated on one of two passenger seats with my flight gear piled unceremoniously by my side. A forty-five-minute flight has me back at Korat barely an hour after the rest of Sixgun flight has finished debriefing. Again I've seen that F-105s and their pilots are a valuable commodity. There's been no time to look for the son-of-a-bitch who established the wing policy giving local birds priority over battle damage. I've probably been saved from an assault charge.

* * *

Some explain dive-bombing as pure physics. The bomb responds mechanically to the set of vectors that exist at the release point, a precisely calculated point above the ground. If you get to the right place at the right altitude, airspeed, dive angle and G-load, the bomb will follow the planned trajectory and, voilà, hit the target. The bomb's weight and shape influence the drag on the bomb and therefore how rapidly the flight path converts from that of the aircraft to a straight descent. Of course, the temperature and pressure altitude at the target will impact air density and drag on the bomb, as well as true airspeed of the aircraft based on flying to a given indicated airspeed. Calculate all of the factors together and you can arrive at a sight setting that displays the pipper properly depressed from the aircraft's flight path to show where the bomb will hit. Oh, and then there's wind. The aircraft moves in the air mass. If the wind is from the north, the aircraft will be moving over the ground toward the south at whatever speed the wind imparts.

Put it all together and you can hit your target. All it takes is for a few things to come together. You've got to have an accurate weather forecast to know the wind and the effect of density altitude on your airspeed. Then you've got to hit your dive angle exactly. You'll need to be at just the right airspeed, of course, and you must pickle the bomb off at the preplanned release altitude with no pushes or pulls on the control stick. The pipper will have to be off the target exactly the right distance upwind to compensate for drift at release. It takes incredible skill and lots of practice to do all of these things precisely and consistently on a controlled gunnery range with lots of reference landmarks. It is virtually impossible in combat, where nothing is certain and hundreds of people are shooting at you.

That leads to the "magic and mirrors" theory of dive-bombing. If you study how various errors in delivery affect where a bomb will hit, you will quickly see that you can be more accurate if you lean toward one end of the mistake spectrum. Comparing steeper than planned deliveries against shallow reveals that being shallow results in nearly three times as large an error. Being faster creates a smaller error than being slow. Releasing below planned altitude gets you closer than releasing high. If you can find the target you will stand a better chance of hitting it by being steep, fast, and pressing. Closer is better.

I was spare for a strike on yet another POL storage area. This one was just over Thud Ridge, halfway between the ridge and the steel plant at Thai Nguyen. Preflight is normal until the point after engine start, when I check the gun sight. I have nothing. None of the modes work. Nothing functions in air-to-air mode. Nothing responds in air-to-ground. Circuit breakers checked, but still no sight. It may be burned out bulbs, but there is no time to check or replace them. Could both filaments burn out simultaneously or is it a problem somewhere else in the electrical circuitry? "Laredo, check." It's taxi time.

"Laredo Two."

"Three."

"Four."

"Spare."

We taxi. In the arming area we've got guests today. The wing chaplain stands just beyond the maintenance and munitions crews with Arthur Godfrey. The red-headed, freckle-faced radio personality is decked out in his familiar Hawaiian shirt. It's all there but the ukulele. Well known as a pilot himself, Godfrey is fascinated by the activity, the noise, the turmoil, and sheer menace of the huge airplanes. He watches intently as, one by one, the aircraft are inspected for loose panels, fuel or oil leaks, cut tires or evidence of malfunction. He stares as the armorers pull safety pins from the bombs and fuel tanks, then open the gun-bay doors to connect the electrical leads and arm the Vulcan cannon. He watches, without understanding what it means, as I see the maintenance crew leader walk to the nose of the number two aircraft and display a prominent thumbs-down indicating that the aircraft has a malfunction and will be turned back. Godfrey waves good-bye with a stupid grin, as though we are simply leaving on a pleasure cruise. The chaplain blesses the airplanes with a theatrical sign of the cross as we turn to take the active runway. I'm now Laredo Two.

I've got an airplane that, with no gun sight, is technically not mission capable, but it never occurs to me not to go. Four airplanes are the standard package. Four airplanes have mutual support and good lookout. Four airplanes bring more bombs to the target and improve the odds of not having to go again tomorrow. Laredo needs four airplanes and I'm Laredo, even with no gun sight.

The weather is good for a change, but the defenses are enjoying the sunshine at least as much as we are. There is already one airplane down in the target area as we cross the Red. The Weasels have fired all of their Shrikes and are now trying to keep the SAMs away by faking attacks on emitting radars. Disco is garbaging up the radio as usual with long, drawn out warning calls that don't mean anything to anybody, but they raise the tension level. We crest the ridge just ten miles north of the target, echelon the formation to the left, and fan up for a roll in to the right.

With no sight, I simply estimate a point on the combining glass about two inches above where the end of the pitot tube is visible. I pull down a bit steeper than normal, let the airspeed build with the throttle parked firmly forward, and press the target until I've got an entire faceful of pavement, pipes and, I hope, POL. I pickle and pull, depending on six Gs to make the recovery without adding my own airplane to the load of delivered iron. I come off to the south, then rake back hard right to watch the blast and the rising fireball of a huge secondary explosion. Above the target, Laredo Four is still on the bomb run. I hope he's got gun-camera film to catch the hits and ensure we don't have to come back tomorrow. I got the target. Even without a sight, I'm glad I came today.

I've got Laredo Lead ahead, and I get back into formation just as we cross the Red west of Phuc Yen. I can see Three and Four back at seven o'clock coming fast into position. It takes only seconds and we're back across the river aimed for Laos and then home. The cost today has been two airplanes down in the target area, but Laredo has gotten in and out, and I've applied the magic theory of dive-bombing with great effect. Two days later I get a note from intel indicating they've got some good film of an F-105 at remarkably low altitude delivering some bombs. It could only be Laredo Two.

CHAPTER 16

Pilots Flying Fighters

Someone has posted a sign at the entrance to the Officers' Club. "Through these doors pass the world's greatest pilots." It's a noble thought, but we're all aware that it can't be totally true. Certainly there is greatness in the group. I've got little doubt about that. I owe my life to the talent, experience, leadership, and skills of some incredible fighter pilots. I've seen greatness develop in my classmates from Nellis as well. There is confidence and maturity now where initially there was only pilot skill. But the sign offers lots of room for question.

Are all of the world's greatest here at Korat? No, of course not. There are some greats over at Tahkli and definitely some greats flying Phantoms at Udorn, Ubon, and Danang. And what about the lack of a modifier for "pilots"? Does the sign mean fighter pilots or does it also include transport and support pilots? Are they great too?

The sign leads to barroom debates. We sit around tables over drinks trying to decide who is great and who isn't. Should we demand that the sign be changed to read "fighter pilots," or is it proper to be more inclusive? And if the sign is changed, what is a fighter pilot? The lieutenants who've known no other life since graduating from pilot training are nearly unanimous in declaring fighter pilots as great. We scrambled hard in competitive flying and academics to earn a seat in a hot jet. We had the talent and ability to prevail. It took study and effort and a bit of the luck of the draw, but now we're fighter drivers, and we know we're good.

The senior guys who have been in tactical aviation for much longer are less convinced, observing that several of the

237

instructors we flew with at Nellis are now operating as forward air controllers in small, unarmed, propeller-driven planes. They aren't flying fighters, but we knew them as fighter pilots, didn't we?

Recent graduates of the short training program who previously had been bomber and transport pilots or Training Command instructors are eager to jump on the greatness bandwagon with the lieutenants. They're flying fighters now, so they're fighter pilots, and by definition they are great.

Wimpy Peake downs his whiskey and leans forward to share the wisdom gleaned from his sixteen years in the Air Force. "Listen guys, flying fighters is an assignment. No more and no less. Sometimes you've got to be lucky and sometimes it helps to be good, but you're only there when the Air Force lets you be there. When you've got the assignment, make the most of it. Enjoy it. Work at it. But remember, the Air Force works in three-year increments, so that's the longest you might be in the assignment. Your next job might be more of the same, or it might be pushing a desk. You might find yourself wearing a tie and plastic shoes standing behind a briefing podium in a headquarters somewhere while the current crop of hotshots thinks you're a second-class citizen. Then they are flying fighters, and you're just pond scum."

It dawns on us that Wimpy's right. Just because we're flying fighters now, doesn't mean we'll be flying fighters next year. Assignments are beginning to come in for those of us getting to high mission counts. The experienced, older guys who've been in fighters for a long time are heading back to the 105 training unit to serve as instructors, but no clear pattern has emerged yet for lieutenants with one hundred missions. We might be fighter pilots today, but something else next year.

Wimpy waves his arm in a circular motion to the bartender to pour another round for the table. The philosophical discussion is fueled by Johnnie Walker Black on the rocks and Beefeater gin with a splash of tonic. He begins to expound. "Flying fighters is simply an assignment, but being a fighter pilot isn't. Being a fighter pilot is a state of mind. It's an attitude toward your job, toward the mission, toward the way you live your life. You don't have to fly fighters to be a fighter pilot. You've simply got to have the attitude. There are fighter pilots driving B-52s and fighter pilots hauling trash. They may not have the flash and glamour, but they are the best they can possibly be at the job they've got to do. There are pilots who fly fighters and there are fighter pilots. You guys want to be fighter pilots, not pilots flying fighters. Look for the difference." This is profound stuff for the Korat bar.

It makes sense to me. I've thought a lot about Butterfly 44 since that day in northern Laos. Even though he flies a Pilatus Porter, that FAC clearly fills Wimpy's definition of a fighter pilot. More important, Wimpy's definition explains a lot about the people I see around me. It explains my own experience at Korat. When I arrived, I was, without doubt, a pilot who flew fighters. I was qualified in the aircraft, but it would have been hard to fit the description of fighter pilot that we're talking about. I wasn't sure whether I was a fighter pilot yet. I looked around the table and saw a group of people who all flew fighters but who weren't all fighter pilots. Some were, some would be, and some might never make the cut.

The guys from McConnell when I first arrived at Korat hadn't been fighter pilots. Oh sure, some were, but most were pilots who flew fighters. It didn't matter that they had been flying fighters for a longer time than most; they didn't have the attitude that Wimpy was describing. The guys who had come from Europe and Nellis seemed to have a high percentage of fighter pilots, but there was no telling about the new crop of retreads. It was tough for them, with very little time in the airplane and the responsibilities of rank and leadership thrust upon them. The delicate balance between flying skill and tactical judgment was difficult to learn. Learning to subordinate your own fear was even more problematic. I knew now that everyone faced it in some degree. How you dealt with it determined whether you were a fighter pilot or simply someone flying fighters.

The flow of retrainees from the short courses had begun to

affect our losses. Filling the squadrons throughout Southeast Asia took a lot of manpower. We were getting the bodies, but we were no longer getting the skill levels. You couldn't prove it, of course, but things were happening that didn't bode well for the future. We had four squadrons of F-105s at Korat now, the 421st, 469th, 34th, and we'd recently added the 13th. Tahkli had three. Each day, the strike packages got a little bigger and each night as we sat around the squadron dining table, the news of the day's losses would come up. Names would be mentioned, and in most instances only one or two of us at the table would recognize them. They were simply losses. New guys who had signed in, flown a few missions, and then were shot down before anyone really began to know who they were. They were faceless names that we might have been sitting next to at that morning's briefing.

Occasionally, someone we knew well would be hit. Then we would want to know the details. Where was it? What was he doing? Was there a chute? Was there any hope of pickup? Usually the answer was no. Glen Nix had returned to Korat to finish his missions. He'd been flying with the 13th on a simple armed recce sortie into Pack I. He'd been hit and bailed out, but no one had been able to talk to him on the ground. As his wingman made passes over his parachute, each succeeding flyby saw less and less of Glen's canopy. Someone was dragging it in and hiding from the aircraft overhead. Nix had been taken prisoner. The guns had finally gotten the cocky warrior. As I walked from the club back to my room that night, I stumbled several times, not seeing obstacles in my path. My vision was blurry and my cheeks were wet. It must be something in the air. I wasn't crying. There were no sobs, simply tears running down my face as I thought about that first night at Korat when I'd met him and he'd warned me about the guns.

Joe Vojir and I, each with mission counts in the mid-eighties, were tacked to the wing of Maj. Burris Begley and Maj. Ken Whittemore. Both were products of the short course, and each had become a flight lead based on his senior rank and having completed twenty missions. Whittemore had been a B-52 pilot and Begley had been in fighters long ago, but had spent the last ten years as a staff adviser to a National Guard unit. While Whittemore worked hard to learn new skills in fighters, Begley seemed never to have had them, despite a log book that showed considerable fighter time in years past. Whittemore showed confidence while recognizing his shortcomings. He understood his weaknesses and was working to fill those gaps and become a good fighter pilot. Begley, on the other hand, seemed unaware of his timidity and inability to lead competently. We quickly dubbed him Mister Magoo. He was short, bald, and wore wire-rimmed glasses. He moved with the same sort of blundering incompetence as the cartoon character. He was leading us to a matériel storage site and staging area in Pack V. Somehow I had the feeling that Wimpy had scheduled Joe and me as baby-sitters for the trip.

We got our gas and dropped off the tanker heading straight north in a brilliant blue sky. Off to the east were banks of clouds that had kept us out of the Hanoi area, but our target would be clear and easy to find. There were guns and the possibility of MiGs, but it was unlikely that there would be much of a SAM threat. It wasn't a milk run, but it wasn't going to be a white-knuckle mission either. We were barely across the Black River when we heard the call on guard.

"Mayday. Mayday. Tempest Three is hit. I've got a fire light on the right engine and am shutting it down. I'm headed south from the target area." Tempest, an F-4C, was in trouble. I had immediately flicked the radio selector to DF when I heard the Mayday call and the bearing pointer had swung to the nose of my aircraft. We were heading straight toward him. I waited to hear what the rest of Tempest flight was going to do. I could have waited forever. The rest of Tempest flight wasn't going to help at all. They appeared to be more concerned with their own survival.

"Tempest Lead, this is Tempest Three. I'm climbing out from the target. I've got the right engine shut down. Say your position." The whole world waited for Tempest Lead to reply on guard channel, but there was only silence. Tempest Three had been abandoned. "Mayday. Mayday. Tempest Three's got a fire light on the left engine now. We're going to have to get out. Any aircraft, this is Tempest Three." Things were going from bad to worse. A fire on one engine of the two-engined Phantom might be isolated easily in peacetime flying, but in combat where the fire usually meant battle damage, seldom more than a few minutes would elapse before the disintegrating engine threw sufficient parts through the aircraft keel to disable the second engine. I watched Begley's head in the lead aircraft. He was fixed, staring straight ahead.

"Anchor Lead, this is Two. I show Tempest ahead of us. Suggest we go to guard and see if we can help him." I hoped I could jolt Magoo into some action. Things were going to happen fast it appeared and it would be comforting for the two guys in Tempest Three if they knew someone was around to help before their airplane became unflyable. It was too late. Before we did anything, Tempest Three called that they were ejecting.

I couldn't get anything on radar, but the DF pointer now had a steady source as the emergency beepers in the parachutes began to howl. The pointer showed them just to the left of our flight path. "Anchor Lead, Two. Suggest we go to Crown and see if we can get some rescue headed this way. Do you concur?" I needed to prod Begley into some response. It looked as though he intended to fly past the ejection and continue on to the target. We were nearly on scene. We've got full loads of ordnance if it's needed, and we've just dropped off the tanker, so we've got plenty of gas. We need to take charge.

Reluctantly, Begley responded. "Anchor, let's go channel fifteen." We switched and checked in. "Crown, this is Anchor . . . uhhh. It looks like Tempest Three has bailed out . . . uhh." He waits for Crown to tell him what to do. He seems lost without a plan, wasting precious time that could mean the difference between life and death for the two pilots descending in their parachutes.

"Roger, Anchor. This is Crown. Copy the bailout. Have

you got the survivors in sight? Say your position and state."
Crown, the rescue coordinator, seems to be ready for action.

"Anchor Lead, Two. We ought to come left. The beepers
are showing off our left wing now." We were over steep
limestone mountains, between the Black and Red Rivers.
The area was sparsely populated with few trails, but it could
have some small pockets of enemy militia. It wasn't a bad
place for a rescue effort, if we could get things moving and
spot the survivors. My leader eases into a left turn. We keep
turning. "Anchor, roll out," I call, wondering if he has any
idea how I know where to go. "Anchor Lead, Two. Can I
give Crown the info?"

"Okay, Anchor Two, give them the coordinates if you've
got them," Begley grudgingly authorized. I wonder what
his Doppler is showing or whether he even updated it after
takeoff.

"Crown, this is Anchor Two. We've got four 105s with
twenty-four 500-pounders and twenty mike-mike. We've got
about thirty minutes of playtime, and we appear to be closing on the survivors' location. Present position is 21 degrees
20 minutes north, 104 degrees 10 minutes east. Can you get
the Sandys and Jolly Green headed this way? We'll try to
spot the survivors and provide cover until then." The good
weather was helping; we could see the ground clearly.

Crown acknowledges my call and tells us that Anchor
flight is designated the on-scene commander until the Sandys
arrive. We'd be getting a pair of A-1Es, call sign Sandy 51
and 52, and a pair of Jolly Greens. They estimate about
twenty minutes en route to our location. Until then, we are in
charge.

Vojir breaks in, "Anchor Lead, Four. I've got a tally on
smoke, near the top of the ridge at right one o'clock about
ten miles. Could be Tempest." We ease toward the smoke,
still at eighteen thousand feet in a four-ship spread. Joe continues, "Anchor, we need to send someone low to see if we
can make contact with the survivors. Suggest that Anchor
Three and I go down and establish a low cap."

Begley says "Roger" but doesn't give the order. Joe closes

on his element leader and waves a hand signal pointing down. Whittemore takes the hint and rolls off toward the smoke. I watch as the pair of 105s begin trolling back and forth along the hilltops, working carefully to avoid direct overflight of the wreckage. Then, a voice on guard, obviously stressed but alive.

"Mayday. This is Tempest Three Bravo. I'm on the ground and can hear aircraft overhead. Say your call sign." It's the backseater from the F-4. We're in the right area.

Joe acknowledges the call. "This is Anchor Four. We've got four 105s over you. Sandys and Jolly are inbound. Estimating about twenty minutes. What's your condition?" Joe is talking to the backseater on guard, so I'm able to tell my lead on Crown frequency that we should establish communication with the inbound rescuers.

"Anchor, let's set up an orbit at an altitude that will let us talk to Crown and the Sandys. We need to ease up a bit higher and throttle back to save fuel." I'm beginning to plan for a longer stay in case problems develop. If we can save sufficient fuel, we can swap places with the low element in twenty minutes and keep fast movers overhead a bit longer.

"Sandy Five-One, this is Anchor Two. Do you read?" I start calling without waiting for Magoo.

"Roger, Anchor Two. Loud and clear. We're haulin' ass your way. Can you give me a status report?" I pause momentarily waiting for Lead to respond, but he says nothing. I've got to continue.

"Sandy, Anchor Two. We've got the wreckage spotted and voice contact with Bravo. We're a flight of four with 24 Mk-82s and guns and about twenty minutes left. Three and Four are working low cap, and I'm high for communications relay. We'll stay on station 'til you get here. Check with Crown and see if they can get us some gas to cycle back if you need us longer." I try to give the rescue specialist as much information as possible while giving him a radio signal to home on to get into the area.

"Thanks, Anchor. Any report on Alpha?" Sandy 51 is worried about the frontseater. We haven't heard anything yet.

Vojir relays the question to Tempest Three Bravo. From the ground the survivor can't hear the A-1s or any of the comments on other frequencies. Joe asks him to switch his survival radio off of guard channel to the regular rescue frequency of 282.8. The backseater reports that he's hung up in some trees along a steep hillside. He hasn't seen or heard anything from Alpha since he saw the other parachute immediately after ejection. He feels some minor bruises but doesn't report any major injuries. Naturally, he urges us to hurry up.

I move forward on Begley's right wing, trying to herd him into a left turn that will take us south of the crash site to meet the incoming pick-up force. I don't know if it's my effort or simply coincidence, but he eases to the left. I spot movement against the dark jungle canopy below us. "Anchor Two's got visual on a pair inbound, low eleven o'clock. Looks like Sandy." I wait for Magoo to acknowledge.

"Sandy Five-One, check your left eleven high. You've got Anchor One and Two overhead. Head three-two-zero from your position. We've got contact with Bravo about fifteen miles off your nose. Anchor Three and Four are working that area at eight thousand indicated. Say your altitude." I describe all the known players to help the lead Sandy get a picture of the situation.

"Roger, Anchor. Thanks a lot. Tally ho on the high element. Tempest Three, Tempest Three, this is Sandy Five-One. How do you read?" A very relieved Bravo responds that he's got radio contact with the rescue leader.

"Okay, Anchor Three, if you guys will move up a bit and give us the airspace below ten thousand, I'd appreciate it." Sandy takes charge. "Tempest Three Bravo, give me a short count for a steer. Nothing more, please."

"Roger Sandy, this is Tempest Three Bravo, one, two, three, four, five. Five, four, three, two, one. Bravo out." I follow along on my own DF to try to get some landmarks to pinpoint his position. I watch the two incredibly slow-moving A-1s creep along the treetops below us.

"Okay, that's good Tempest. Can you hear us yet?" Sandy has one good radio cut, and now he's working short transmissions to refine the position. The enemy has DF gear too, so he doesn't want his survivor giving away his position if at all possible.

"Sandy Five-One, Tempest. I hear props south of me."

"Good, Bravo. We've got the Jolly about five minutes out. If you could prepare a smoke now, but don't fire it until I tell you. All right?" Tempest Three acknowledges that he's ready.

"Anchor flight, this is Sandy Five-One. Crown says I've got Chevy inbound to relieve you. You guys can head to the tanker. You'll be on Red One-One and they'll top you off if we need more help. Thanks for guiding us in and getting things rolling here. Sandy Five-One is now the on-scene commander. I'll take it from here."

Begley acknowledges that we are relieved and eases southbound. Whittemore and Vojir start climbing to rejoin. As we head out of North Vietnam, we continue to listen to the rescue. The Jolly Green has arrived, and the Sandy talks him into position over the survivor. Tempest Three Bravo pops his orange smoke flare, and the helicopter moves in for the pickup. Hovering atop the jungle canopy, the penetrator is lowered and the pararescue man rides down the cable to aid the pilot. As they hover, the jungle erupts with gunfire. Automatic weapons and machine guns fire at the chopper, helplessly stationary, linked to the ground by a cable and winch. The PJ struggles to untangle the parachute harness and wrap a belt around the survivor. He's got him now and signals thumbs up. The helicopter rises, scrambling to get above the gunfire. Trailing the cable below with two men swinging at the end, the Jolly moves forward. Shots ricochet from the steel beam of the winch and whistle through the open doorway of the rescue copter. Then, they're clear. They radio to Sandy 51 that they've got the survivor aboard and are heading outbound. I breathe a sigh of relief. We've got the first one.

Sandy 51 is working the area as the Jolly heads outbound. The second helicopter is orbiting nearby, waiting to see if contact can be established with Alpha. Chevy is putting bombs on the spot where the pickup was made, hoping to silence the guns if Alpha can be found. As we level off at twenty-eight thousand feet, the last we hear from Sandy 51 is the call, "Tempest Three Alpha, if you read come up voice or beeper. Tempest Three Alpha, come up voice." There is no response.[1]

As we approach the refueling track, Lion advises us that we won't be needed anymore. We head for Korat. After landing, the debriefing is terse. Begley says little about the flight. We finish up the paperwork and Vojir and I head to the lounge for a cup of coffee. Twenty minutes pass as Joe and I talk about the mission. Sergeant Morgan sticks his head in from the hallway and says, "Major Loyd wants to see you two."

We report to the operations officer in his office. Loyd looks us up and down. He clearly has something on his mind, but we don't have a clue what it might be. Then we know. "Major Begley was just in to talk about you guys."

Simultaneously, we both respond with a combination of contrition, ignorance, and humility that always works to protect lieutenants when they're about to get an ass-chewing. Together we say, "Sir?" The rising inflection seeming to indicate that we don't have the slightest idea what this is about.

"He says you guys took over his flight this morning. You were Two, Raz, and you were Four," Loyd gestures at Joe. "How the hell do you take over a major's flight? What was going on? What's your story?" We're not sure which of us should respond. We look at each other, and then I take the lead.

"There was an F-4 in trouble, sir. We were close by, and it looked as though they needed help. Major Begley seemed reluctant to act. We thought it was a good idea to get things rolling before it was too late." I start to plead our case. Vojir jumps in and adds to the explanation. Loyd sits back in his chair and nods slowly.

"Did they get them out?" he asks.

---

1. Tempest 3 came from the 433rd TFS at Ubon. The aircraft piloted by Capt. W. R. Andrews (KIA) and 1st Lt. E. W. Garland was downed on 5 October 1966.

"No, sir. Only the backseater. We never got contact with the nose-gunner. The Jolly got shot up pretty good during the pickup. They called the rescue off before we got back to the tanker." My summary satisfies the boss.

"Good job, guys. I'll clear this up with Begley." Loyd dismisses us, and we're pretty certain that he's got the picture. Vojir and I salute smartly and get while the getting is good.

Being in trouble in a singleseat fighter and not having your flight members around to support you is a frightening concept. I'm trying to understand where the rest of Tempest flight had gone, and why Tempest Three wound up on fire and alone over enemy territory. Nothing seems to explain it. I consider the possibility that different criteria apply in two-seat aircraft but immediately abandon that idea. I'm happy to be where I am and flying with the guys in the 421st. I'm comfortable that my flight leads and other wingmen will be there for me, just as I know that I'll reach as far down as I possibly can to help them. I wonder if the incident with Tempest flight was a momentary aberration or if it signals something that will happen again.

Two weeks later I got my answer. I was on a two-ship with Ken Frank checking out the roads around Mu Gia and Ban Karai Passes in Pack I. We had dropped on a suspected storage area that intel had indicated on our maps, but there wasn't much in the way of results. As we were climbing out to head home, there was a call on guard. It was Avenger Three, an F-4. He had both engines in idle and his throttles weren't getting any response. It didn't take an aeronautical engineer to know that a flat-nosed, pug-ugly airplane like an F-4 wouldn't fly for very long without power.

Avenger Three had come off a target in the Steel Tiger area of southern Laos with both engines throttled back. I didn't know what they taught people in F-4 school about dive-bombing, but I knew from my own experience that the throttle never came back very much on a combat mission. If anything, there was always a distinct forward pressure on that particular control. I could never get going fast enough. Avenger Three apparently thought he was going too fast. When he pulled off the target area and pushed the throttles back up, nothing happened. He zoomed off the target area and immediately switched to guard channel and started advising the rest of the world about his imminent bailout. Avenger Lead, Two, and Four rejoined and went home to Ubon. I couldn't believe that we were going to be capping another abandoned Phantom crew.

It was almost reflex action to switch to DF as soon as the beepers started. Ken Frank's turn told me he was doing the same thing, pointing the nose at the ejection scene. He rocked his wings, signaling me to route formation where I could see hand signals, then tapped his helmet and flashed one finger then all five. I changed the radio to channel fifteen and waited for the check-in. "Crown, this is Condor. I've got a pair of 105s with guns and about fifteen minutes of fuel in the vicinity of Avenger Three. Condor Two, check."

"Two," I replied. He wasted no time. We were already close enough to see the column of smoke rising from the crashed Phantom. The beepers were still blocking radio communication on guard, but they should be turned off as soon as the pilots got on the ground or in a position to reach the toggle switch on the small transmitter.

"Roger, Condor. This is Crown. If you can establish contact with the crew it would be a big help. We're getting the A-1s and Jolly airborne now out of NKP. We'll coordinate with Cricket to get the next inbound set of fast movers to relieve you, but for right now, you're it." Once again we are the quickest link to the rescue forces. I switch my TACAN to Nakhon Phanom to see how far the rescue guys have to come. We were only seventy miles out.

The crash scene was in relatively flat country, with small villages and rice paddies nestled among softly rolling hills. It looked like the hill country of Texas but with a lot more water and much darker trees. Depending upon where the chutes landed, getting these guys out might be fairly easy. The fact that they had been dropping bombs nearby was strong evidence that there weren't many friendlies in the neighborhood. Trees and hills would be good news; hootches and farm fields would be bad.

The beeper howl is clearer now. At least one of the Phantom crewmen has turned off the automatic emergency transmitter. With both beepers going there was a continual squeal from the radio making guard channel virtually unusable. With only one beeper going the channel isn't totally clear, but the noise is tolerable. I hope that we can establish some communication with the guy on the ground. Frank has us in a slow left-hand orbit at twelve thousand feet, so we must be close to overhead now. It would really help if the other guy would turn his beeper off. I'm reluctant to turn off the guard receiver because we might miss important calls. "Avenger Three, this is Condor Lead on 364.2. Do you read? Avenger Three, do you read Condor?" Frank is trying to establish contact, and we're both hoping the guy is able to talk to us. Then we hear the tinny sound characteristic of the handheld survival radio. We've got contact with one of them at least.

"Condor, this is Avenger Three Alpha. Do you read me?" It's the frontseater.

"Roger Avenger. We're overhead with a pair of 'Chiefs, what's your condition?"

"Condor, Avenger is hung up in a tree. I'm okay, but not sure how to get down from here. I lost sight of Bravo during the descent. I think he's about a mile east of me but I can't tell for sure."

Frank has been using the DF on Avenger's transmission and now he steepens up the left turn and descends to see if we can spot a chute. We swoop down to barely one thousand feet over the trees and then there's a flash of white and orange draped atop the jungle. We roar by and can hear our own jet noise when Avenger calls, "Is that you Condor? Two guys just went overhead."

"Rog Avenger, we've got your chute and a good fix on

your position. Stay right where you are if possible. We've got the Jolly just a few minutes out. We're going to try to spot Bravo now." We ease up a little bit and start to orbit east of the chute.

"Mayday. Mayday. This is Avenger Three Bravo. Does anyone copy?" It's taken a few minutes longer, but now we've got the backseater on the radio.

"Hello Bravo, this is Condor. We've got you five-by. How you doing?" Frank wants to get another transmission to home on the second crewman. It's hard to follow the needle on the DF and maneuver our jets in tight enough turns to really fix a position, but the more info we can give the Sandy Lead when he gets here, the more likely we'll have a successful pickup.

The A-1s arrive on the scene sooner than we expected, so we'll have enough gas to help them if they need some strafing. I can tell by our fuel state that Major Frank has already decided that we'll recover at Ubon rather than return to Korat. We'll stay overhead as long as we possibly can. Frank briefs the Sandy and gives him a detailed description of the position of the two downed crewmen. We ease up above eight thousand feet to stay out of the way and maybe save some fuel.

Sandy spots the backseat pilot and calls that the helicopter will pick him up first. The Jolly Green comes into the area, and it seems like only seconds before he's asking the survivor to pop a smoke. We can see the bright orange cloud drifting out of the treetops. There's little wind, and it looks like an easy pickup until a 23-mm cannon hidden on the edge of a nearby field opens fire. It looks as though they've been waiting for the slow-moving chopper to come along. The two A-1s roll in on the gun and fire their 2.75-inch rockets, trying to stop the gun as the helicopter hovers over the downed pilot. To us in our jets it seems like seconds but for the Jolly crew it must be an eternity until Bravo is on the penetrator and being winched aboard. The helicopter moves forward and starts to the location where we've spotted the frontseat pilot. It will be over in just a few minutes now. Then the radio crackles and we hear, "Hey guys, this is Jolly One-One. I've apparently taken a hit in the transmission. I'm gonna have to put this bear down right away. It looks like there's an open field ahead."

We can see the huge helicopter trailing a thin gray line of smoke as he descends straight ahead into a clearing. The second helicopter has come in from the west and is almost in formation as the first Jolly touches down. We watch as one figure in a flying suit comes running down the ramp at the back of the chopper then races across the hundred yards separating the two rescue birds. Then five more figures emerge and make the run. Orbiting overhead we can't tell if there is gunfire or silence as we watch the scenario unfold. The A-1s have passed over the field and circled back now to fall into formation on each side of the backup Jolly as he lifts off. Without a moment's hesitation he heads toward the second survivor.

Jolly Green One-Two hovers over the chute and in less than two minutes snags Alpha and gets him into the chopper. From our high station we relay the information to Crown, the rescue command post. The helicopter is outbound and it looks as though we've had a win for the home team. Then Crown has one more request. "Condor or Sandy, this is Crown. We've got word from Seventh Air Force that we need to do something about that downed Jolly. Can either of you get back in there and destroy it so that the classified radios and stuff don't get recovered by the bad guys?"

I look at my fuel gauge and see that we're down below two thousand pounds, which will just get us to Ubon. We won't be doing any strafing now. Before we can respond Sandy 31 acknowledges that he and his wingman will destroy the helicopter. Major Frank and I start a turn to the southwest and climb out to head for Ubon. Then we get one last radio call. We can't believe what we hear, and there's not a thing we can do. We're out of gas, and it is done. A quivering voice reports to Crown, "This is Sandy Three-Two; Sandy Three-One has crashed while strafing the Jolly. No chute, no beeper, no survivor."[2]

We land at Ubon and do a quick debrief while our jets are refueled for the short flight back to Korat. It's inevitable that we ask at the command post what happened to the rest of Avenger flight. The intelligence sergeant can't offer any insight into their actions other than to note that they reported the loss of Avenger Three in the target area. Frank and I don't talk about it, but as we walk silently back out to the flight line we're both thinking about the events of the last two hours. We've seen good men reach deep to do remarkable things to save a brother warrior. And we've seen one man die today. We don't know if it was a lucky shot by an enemy gunner or a momentary lapse in concentration by an emotionally drained pilot that caused the loss of Sandy 31. We'll never know. One thing we do know, however, is that we've again seen that there are fighter pilots and pilots who simply fly fighters.

2. Avenger 3 was out of the 433rd TFS at Ubon. The pilot Maj. L. Breckenridge was recovered uninjured. The backseater, 1st Lt. J. E. Merrick was recovered with minor injuries. The A-1E pilot was Capt. D. R. Wagener (KIA). The events took place on 20 October 1966.

CHAPTER 17

Endgame

For most of the summer we'd been regularly flying Iron Hand missions. The handful of Wild Weasel birds that had survived the first few weeks of their deployment had been going downtown every day supporting the strikes in the Red River Delta. We had barely enough of the specialized airplanes to fill the daily schedule, but they had demonstrated such effectiveness that no one wanted to enter SAM territory without them. Single-seat D-models accompanied them on every sortie, usually with the number two airplane carrying a pair of Shrike missiles and the element loaded with CBU-24, cluster bomb units. The Weasels were always "first in, last out," leading the way, shielding the first flight of bombers, flying as a barrier between the strike force and the most likely source of launches, then scouring the area near the target for missile sites and finally trailing the last bomb droppers back out.

There were no bad Weasels. The quality of leadership reflected the fact that this initial group of specialists had been handpicked volunteers, all with lots of experience in the airplane and many with prior missions as strike pilots. They were quick to learn what worked and what didn't, and they were continually engaged in a game of cat and mouse with the enemy gunners. As quickly as the Weasels would take advantage of the classic sequence of radar emissions to find and destroy radar vans and missile launchers, the bad guys would devise a new way of gaining the necessary targeting info for their weapons without disclosing their position. Move and countermove, each side trying to gain an advantage over the other with the prize being life for another day and the penalty of loss being death or an indefinite period of imprisonment.

We learned that the Fan Song radar could detect a Shrike being fired, which tipped the enemy to turn off the radar and deny our missile a source to guide on. The Vietnamese developed a technique of feeding initial guidance info to the SA-2 from early warning radars, then firing their missile and turning on the guidance signal only after the weapon was airborne. We countered by attacking more sites visually, following the smoke trail of the missile back to its source then peppering the area with canisters of CBU. The air-bursting dispensers would scatter six hundred baseball-sized bomblets over the entire missile site. On impact the bomblets would explode, spreading shrapnel pellets at rifle-bullet velocity throughout the area, penetrating the thin skins of radar vans, missiles, and SAM operators with equal effectiveness.

Everyone in the squadron had a turn in the barrel. When we got to fly with the Shrikes, we learned a lot about the electronic environment of the war. The APR-25/26, with its flashing warning lights and buzzing missile tones, had been enlightening, but the Shrike raised the awareness to an entirely new level. The RHAW gear presented processed signals detected by antennae on the aircraft, then interpreted by a small electronic box, and finally displayed in condensed format on the TDU and vector scope. The Shrike, on the other hand, was the real deal, no middleman involved. The missile-seeker head received radar signals and dumped them to us immediately as pure audio. The beeps and buzzes were just like listening to the local DJ on the radio, except that it wasn't the latest in rock and roll music you were hearing. It was the entire air defense system of North Vietnam looking for you, finding you, and measuring your location precisely, then locking onto you and collecting information for a weapon that was going to come to kill you. The ultimate crescendo of the hit parade was the guidance signal that was directing the guns or the SAM. It was often a whole lot more than you wanted to know, and it was a bit disconcerting to realize how much was going on around you electronically that you were unaware of, even with the RHAW gear.

The Shrike linked information about its own capability to reach a radar target directly to the aircraft's attitude indicator by presenting directional cues through the pitch and bank steering bars. The missile could be lofted to reach longer range targets, fired level, or even pointed down to stuff a little present right down the radar operator's antenna when you got close. The Weasels would explain that you needed to visualize a "basket" over the target. From a distance you would be shooting from three-point range, as you got closer you could easily lob the missile into the basket, and when you were really hot, you could jam it from above the rim. The pitch and bank steering bars guided you to turn left or right, pull up or pitch down. Follow the bouncing needles and see who lives longer, you or the guy trying to shoot you. It was an exciting game.

We'd learned a surprising lesson about survivability during the hundred-mission tour. Although we knew that the first ten missions were deadly because of fear, lack of experience, and unfamiliarity with the whole pattern of the war, we were more surprised to learn that the last ten missions were almost equally as dangerous. There were several things going on as we got near the end of the tour. For some there was an increase in timidity that could be just as dangerous as early mission fear. You'd come so far and gone through so much that you started being just a wee bit more careful. That led to indecision and apprehension and those could be dangerous. With the end in reach, it wouldn't do to hang it out too far.

There were other guys who felt an uncontrollable need to get in their last licks. With only a few missions to go, they felt pushed to end the war on their terms. Press a little harder, stay a little longer, drop a little lower, do a bit more damage. Either way, the stats showed that the worst parts of the tour were the first ten and the last ten. Schedulers tried to ease off for guys in the home stretch. If the daily frag allowed, they would try to slip high timers into Skyspots, or Pack I road recce sorties, the kinds of missions that didn't take you into SAM and MiG country but which still were counters. Some guys asked that the rule be ignored, while others hovered over the scheduler's desk repeatedly reminding him that they were in the sanctuary zone. I chose to simply chew on the inside of my cheek and keep my mouth shut. I'd take what came my way.

Stories of guys getting shot down with mission counts in the high nineties raised lots of superstitions. No one was going to get a new flying suit or change a G-suit during their nineties. If you wore red socks, you kept doing it. If you zipped the left leg of the G-suit first, you didn't change the pattern. It was out of the question to request a port call for transportation back to the States and, even though you might have an assignment back in the world, you weren't about to do even the first step of out-processing. You didn't pay your club bill early, didn't close out your supply account, didn't bring your B-4 bag out of the back of the closet, didn't even clean the papers off the top of your desk. Until number one hundred was in the log book, it was business as usual, no future after today, no plans beyond the next mission. It was simply the prudent thing to do.

All the guys in my class out of Nellis had assignments. Richter was waiting for approval for his second hundred. He fit the pattern of guys trying to get in their best work before they finished. He wanted to win the war and hurt the enemy badly, and until he got the word that his extension was going through, he was fudging his flight records, logging missions into North Vietnam as noncounter Laos sorties. He'd been hovering between ninety-six and ninety-eight missions for nearly ten days. His friends were ambivalent about his goals. We wanted him to get what he wanted and do what he loved, but we knew instinctively that it wasn't a good thing.

Hackford, Harvey, Hallmark, and I all had assignments back to Air Training Command to be T-38 instructors in undergraduate pilot training. Spelius and Pete Foley were going to Air Defense Command, Spider to fly F-101s and Foley to the jazzy F-104 squadron just outside Miami. Bill Ricks would fly the 105 at Kadena, Okinawa, and Nels Running was headed to Williams in the F-5 training squadron that taught foreign military pilots how to fly the tiny Northrop aircraft. In general we were all reasonably happy with our follow-on assignments. All we had to do was finish the hundred.

The squadron was going through another cycle of change. Just as so many of the McConnell troops had finished their tours in a cluster, now six months later there was another changing of the guard. The lieutenants and the senior guys from Europe and Nellis who had survived so far were wrapping up the count. The new guys replacing us were older; most were coming through the high production short course. There weren't going to be any more recent UPT grads for the foreseeable future. Experienced F-105 pilots were also still flowing through the pipeline. If there were someone in the Air Force with an F-105 rating who hadn't yet been to the war, they were living on borrowed time. They were coming and it would be soon. For now, the experience level was going through another cycle. High timers were on the way out and new guys with a deer-in-the-headlights look in their eyes were showing up each day.

It was time. It was the final mission. I had ninety-nine hash marks on the band of my jungle hat, starting at the right front and winding around almost to the back. Buried in the reddish Korat dust clinging to the sweat-stained areas at the far end of the line on the back of the band, I had ten more hash marks reflecting the ten noncounter missions to Laos. I'd drawn a couple of the marks in red rather than black to signify the days that were just a bit more intense than they should have been. Now, it was the fourth quarter, two-minute warning, and time to try to draw that last diagonal that would make the whole set add up to a magical one hundred.

Spider Spelius, Bill Ricks, and I were all up for the big one. We'd each finished ninety-nine, and Wimpy thought it would make the schedule look better if we all flew the final trip together. The one place where three guys could easily fit into the schedule was on a Weasel sortie. We had a couple of strike flights on the squadron's frag, but it didn't seem fair to detract from our big mission by putting someone else from the squadron in our flight. We got penciled in to Hotrod flight, an Iron Hand sortie escorting a strike package against an oil storage area and shipment center at Viet Tri, a hot spot just up the Red River from Hanoi. It was a Pack VI mission, but just barely. Viet Tri was only a few miles across the dividing line from Pack V, out in the flats and definitely within the SAM defenses, but getting to the target required only a short dash across open country and then a few moments of terror returning to the safety of the hills. For us, a lot depended on how the Weasel handled the job. We could find ourselves out in the middle of the delta in the classic Dr. Pepper scenario with missiles at ten, two, and four o'clock, or we might simply hover in the shadow of the mountains and dash out into the flats only if the SAMs began to seriously threaten the strike force. There was a whole bunch of ambivalence in how we viewed what we were going to be asked to do. We didn't want to wait any longer to get our hundredth mission, but we weren't sure if being up at the pointy end of the spear for as long as required on a Weasel mission was a really good idea either. No one was going to mention a word about ten mission sanctuaries to Wimpy. It was the schedule. We would fly it.

The Weasel was John Hill, a soft-spoken guy with a steady confidence that made you feel that he wasn't going to get you killed as long as you did the job. He wasn't going to get you killed if he was protecting you from SAMs while you dropped bombs, and he wasn't going to get you killed if you were a lieutenant flying his wing as he did his job of zapping SAM sites. He didn't need to say it. You simply knew that he wasn't going to get you killed. In fact, you knew that he had no control over whether you were going to get killed or not. You hoped he wouldn't get you killed, and you believed that he wouldn't do anything stupid. Would bravery be stupid? We wouldn't know for a while.

Spider flew number two and carried a pair of Shrikes. He would have to listen to the high intensity whistle and squeals for three hours or as long as he still had the missiles aboard.

Ricks flew Three, and I flew on his wing. We each had a half-dozen Mk-82s fused for instantaneous detonation, right at ground level for maximum shrapnel effect on the SAM sites we might attack. The weather was briefed as good in the tanker tracks and deteriorating as we would proceed farther north and east. The early morning weather recce flight across the Red River Delta had found the area with broken clouds then a solid undercast over most of Laos. We didn't care if anyone got to the target or not on this particular day. All we needed was to poke a nose across the North Vietnam border and come home with a counter. Nothing more.

We were supporting flights from the 469th, the 13th, and from our own squadron. Major Begley was leading the 421st bomber flight with a new arrival from the short course, Maj. Bob Cline, on his wing. His element had Maj. Ken Whittemore leading Capt. Bob Loken. Whittemore had the high mission count for the foursome, and Loken was the most capable aviator, despite having spent most of his Air Force career as a bomber pilot. Cline was too new in the unit for anyone to know much about his capabilities. And, of course, everyone knew Magoo.

The weather was exactly as advertised, at least over Laos. From the tankers we could look down and see a fluffy white blanket covering the landscape, shielding the emerald jungle and rocky karst from view. Flat and level, it stretched from horizon to horizon. Far to the north, however, the weather looked like it might be different. There were higher clouds and slashes of sunlight through the murk. There appeared to be an end to the undercast far ahead of us that might allow the force to get through to the target. We dropped off the tankers and headed northward. Hotrod flight hedged to the right of the inbound track, forming a shield from the SAM sites that were already beginning to light up the RHAW. Anything fired at the bomb droppers would have to get through us. We'd play missile catcher all the way in and, if we could, we'd turn on anyone with the audacity to challenge us and dump capitalist iron on their commie missile site.

By the time we got to the Black, it was clear ahead but dark below us. Scattered clouds to the west got gradually thicker, larger, and darker as we scanned from left to right. To the east of us, out over the delta, rain squalls were dumping on the villages and rice paddies. Whether Viet Tri would be open for bombing business when we arrived was unknown. Hotrod dropped lower and started nosing toward a familiar SAM location between Viet Tri and Phu Tho, along the banks of the Red. Site batteries got moved around a lot, and a site occupied yesterday would seldom be occupied tomorrow. We knew the guy had fired in the past, but we had no way of telling if he'd come up against us today.

We had another site listed on our maps beyond the target area, just short of Phuc Yen. Hotrod would troll through the area as bait to distract the defenses while our running backs came through the middle, carrying the ball to the target. If anyone came up to challenge us, we'd attack. Spider was up nearly line-abreast with Hotrod Lead, maneuvering less than a thousand feet off his wing, ready to fire a Shrike if Hill should need it. Ricks and I stayed offset about 30 degrees from the lead element and about six thousand feet out — far enough back to see a target that had shot at the Weasel and still have enough room to maneuver to bomb it.

The first flight, from the 469th, called that they couldn't get to the target. The bad weather was directly over Viet Tri and there was no way to operate under the rain squall. They were heading back up the Red River to look for targets along the road and railroad that paralleled the river. One down and two to go. We could be on our way as soon as the other two flights called outbound.

The second flight called that they also were diverting. With barely a pause, we heard Magoo announce that his flight was aborting the run on Viet Tri as well. Hotrod Lead advised the strikers that we'd clear behind them and follow them up the Red providing cover from any threats. We turned the flight toward the northwest and circled back outbound. We were over Phu Tho and everything was quiet. Nothing but an occasional buzz of a Fire Can. No SAMs.

It didn't take long before everyone had dropped their ordnance but Magoo's flight. They were working their way up the northwest railroad, looking for targets to expend on. There were plenty of road intersections and rail bridges along the way, crossing creeks and streams draining into the Red so it shouldn't have taken long. Hotrod was wisely leading us around to the south of Yen Bai, hugging the mountains along the southwest side of the valley. Whether they were the target or not, the folks at Yen Bai always seemed to be manning their guns and always had time to throw up a flak barrage. It was a good place to avoid.

Begley's voice came over the radio announcing that he had spotted a train, and the guys should come around first for bombs and then to strafe. A chill ran down my spine. I wasn't positive but based on timing and where we had all been throughout the mission, it was very likely that Begley was leading his flight into an attack on a notorious flak trap. The burned out hulk of a locomotive had been parked on a rail siding up the river from Yen Bai for as long as I'd been at Korat. A nest of 37- and 57-mm guns surrounded the area, all focused on the dive angles that flights would use to attack. It was a big rat trap with a train for bait. I hoped I was wrong.

Hotrod maneuvered along the valley's south side, scoping out the river valley and watching for emissions from radars that would signal SAMs or guns. We heard Begley's flight call in on their bomb passes and then call in for strafe. It took only seconds, then Loken called off the target. "Cobalt Four is hit. I'm climbing out southbound with a fire light."

Whittemore was right there. "Cobalt Four, Cobalt Three has you in sight. Continue climbing. I'll catch up in just a second." We heard nothing from Cobalt Lead or Two. Whittemore continued to update Loken, "Cobalt Four, you're trailing smoke and it looks like a bit of flame from the tail section."

Hill waited for a break in the transmissions, then jumped in. "Cobalt Four, Hotrod's nearby and we've still got ordnance. We'll stay with you as long as you need." We all started scanning the sky ahead, looking for the slightest sign of Cobalt Four. Ricks got the visual first. Cobalt Four was about ten miles ahead and climbing slowly, a dark dot with a wispy gray smoke trail, silhouetted against the clouds on the horizon.

"Cobalt Four's got the AB going now. I've had an explosion and I've got a main airline overheat. The AC generator's off and PC-1 hydraulics are zero. I don't know how long she'll stick together." We'd learned early on that the main engine didn't know or care whether the afterburner was going. As long as fuel was available and air was flowing through the engine, even if it was flamed out, the AB would keep pushing, and it might make the difference in getting to a safe bailout area. We had no doubt that Loken would be bailing out. Even at our distance we could see flame trailing from his airplane.

Ahead of Bob, the clouds began over Laos. He could bail out farther north than he might want but have clear sky overhead for a rescue, or he could proceed south, hoping the airplane would sustain him long enough to get to Thailand. Bailing out into the solid cloud deck beneath would mean that rescue forces wouldn't be able to find him until clear weather moved in. It was his call, and pulling the ejection handles wasn't easy without first exhausting every option.

"It looks solid ahead, guys. I'm going to have to get out before I get over that stuff. You with me, Cobalt Three?" It sounded as though he had decided. Whittemore acknowledged that he was there off Bob's right wing. "Okay, here goes. Wish me luck."

Hotrod pressed toward the ejection scene. We could see the flaming aircraft clearly now, tumbling end over end, then pinwheeling, and finally breaking up just before it hit the jungle floor. Just to the west of the airplane we could see Loken's chute, incredibly small, descending slowly. Hill asked Whittemore if he had gas to stay overhead, or if he wanted to head out to a tanker while we capped Cobalt Four. Ken needed gas, so he headed out. Hotrod flight began orbiting the descending chute.

When Cobalt was first hit, the call went out on guard channel to get the rescue forces headed north. A pair of Jolly Greens and a flight of A-1s had been on airborne alert near Channel 85, a remote mountaintop TACAN station in Laos, almost at the North Vietnam border. Guiding the Sandys in while we had a visual on the parachute was easy. We watched Loken descend on the jungle, and we called out co-ordinates and TACAN bearings to bring the rescuers close. It took about ten minutes for Bob to descend, each minute bringing the rescuers nearer. The decision to eject prior to overflying the cloud deck was a good one, even if he didn't make it voluntarily.

When Loken hit the trees, we all tried to spot a ground reference that we could use to keep track of exactly where he was. Sandy One-One was on the scene now, and the Jolly was only minutes behind. John Hill moved Hotrod flight up into a higher orbit to stay clear and save gas. If we were needed, we still had the bombs. Loken had his survival radio out and was eager to talk.

"Sandy, Sandy, this is Cobalt Four."

"Roger, Cobalt. You've got Sandy One-One overhead. Jolly's about five minutes out. What's your status?"

"Roger Sandy. I'm hung up in a tree."

We were getting low on gas, particularly Ricks and me. We were still hauling bombs and the weight and drag took a toll. Hotrod Lead asked Sandy if we could head out to a tanker. With the Sandy overhead, we could still react quickly even if we were halfway to the tanker, and if the rescue got more complicated, we would be better able to support if we had more fuel. Sandy 11 agreed that we ought to go for fuel.

Hotrod headed southbound to the tanker, listening on the way to what sounded like a Bob Newhart comedy routine. We quickly lost the ability to hear the low-powered survival radio from the ground, so we only heard the Sandy talking to Bob. He would repeat what Loken said before answering each time, giving the impression of one of those stand-up acts where the comedian simulates a phone conversation.

"Roger, understand, you're in a tree. What can you see?"

"Rog, you're on the top of a hill looking down at a village."

"Okay, do you see any people? You do see people. What are they doing?"

"They're wearing black pajamas and carrying guns? Right, they've got guns."

"No, I don't know if they're friendly. We've got both kinds in this area. Have they seen you yet?"

"They've seen you. No, I don't know if they're friendly. What are they doing now?"

"They're walking up the hill toward you. I don't know any way to tell if they are friendly or not. How close are they?"

"They're right next to you? What are they doing?"

"They're shaking your hand? Okay, they're friendly."

"They want you to come with them? I'd try to avoid that. They're pointing at the village? Can you stay on the hill?"

"Okay, I guess you've got to go with them. Keep your radio. We'll have the Jolly overhead in just a few minutes."

We cruised southbound listening to the incredible dialogue, hoping that things would work out and that it wasn't simply a ruse to hide the captured pilot somewhere from the rescue forces that were even now overhead. The tanker was just a few miles ahead and we had to leave the frequency for refueling. Hill led the flight into position and slid quickly onto the welcoming boom. Spider, Ricks, and I rode steadily in formation on the tanker's right wing. Hill came off and Spelius dropped back then eased forward to start taking gas. He'd been on the boom for less than two minutes when we got a radio call from Crown. It was good news. Loken was safe and in the Jolly. The rescue was terminated. We were all released to go home. Spider dropped off the boom, full of fuel. Ricks slid back off the wing and smoothly rolled into position behind the boom.

"Uhhh, Hotrod, this is White Three-Five. We've got orders to head home. We won't be able to give you any more gas. The rescue is terminated, survivor's in the chopper, and we aren't authorized to pass any more fuel."

"Okay White Three-Five, understand, but could you just spare a couple of thousand pounds each for my number Three and Four?" Hill was looking out for us.

"That's a negative, Hotrod. We've been ordered to suspend refueling operations and RTB, can't do anything for you. Sorry."

We were in a sticky situation. Lead and Two were full of gas, while Ricks and I were sitting with low fuel and a load of bombs still hung from the centerline. Hill dropped back from the tanker, rocked us into close formation and flashed four fingers at us, displayed horizontally, the signal to switch to radio channel nine. We switched and checked in on Lion control. "Hotrod ops check, Lead has fourteen thousand," was the first radio call.

"Two's fourteen five," was Spider's call.

Ricks indicated he had three thousand, and I had twenty-five hundred pounds of gas. We needed to make a run across the controlled jettison range at Udorn to dump the bombs before we could land anywhere. Hill asked Lion to vector us to the dump.

The pass was simple and efficient. We were directed by radar, just like an instrument approach, to line the flight up over a safe area to drop the bombs without hurting people or property. We had to go low and slow to ensure the accuracy of the run and that was costing us valuable gas. The smart thing to do after the jettison run was to land at Udorn to refuel. With bombs off, Hill called the flight over to our squadron frequency. "Okay, guys, I know Three and Four are short of gas. It's your last mission. What do you want to do?"

Spider said he had plenty of gas, so it was up to us. Ricks said he thought he could make it. I looked at the gas gauge and saw fourteen hundred pounds remaining. I said, "The party's at Korat. Let's go home." Hill nodded his assent and eased the throttle forward. We started a climbout toward Korat.

Level at eighteen thousand feet, I had eight hundred pounds left. Minimum fuel for a safe landing when you were in the traffic pattern was fifteen hundred pounds. At one thousand pounds you were supposed to declare emergency fuel to ensure traffic priority. We were eighty miles north of Korat. I declared emergency fuel.

It's easier on the gas to lead than to fly wing. You don't

need to move the throttle as much and you can concentrate on being smooth. Hill realigned the flight, putting me in the lead, with Ricks flying Two. Spelius flew Three, and the two-seater flew the number Four position. I concentrated on milking the altitude down, smoothly translating every foot of descent into the maximum forward movement. While Ricks and I nursed our gas, Hill and Spider were in after-burner with the speed brakes extended, trying to burn off enough fuel to get down to landing weight. It was just one more incredible image in a totally ludicrous war.

The Korat approach controller acknowledged my emer-gency fuel state, and asked if we would like to be broken up for individual straight-in approaches, the most economical way to get on the ground. I said, no thank you, we were going to fly a four-ship down initial. The controller quietly ac-knowledged my choice and probably began preparing his de-fense for the court-martial that would ask him why he let two emergency-fuel jets fly an overhead pattern.

We turned initial for runway 06. I hit the break with four hundred pounds remaining. Gear and flaps down, then roll into the base turn at 220 knots. Two hundred pounds of fuel remaining as I approach final. There's no go-around, there can be no overshoot, I can't screw it up and neither can Ricks. I roll out and slow to 190. I set down on the left side of the runway with a wisp of tire smoke and pull the drag chute. I can see Ricks's airplane in my right rearview mirror as he touches down behind me. I roll out and clear the runway. We're all home. We're all alive.

Hotrod flight pulls out of the de-arming area and onto the long parallel taxiway back to parking. Ahead of us half a dozen trucks are on the taxiway. The lead truck has a huge flag unfurled in the back with that red, white, and blue one-hundred-mission patch shield on a bright red background. There's a fire truck with lights flashing and the siren going loud enough that I can hear it over the sound of my own en-gine. Guys from the squadron and the intel shop and mainte-nance are in the back of the various trucks, some are waving orange smoke flares. I move over to the left side of the taxiway and let Ricks come up parallel on the right. A glance in my canopy mirror shows Hill and Spelius paired up close behind us on the taxiway. I give Ricks the finger and he nods and we both reach down and pull the handle to extend our refueling probes. We give the world the finger. We've done it. We've finished one hundred missions.

The trucks lead us to a cleared spot on the ramp where the four airplanes move into parking position side-by-side. A wave down the line of jets and all four engines are chopped simultaneously and the sudden silence is overwhelming. Tech Sergeant Church is there with the ladder, and the first one up is Bill Loyd with a bottle of champagne and a handshake. I tell him about Loken's rescue, and he lets me know that Bob Cline is missing. Begley came home alone and doesn't know where or when his lost wingman disappeared. Cobalt had lost two airplanes, not one.

Loyd moves on to congratulate the other two lieutenants. One of the maintenance officers comes up the ladder to shake my hand. I ask him if he has ever seen an airplane with so little fuel remaining that the gauge doesn't move off zero when the battery is turned on and off. Later that night he will tell me that out of curiosity he had the fuel sump drained and got only ten pounds of JP-4 out of the bird. Less than a gallon and a half. Maybe another thirty seconds of engine running time remained.

Sergeant Leonard from the parachute shop meets me at the foot of the ladder with a new flying suit, adorned for the first time since I've been a member of the 421st with a squadron patch, and on the left shoulder, incredibly, there's that shield. The one-hundred-mission patch is mine. I let him take my parachute, then I zip out of my survival vest and G-suit. I shrug out of my sweat-soaked flight suit and pull on the new suit. Willing hands pick up my gear and throw it in the back of one of the pickups. All I've got to carry is my champagne bottle. I take a moment to look back at the airplane. It's still beautiful. Big, brutish, and powerful. I've flown my last flight in an F-105. I'll never again climb up that ladder and step into that now familiar cockpit. It's a bittersweet moment.

Debrief is quick, with John Hill volunteering to take care of the paperwork and other details while Spider, Ricks, and I pose for pictures in front of the squadron building. My face hurts from smiling and laughing so much. The three of us are giddy, shaking people's hands, and patting each other on the back. For the first time in six months we are certain that we will live through tomorrow. And the day after that. We've finished.

The following night there is a gathering at the club. It isn't a formal dinner, simply a few drinks around tables pushed together in the bar. The guests of honor, the one-hundred-mission lieutenants get to ring the bell several times and buy for the assemblage, a packed house with an incredible number of people crushing into the bar. It is money very willingly and eagerly spent.

Loken is already back at Korat and regaling the group with tales of his encounter with the citizens of the North Vietnamese village. They had taken him down the hill, shaking his hand and patting him on the back. Clearly more capitalist than communist, they had offered him several drinks of their local home brew in the few minutes before the rescue chopper appeared overhead. As payment for their hospitality, he'd left his gun, chute, G-suit, and survival vest with them, taking only his radios to ensure they wouldn't fall into enemy hands and be used to decoy rescue forces on future missions. He confessed to being somewhat tipsy by the time the chopper snatched him up. The local moonshine was pretty good, he admitted, but he was glad he didn't have to endure it for more than a few drinks.

Afterward, at the squadron dining table, Major Tracy congratulates us and Major Loyd presents each of us with a squadron plaque. A brass shield on a polished teak base, engraved with an outline of Southeast Asia, and with a small silver plate acknowledging one hundred missions flown over North Vietnam from 3 May to 3 November 1966. As he speaks, however, Loyd cautions us that while we in the 421st know what the plaque means, few others ever will. We who have been together know what one hundred missions over that hellacious jungle and river delta cost, but we should not expect that our wives, family, and friends will know or understand it. We take our plaques and sip our drinks and thank our God that we are alive. We would worry about whether anyone else understood it much later.

As I'm packing the next morning in our room, Bill Ricks brings a small book out of his dresser. It's his journal. He's kept a very brief calendar for the six months we've been at Korat, each day simply marking down the losses of F-105s. Simple lines, entered in a table, but each one indicates a change in a man's life. Some are rescues, some are deaths, and some are imprisonments. Some of the lines mean that there are widows and orphans somewhere back home. Some mean years of pain and loneliness that lie ahead for friends and families. Each tiny black mark in the diary has a story behind it. Bill counts them up, slowly turning the pages. He turns to me and announces that we've lost more than 100 percent of the airplanes assigned to Korat. We've lost a whole wing, four squadrons worth of F-105s in just six months. The flow of replacements has kept us in operation, but the magnitude of the numbers is stunning. We look at each other and say nothing.

Two days later I was on my way back to the States on a Pan-Am flight out of Bangkok. Spelius was on the same flight, and John Casper had finally gotten orders to return home as well. The three of us spent a night in the bars of Bangkok and then boarded the airplane to return to the real world with three very real and intense hangovers. We stopped at every airport on the Pacific Rim going home. First Saigon, then Clark in the Philippines, Okinawa next, then Tokyo, finally Anchorage, Alaska, and then Travis Air Force Base in California. We watched the sun rise and set three times on the flight and gagged down three of those burned TV dinners. When we got to Travis at nine o'clock at night, we had a plan.

We all had flights out of San Francisco early the next morning. We'd rent a car at the Travis terminal, head into

'Frisco, catch a dinner, and hit a bar or two then check into the airport by dawn. Back in the States. It was great. We walked up to the Hertz counter. We asked for a car. The clerk checked our driver's licenses. "Sorry," he said, "you guys are too young." Right. Among the three of us we've got 226 missions over North Vietnam, three ejections, two Silver Stars, five Distinguished Flying Crosses, twenty-three Air Medals, three Purple Hearts, and we're still too young to rent a car.

We wound up taking a cab and sleeping curled up in plastic chairs in the airport waiting for dawn, when the coffee shops would open up and we could get breakfast. Loyd was right, no one understood.

CHAPTER 18

"We Have Met the Enemy and He Is Us"
— *Pogo Possum*

Karl Richter died six months later on what was officially his 198th mission over North Vietnam. Leading a two-ship into the familiar area of Route Pack I, Karl took a hit on a dive-bomb pass and was forced to eject. During the ejection he suffered compound fractures of both legs. An intense rescue effort snatched Karl out of the jungle, but shock and loss of blood were too severe and Karl expired in the chopper. The aircraft that he had bailed out of was 62-4334, the Bat Bird.

Glenn Nix spent six and a half years in captivity in North Vietnam. Burris Begley was shot down and died less than a month after my hundredth mission. Wayne Fullam rode an airplane into the jungle asking with his last words how he could get the nose of the aircraft to come back up after hydraulics were gone. Fred Tracy, Bill Loyd, Wimpy Peake, Bob Loken, Ken Frank, Bob Phillips, Ralph Beardsley, Ken Whittemore, Bob Dundas, and others completed their hundred mission tours.

The losses were appalling. The class of nine that had been six weeks ahead of mine at Nellis lost four. The class that followed me lost five out of nine. The first short course class of "universally assignable" pilots lost fifteen out of sixteen, all either killed or captured. My group of nine had three shot down during the hundred missions but all were recovered successfully and went on to finish. Karl was our only loss, and that was on his second tour. The *Newsweek* statistic that a 105 pilot was shot down on average once every sixty-five missions was true. For every five pilots that started the tour, three would not complete it.

After Richter died, Pete Foley was the first to go back for a second tour. The war was still going on and it was only appropriate that his airplane bore the name Foley's Folly. Nels Running couldn't stay in the peacetime environment of training pilots in the F-5, so he also returned to the war for a second tour. Bill Ricks, flying the few remaining airplanes in Okinawa, followed the pattern first transitioning to the F-4 Phantom and then heading back to combat. I was no exception. Although I had vowed never to take those risks again, I too had become addicted to the adrenaline rush of stealing hubcaps. I returned to Korat, flying the F-4E, hitting the same targets, drinking and eating at the same club, with the same bartender, and living in a hootch less than forty yards from the one I had been in during my first tour, six years earlier.

No one had to go back. Under the Air Force policy of "no involuntary second tours," we could have stayed in peacetime jobs indefinitely, but we were drawn back into the war strictly by our own choice. We rationalized as best we could, citing patriotism and the MacArthur mantra of "duty, honor, country." But by the time we returned, we knew that patriotism had nothing to do with it. Our country had demonstrated quite clearly what it thought of the war and the people who fought it. There was no desire to win the war and there was no identification of national interest in Southeast Asia. We looked around and saw a generation of long-haired, slogan-chanting hippies, concerned exclusively with themselves and unwilling to undergo the discomforts of defending their country. The prevailing philosophy was expectation, not obligation. The function of society was to meet the needs of the weak, providing food, clothing, shelter, drugs, and sex by taxing the evil, wealthy rich and distributing to the poor, peace-loving masses. If there were ever a threat to the Republic, someone else would defend us. Hell no, they wouldn't go. But we went anyway. In truth, we loved it.

Ask the man on the street what a fighter pilot is, and he's liable to look at you blankly. He may offer a Hollywood view of John Wayne in *Flying Leathernecks* or Robert Mitchum in *The Hunters*. It could be that he's heard of McConnell or Bong, Jabara or Gabreski. Maybe he's heard of some folks from the Vietnam years like Ritchie or Madden or Olds. But press the guy for a description of a fighter pilot and he'll probably draw heavily on stereotypes. Give him some help with a list of attributes and it's a sure bet that you'll get things like brave, patriotic, young, fit, and daring. You may also get traits like arrogant, obnoxious, conceited, and cocky. Whichever answer you get is partially right and partially wrong.

Fighter pilots come in all sizes and shapes. Some are young, some old. There are sons and husbands, fathers and grandfathers flying tactical aircraft. They span the spectrum from brave to cowardly, from skilled to inept. Some are eager warriors, and some are reluctant. Chance and the luck of the draw bring them together. They may fly high performance aircraft for years and never face the challenges of combat, or they may be thrust into war continually throughout their careers. Regardless of when, where, why, or how, they fight when asked to on behalf of their country. They deserved much better than they got.

It's thirty-five years since that summer of '66, and the view of the war today is only slightly clearer than it was then. We don't know yet why we were there or what the objective was. We can't define a national self-interest for involvement in Southeast Asia, nor has anyone told us why we squandered such a valuable treasure of manpower and machines. We should know, but we don't. Many attempts have been made to explain it all, but they're either self-serving excuses posing as the memoirs of the senior decision makers or detailed rationales for pacifism by professors who opposed the war and taught their students to think the same way. As with so much of history, the explanation depends on the observer's particular perspective rather than the facts at hand.

Looking at the various levels of involvement in Rolling Thunder, we can see the lieutenants doing what was asked of them without question. We trusted our leaders and our senior decision makers to give us a mission with a purpose. They had a moral obligation not to waste our lives without meaning. They would decide when war was necessary and what we had to do to win it. In return for that, we would risk our lives and do the job. We would fly and fight because, as the sign in the Korat briefing room reminded us daily, that was the mission of the United States Air Force. All we asked was that we be allowed to win.

The captains and majors had the benefit of experience. Some had been in Korea and faced the challenge of overcoming their fears in that earlier war, but all of them had the hours of flying time that helped them handle the tasks thrust upon them. They fought and died, doing the job that they had been asked to do. They led the trusting lieutenants, sometimes competently, and sometimes reaching too far. Occasionally they failed, but they did the best they could.

The colonels and the generals were the failures. They let us down by failing to challenge our country's political leadership. They had an obligation to follow the orders of the duly elected administration, but they needed to demand clear tasking and reasonable rules under which to conduct the war. It's too easy to attribute the mismanagement of the war to a timid foreign policy and a reluctance to risk confrontation with the Soviets and Chinese. If one isn't willing to win, then one shouldn't risk defeat. Fighting with no purpose is the true immorality of war because it means you are asking your citizens to die for no reason other than winning the next election or making profits for a major multinational corporation. Dying for one's country is no longer noble when your country doesn't care either way about the outcome, and it becomes a travesty when your war is being waged in conjunction with the latest presidential campaign. Turn it on when you're high in the polls, and turn it off when your richest contributors gather in protest. Several hundred aircrew members languishing in North Vietnam prisons? No problem. They won't be voting, and the majority of people don't think they were doing the right thing anyway.

The obvious enemy that took such a heavy toll on the F-105 force during Rolling Thunder was the North Vietnamese. Armed with an incredible array of defensive weaponry, they fought for their very lives, with no end-of-tour date and little choice in the matter. Their nightly television shows weren't focused on the latest protest march at the university, and the only celebrities protesting the war weren't Vietnamese; they were Americans opposed to their own country's policies. The guns, the SAMs, and the MiGs were the threat, but they weren't the tools of the real enemy.

The real enemy was us, ourselves. We couldn't be beaten by a third-rate country on the other side of the globe, no matter how well equipped and motivated they might be. We could only be beaten by ourselves. You didn't have to be killed by flak or missiles; you could more easily be killed by lack of leadership, flying the wing of a suicidal pilot on a mission from God to defeat world communism single-handedly. You could be killed by an incompetent who shouldn't have been in a fighter cockpit, but who was placed there by a personnel system that thought it was doing the right thing. You could be killed by a wing commander who felt an obligation to put priorities for traffic ahead of common sense in an emergency. You could be killed by a fuel tank that had not been lubricated and was so corroded that it didn't function properly. You could be killed by weapons that didn't function properly or equipment that wasn't reliable. You could be killed by an unrealistic competition with your sister service that placed daily statistics ahead of meaningful missions. You could be killed by a bomb shortage, which couldn't be publicly acknowledged but which put more airplanes with fewer bombs at risk. You could be killed facing a hail of flak for a worthless target. And you could be abandoned by your country, languishing in a POW camp for years, as part of the 1968 presidential campaign. You could die so very many different ways.

But you could also live. You could find yourself capable of things well beyond what you thought you could do. You could learn of fear and coping with it. You could know what bravery looks like and what cowardice costs. You could change in subtle ways that would affect the rest of your life, causing you to stand just a bit taller than you had before and leading you to feel just a bit sorry for those who hadn't gone where you had been.

Appendix

F-105 Combat Theater Losses—April–November 1966

Date	Type	Tail #	Crew	Area
4/15/66	F-105D	58-1158	Capt. J. A. McCurdy	Thailand
4/19/66	F-105D	62-4330	Lt. L. A. Adams	Route Pack 1
4/20/66	F-105D	60-0442	Capt. J. B. Abernathy	RP1
4/22/66	F-105D	62-4409	Capt. C. Boyd	RP6
4/23/66	F-105D	61-0048	Maj. B. J. Goss	RP6
4/23/66	F-105D	61-0157	Capt. R. E. Dyczkowski	RP6
4/24/66	F-105D	61-0051	Lt. C. W. Cooper	RP6
4/24/66	F-105D	62-4340	Lt. J. Driscoll	RP6
4/29/66	F-105D	62-4304	Lt. D. W. Bruch	RP6
5/5/66	F-105D	61-0147	Lt. K. D. Thomas	RP6
5/6/66	F-105D	61-0179	Col. J. Lamar	RP5
5/8/66	F-105D	62-4236	Lt. J. Ray	RP6
5/10/66	F-105D	59-1819	Lt. G. L. Clouser	Laos
5/10/66	F-105D	61-0135	Capt. M. Mahrt	RP5
5/10/66	F-105D	62-4255	Capt. J. E. Bailey	RP1
5/11/66	F-105D	62-4293	Capt. F. J. Feneley	RP1
5/13/66	F-105D	60-0427	Unknown	Thailand
5/15/66	F-105D	61-0174	Capt. R. C. Balcom	RP6
5/22/66	F-105D	58-1164	Lt. R. A. Hackford	Laos
5/25/66	F-105D	59-1746	Lt. Hunter	Laos
5/30/66	F-105D	61-0142	Capt. D. Hatcher	RP5
5/31/66	F-105D	61-0120	Lt. M. W. Steen	RP5
5/31/66	F-105D	62-4386	Lt. L. Eckman	RP5
6/1/66	F-105D	62-4393	Capt. G. H. Peacock	RP1
6/2/66	F-105D	61-0160	Unknown	Thailand
6/3/66	F-105D	58-1171	Capt. R. D. Pielin	RP1
6/7/66	F-105D	61-0168	Capt. J. F. Bayles	RP1
6/8/66	F-105D	62-4273	Maj. J. C. Holley	RP1
6/14/66	F-105D	60-0429	Unknown	Thailand
6/15/66	F-105D	62-4377	Lt. P. J. Kelly	RP1
6/17/66	F-105D	58-1165	Lt. W. C. Spelius	RP1
6/21/66	F-105D	62-4358	Lt. J. B. Sullivan	RP6
6/29/66	F-105D	60-0460	Capt. M. N. Jones	RP6
6/30/66	F-105D	62-4224	Capt. R. K. Nierste	RP6

Continued on next page

F-105 Combat Theater Losses—April–November 1966 (continued)

Date	Type	Tail #	Crew	Area
7/1/66	F-105D	62-4354	Lt. B. Campbell	RP1
7/4/66	F-105D	60-0486	Lt. B. L. Minton	RP1
7/6/66	F-105D	62-4254	Capt. E. L. Stanford	RP1
7/6/66	F-105F	63-8286	Maj. R. Hestle	RP5
			Capt. C. Morgan	
7/7/66	F-105D	59-1741	Capt. J. Tomes	RP5
7/8/66	F-105D	61-0158	Lt. R. Browning	RP6
7/11/66	F-105D	62-4282	Capt. L.. Shattuck	RP6
7/11/66	F-105D	61-0121	Maj W. McClelland	RP6
7/15/66	F-105D	59-1761	Capt. C. L. Hamby	RP6
7/18/66	F-105D	60-0453	Lt. G. H. Comfer	RP4
7/19/66	F-105D	59-1755	Lt. S. Diamond	RP6
7/19/66	F-105D	60-5382	Capt. R. E. Steere	Laos
7/20/66	F-105D	62-4308	Capt. M. R. Lewis	RP6
7/23/66	F-105F	63-8338	Maj. G. Pemberton	RP6
			Maj. B. Newson	
7/25/66	F-105D	62-4271	Maj. F. C. Hiebert	RP6
7/27/66	F-105D	61-0045	Capt. J. Mitchell	RP1
8/1/66	F-105D	62-4380	Capt. K. North	RP6
8/4/66	F-105D	61-0119	Lt. A. Rogers	Laos
8/6/66	F-105D	62-4315	Capt. A. Rutherford	RP6
8/7/66	F-105D	60-0499	Capt. J. Wendall	RP6
8/7/66	F-105D	61-0140	Maj. W. Gideon	RP6
8/7/66	F-105F	63-8358	Capt. Larsen	RP6
			Capt. K. A. Gilroy	
8/8/66	F-105D	61-0155	Lt. J. R. Casper	RP1
8/8/66	F-105D	62-4327	Lt. F. Flom	RP5
8/8/66	F-105D	62-4343	Maj. J. Kasler	RP5
8/8/66	F-105D	62-4370	Lt. M. L. Brazelton	RP6
8/12/66	F-105D	61-0156	Capt. D. Allinson	RP6
8/12/66	F-105D	62-4323	Lt. M. Neuens	RP6
8/14/66	F-105D	59-1763	Capt. C. Eaton	RP6
8/14/66	F-105D	61-0197	Capt. C. Franklin	RP6
8/14/66	F-105D	62-4266	Capt. J. W. Brodak	RP6
8/17/66	F-105F	63-8308	Maj. Brand	RP5
			Maj. Singer	
8/17/66	F-105F	63-8361	Capt. R. Sandvick	RP6
			Capt. T. Pyle	
8/18/66	F-105D	62-4312	Unknown	Thailand
8/20/66	F-105D	62-4308	Capt. M. R. Lewis	RP6
8/21/66	F-105D	59-1770	Capt. N. Wells	RP6
8/23/66	F-105F	63-8338	Maj. G. Pemberton	RP6
			Maj. B. Newson	
8/29/66	F-105D	60-0523	Capt. N. Wells	RP1
9/2/66	F-105D	62-4303	Capt. E. R. Skowron	RP2

F-105 Combat Theater Losses—April–November 1966 (continued)

Date	Type	Tail #	Crew	Area
9/4/66	F-105D	61-0085	Lt. T. McNish	RP6
9/4/66	F-105D	62-4369	Lt. R. Bliss	RP6
9/5/66	F-105D	60-0495	Capt. T. D. Dobbs	RP1
9/9/66	F-105D	62-4275	Capt. J. Blevins	RP6
9/11/66	F-105D	62-4282	Capt. L. Shattuck	RP6
9/12/66	F-105D	61-0201	Capt. R. Waggoner	RP3
9/13/66	F-105D	62-4281	Lt. K. V. Hallmark	RP1
9/14/66	F-105D	62-4306	Lt. J. R. Casper	RP6
9/17/66	F-105D	61-0191	Capt. A. Rutherford	RP6
9/17/66	F-105D	62-4280	Capt. D. D. Leetun	RP6
9/19/66	F-105D	62-4287	Capt. D. Waltman	RP6
9/21/66	F-105D	62-4371	Capt. G. L. Ammon	RP6
9/25/66	F-105D	62-4341	Capt. C. E. Cushman	RP6
9/26/66	F-105D	61-0186	Capt. A. Balard	RP6
10/1/66	F-105D	60-0483	Capt. C. G. Nix	RP1
10/10/66	F-105D	62-4300	Lt. Glen F. Bullock	Korat
10/14/66	F-105D	62-4391	Maj. R. P. Taylor	RP3
10/21/66	F-105D	61-0057	Capt. D. J. Earil	RP1
10/27/66	F-105D	60-0431	Maj. R. E. Kline	Laos
10/27/66	F-105D	62-4396	Maj. D. Johnson	RP1
11/2/66	F-105D	60-0469	Maj. R. E. Kline	RP5
11/2/66	F-105D	62-4379	Capt. R. F. Loken	RP5
11/4/66	F-105D	62-4366	Capt. D. Elmer	RP1
11/6/66	F-105D	60-5374	Capt. W. G. Carey	RP2
11/6/66	F-105D	60-0487	Capt. V. Vizcarra	RP1
11/11/66	F-105D	62-4313	Maj. A. Mearns	RP6
11/16/66	F-105D	62-4332	Capt. D. Green	RP6
11/22/66	F-105D	58-1161	Unknown	Thailand

Source: J. M. Campbell and M. Hill, *Roll Call: Thud.* Atglen, Pa.: Schiffer Publishing, 1996, and from Chris Hobson, *Vietnam Air Losses: United States Air Force, Navy and Marine Corps Fixed-Wing Aircraft Losses in SEA, 1961–1973*, Midland Publishing, LE10 3EY, England, 2001. Additional detail provided by F-105 historian Theo Van Geffen. Readers should note that this table lists F-105 losses only and does not include the significant losses of F-4, A-4, F-8, A-1, and other USAF and USN aircraft during the period.

Glossary

AAA Anti-aircraft artillery. Large guns ranging from 23 to 120 mm in bore, often radar guided and massed for the express purpose of shooting down aircraft. Projectiles carry explosive charges and detonate on contact or at a predetermined altitude.

AGM-12B/C Air-to-ground missile guided from the launch aircraft and flown into the target. A first-generation precision-guided munition. Also known as Bullpup.

APR-25/26 Military nomenclature for the first generation radar warning receivers used by the F-105.

BDA Bomb damage assessment. A report of the results of an attack using data obtained from reconnaissance photos or an observer estimation.

bingo Code word used to indicate that fuel remaining has reached the minimum necessary to safely return to base and land. Calculated for normal climb and cruise from the target area back to home base or a post-strike tanker.

Bullpup See AGM-12B/C.

CBU Cluster bomb unit. A wide range of weapons that either dispense bomblets from a fixed unit or drop from the aircraft then open to deploy small baseball-sized bomblets. Early versions such as CBU-2 required low, level delivery. Later mods such as CBU-24,-27, -52, and -58, consisted of a bomblike shell that was delivered from a diving pass and activated by a timer fuse at a preset altitude above the ground.

College Eye Also Big Eye and later Disco. An EC-121 airborne command and control aircraft carrying a large radar. Capabilities included monitoring flight paths of airborne aircraft, monitoring borders to prevent border violations, and vectoring aircraft toward other aircraft. A forerunner of AWACS.

DF Direction finding, often ADF for automatic direction finding. A system in which the navigation bearing pointer points at the source of a radio transmission.

DME Distance measuring equipment. An instrument readout that provides distance in nautical miles from a TACAN station or to a Doppler destination.

DNIF Duty not including flying. A medical term describing conditions in which illness such as the common cold temporarily ground an aviator.

Doppler A self-contained navigation system that does not depend on external ground stations. A computer detects frequency differences in the returns of three narrow radar beams projected below the aircraft. By sensing motion through analysis of these Doppler frequency shifts, the computer calculates movement from a start point and displays both latitude and longitude as well as heading and distance to any coordinates the user has input.

emergency fuel A fuel state in which all remaining fuel may not be sufficient to safely land the aircraft, even if traffic priority is given.

EPR Exhaust pressure ratio. Pronounced "eeyper," it corrects for atmospheric pressure and temperature to ensure the aircraft engine is operating at rated power. Typical for Pratt & Whitney engines.

FAC Forward air controller. A pilot flying a small spotter plane, qualified to direct air strikes by fighters. Used in areas close to ground troops as well as for detailed reconnaissance of specific geographic sectors.

Fan Song A ground-based radar system that provides azimuth, elevation, range, and command guidance for the SA-2 surface-to-air missile.

Fire Can A small ground-based radar used primarily for aiming and ranging anti-aircraft artillery.

frag Abbreviation for "fragmentary order." Units received only part of the daily strike plan, only a portion or fragment of the total operations order. The daily tasking for a wing was called the "frag."

GCA Ground controlled approach. A radar precision instrument approach that gives guidance to both runway centerline and glideslope. Also called PAR for precision approach radar.

GCI Ground control intercept. An acronym used to describe air defense interceptor radar control systems.

GIB Guy-in-back, acronym for the pilot systems operator or backseater in the F-4 Phantom. Also PSO, WSO, or "Bravo."

guard A dedicated radio frequency for emergency communications. UHF guard channel is 243.0 mHz. Also the auxiliary radio receiver used by tactical aircraft.

IP Instructor pilot.

Jolly Green Large helicopter used for aircrew rescue. Also CH-3 and simply Jolly.

judy Brevity code word indicating that the pilot has sufficient radar or visual information to complete an intercept without further assistance from ground radar controlling agencies.

karst Prominent limestone formations, often reaching several hundred feet high, that thrust upward from the jungle.

Klong An open canal or manmade lake used for irrigation and often for waste disposal. Also the call sign of in-theater C-130 airlift missions. Used to denote almost any C-130 in the region.

knot Unit for measuring speed equal to one nautical mile per hour. A nautical mile is longer than a statute mile used in miles per hour. One hundred knots equals one hundred fifteen miles per hour.

LPU   Life preserver, underarm. A harness worn under the parachute with two small pouches containing two compressed gas cylinders that would inflate U-shaped bladders under each armpit for water survival.

M-117   General purpose 750-pound bomb.

M-118   General purpose 3,000-pound bomb.

MER   Multiple ejector rack. A suspension rack carried on the centerline station that had six bomb stations allowing for multiple weapons to be carried from a single aircraft position. Depending on weapon dimensions and weight, the rack was used to carry from two to six munitions. Release was sequenced to avoid weapon interference, and a time interval for release was preflight selectable.

MiG   Any of a range of Soviet-built interceptors from the Mikoyan design facility. Highly maneuverable, lightweight fighters armed with cannon and various air-to-air missiles depending upon type. MiG-17, -19, and -21 were flown by the North Vietnamese Air Force.

MiGCAP   MiG Combat Air Patrol. An air superiority mission dedicated to protecting a strike package from enemy interceptors. Can be flown in orbits in the target area, as escort for bombing aircraft, as a sweep ahead of the strike, or as a free-ranging flight over enemy territory.

minimum fuel   A fuel state in which all remaining fuel may be required to achieve a safe landing in normal sequence with other aircraft. An advisory meaning that delays may result in problems.

Mk-8X   A series of low-profile, low-drag, general-purpose bombs ranging from Mk-81 (250 pounds) through 82 (500 pound), 83 (1,000 pound), and 84 (2,000 pound).

napalm   Also called incendigel. A flammable chemical compound dropped and then ignited by magnesium flare fuses. Described officially as "anti-PAM" munitions, i.e., anti–personnel and matériel.

PJ   Acronym for pararescue specialist. A crewmember on a Jolly Green trained to aid aircrew members being rescued. PJs were trained to swim, parachute, rappel, etc., to reach the ground to aid the downed crewman.

POL   Petroleum, oil, and lubricants. The fuel required to run the machinery of war along with all of the equipment to store, transport, and process it.

RHAW   Radar homing and warning. Generic name for a radar warning receiver. Also called APR 25/26, "vector gear," RWR, and "gadget."

ROE   Rules of engagement. Official rules and guidelines establishing what may and may not be done in the combat theater.

RTB   Return to base. Brevity code acronym for going home.

SAM   Surface-to-air missile. The Soviet-built Guideline missile. Also called SA-2. A large, command-guided, radar missile with a range of more than twenty-five miles.

Sandy   Call sign of rescue support aircraft, usually A-1 propeller-driven aircraft noted for their long flight endurance and wide range of munitions carried. Derived from the mission of search and rescue.

SAR Search and rescue. The mission of finding and recovering downed aircrew members.

SEA Southeast Asia.

solution anticipation A nuclear weapons delivery mode in which the computer begins a bomb-tossing pull-up prior to reaching the optimum range to release the weapon. By anticipating the solution to the bombing problem, the weapon can be released farther from the target and provide the attacker greater separation from the nuclear blast.

stab-aug Stability augmentation. An aircraft system employing sensors to minimize oscillations around all three axes of flight: yaw, roll, and pitch. Supersonic aircraft are inherently unstable, requiring some automated system to aid the pilot in maintaining control. Stab-aug depends on both electrical and hydraulic systems to function. Autopilot tasks are an advanced component of the stab-aug system.

stabilator An aircraft's horizontal tail plane. On supersonic aircraft it is a single moving airfoil combining both elevator and horizontal stabilizer components.

TACAN Tactical air navigation system. The primary means of fighter jet navigation, it depends upon ground-based stations that emit radio signals offering a bearing to the station and a distance from the station. Locations can be described relative to a TACAN station by giving a radial and DME.

TDU Threat display unit. The component of the APR-25/26 that displays the frequency band of detected threat radars as well as status of a SAM launch sequence.

toss bomb computer Also TBC, the weapons delivery computer in the F-105 designed for all-weather delivery of nuclear weapons.

UHF Ultra high frequency. The radio band used by USAF aircraft ranging from 225.00 to 399.9 mHz.

UPT Undergraduate pilot training. The aviation training that prepares an individual to become a military pilot. This generic training results in the award of an aeronautical rating and the coveted silver wings of an Air Force pilot.